POWER, POWERLE
AND ADDICTI

Addiction exercises enormous power over all those who are touched by it. This book argues that power and powerlessness have been neglected in addiction studies and that they are a unifying theme that brings together different areas of research from the field, including the disempowering nature of addiction; effects on family, community and the workplace; epidemiological and ethnographic work; studies of the legal and illegal supply; and theories of treatment and change. Examples of alcohol, drug and gambling addiction are used to discuss the evidence that addiction is most disempowering where social resources to resist it are weakest; the ways in which the dominant discourses about addictive behaviour encourage the attributing of responsibility for addiction to individuals and divert attention from the powerful who benefit from addiction; and the ways in which the voices of those whose interests are least well served by addiction are silenced.

JIM ORFORD is Emeritus Professor of Clinical and Community Psychology at the University of Birmingham. Jim is a long-standing researcher and writer in the addiction field. Amongst his 14 previous books are successful titles on addiction, notably *Excessive Appetites: A Psychological View of Addictions* (1st edition, 1985; 2nd edition, 2001); as well as others on community psychology, including *Community Psychology: Challenges, Controversies and Emerging Consensus* (2008). He is one of the UK's leading addiction researchers and has an international reputation. In 2010 he was awarded the prestigious international E.M. Jellinek Award for his contribution to alcohol and addiction studies.

POWER, POWERLESSNESS
AND ADDICTION

JIM ORFORD

CAMBRIDGE
UNIVERSITY PRESS

CAMBRIDGE UNIVERSITY PRESS
Cambridge, New York, Melbourne, Madrid, Cape Town,
Singapore, São Paulo, Delhi, Mexico City

Cambridge University Press
The Edinburgh Building, Cambridge CB2 8RU, UK

Published in the United States of America by Cambridge University Press, New York

www.cambridge.org
Information on this title: www.cambridge.org/9781107610095

First published 2013

A catalogue record for this publication is available from the British Library

Library of Congress Cataloguing in Publication data
Orford, Jim.
Power, powerlessness and addiction / Jim Orford.
pages cm
Includes bibliographical references and index.
ISBN 978-1-107-03476-1 (hardback)
1. Compulsive behavior. 2. Control (Psychology) I. Title.
RC533.O74 2013
616.85′84 – dc23 2013013117

ISBN 978-1-107-03476-1 Hardback
ISBN 978-1-107-61009-5 Paperback

I dedicate this book to the memory of Professor Griffith Edwards, who died in September 2012 as the book was just about to go into production. I would have liked him to read it and I would have been anxious to know his opinion. He was the single person of greatest significance in my career and was an inspiration to me as to so many others.
He was a giant in the addiction field.

Contents

Preface

This book is exploratory. There is no single body of knowledge correspond-ing to power, powerlessness and addiction; I have had to make it up as I went along. The idea for this book merges two streams of thought which have dominated my career in psychology. One of those is addiction studies where power is scarcely ever explicitly referred to. The other is community psychology, for which power and powerlessness are central concepts. Writ-ing this book has, therefore, served a personal purpose in uniting the two halves of my professional life which might otherwise remain disconnected. I might go further and argue that in order to explore the relationship between power and addiction it is necessary to bring together theory and research arising from different scientific traditions: on the one hand the biomedical, public health and epidemiological and on the other the social sciences. The former have dominated addiction studies while the latter have played a much lesser role. One feature of my earlier book on addic-tion, *Excessive Appetites* (Orford 2001), which left me dissatisfied was its emphasis on the individual and its relative lack of attention to the social. The present book is a partial attempt to put that right.

Although power is rarely mentioned when addiction is discussed, it had long occurred to me that power and powerlessness were never far below the surface and, once you were looking for them, they often appeared. The very concept of dependence, often used as a synonym for addiction, implies a loss of power. Indeed, acknowledging one's powerlessness is considered by Alcoholics Anonymous and other 12-step groups to be a requirement for recovery. The experience of family members and others closely affected by other people's addictions – something that my colleagues and I have made a special study of – can well be thought of as an experience of powerlessness. Once the focus moves beyond the individual and the family to consider the complex network of connections involved in the supply, legal or illicit, of substances and activities to which people become addicted, then the exercise of power and the creation and exploitation of the powerless are impossible to avoid. All those manifestations of power, overt or hidden, malignant or benign, and others, are discussed in the chapters which follow.

In defence of the word 'addiction'

Terminology in this field is itself controversial. I use the common term 'addiction' throughout this book although I try to avoid as much as possible using terms applied to individual people, such as 'addict' or 'alcoholic', labels which have been associated with stigma and which can carry pejorative connotations. I have also tried to avoid a number of terms which have become popular in official circles and which appear to be less pejorative but which in fact serve to reinforce the focus of responsibility for addiction on to the individual who experiences it at first hand, in the process shifting the focus of responsibility away from everyone else who is connected with addiction in some way. The expressions 'drug misuse(r)' and 'drug abuse(r)' are such terms. Similar in their implications are the now-popular terms such as 'sensible drinking' and 'responsible gambling' with their clearly implied opposites – drinking which is not sensible and irresponsible gambling. Other terms such as 'drug dependence', 'problem drinking' or 'excessive appetites', are alternatives, each with their own slightly different take on the matter. In this book I fall back on the word 'addiction' because it is one that is both in wide public use and is common currency in the expert literature on the subject as well. For my purposes it is also a good vehicle for introducing the theme of power and powerlessness, as I hope will become clear later. 'Addiction' does, however, carry a number of dangers. It can easily be taken to imply a definable illness, distinctively different from normal experience, and most likely explicable ultimately in terms of biological vulnerability, probably involving some genetic predisposition and possibly brain abnormalities. In my view the opposite of all those is true. Addiction is best thought of as a process; at any one time it is represented in the population in terms of a continuum (several continua in fact), with many more people mildly or moderately addicted than severely so; and its causes are legion, probably involving many genes which interact with numerous environmental factors in complex ways which vary by time and place. I hope it will not be thought that, by using the expression 'addiction', I am trying to over-simplify what is in fact a very complicated subject.

I need also to make a point about the diversity of addiction and to explain why I have concentrated on three forms of addiction, to alcohol, drugs and gambling. They constitute, for me, the 'big three', with many features in common. Each involves an activity which is indulged in, or a commodity which is consumed, to put it in other terms, for positive, rewarding purposes, supplied, legally or illegally, for such ends. Each is potentially addictive and, therefore, dangerous and excessive indulgence is associated with disruption to the person, the family, and beyond. They are not the only dangerous activities to which people can get addicted, however. Smoking tobacco cigarettes is one of the strongest and most difficult-to-break addictions and I could be criticised for not making it more of a focus. It is certainly one of the main addictions and arguably the one that wreaks the most havoc worldwide. But its harm profile somewhat differs from that of the big three: in particular, its effect on family life, which is one of the principal domains on which I have drawn, differs. There are other forms of addiction which could have been included and which might have served to deepen my exploration of the connections between addiction and power. In *Excessive Appetites* I included binge eating and sex addiction and there is now a body of work on shopping addiction and a rapidly expanding literature on internet addiction. But I judged that this was not the place to discuss what should and should not be included as an addiction and that I had enough work to do exploring how power figures in an account of alcohol, drug and gambling addiction.

The structure of the book

Chapter 1 orientates the reader to the breadth of topics to be covered in the book by means of presenting three hypothetical cases: a middle-aged man with an alcohol addiction; a young woman with an illicit drug addiction; and a woman with an addiction to gambling machines. Although each 'case' is hypothetical, they are based on an amalgamation of my research and reading and are, therefore, designed to be as realistic as possible. As well as serving to introduce the three principal kinds of addiction which will feature throughout later chapters, these three cases begin to introduce the idea that one person's addiction is connected, in relations of power, to the lives of many others, including those with whom the addicted person lives or works, other relatives, friends and acquaintances, people who deal in addictive commodities locally and at greater distance, as well as those who treat and support those with addictions. Offering hypothetical examples in this way presents a problem because it runs the risk of reinforcing stereotypes and failing to do justice to diversity. I considered trying to reflect more cultural and historical diversity in the examples presented in this chapter. But in the end I decided that to do so effectively was impossible and that it was preferable, and sufficient for making my point, to offer three examples of people who, as will be evident to the reader, are living in the late twentieth/early twenty-first century in the European country where I myself live and work. From time to time in the rest of the book references are made to the three cases described in Chapter 1.

Chapter 2 focuses on the experiences of people who themselves become addicted, re-interpreting that experience as one of diminished autonomy or increased powerlessness. It draws on psychological theories of addiction which see it as the development of a strong and difficult-to-break habit. Concepts such as habit development, erosion of restraint, and the development of conflict and its consequences are those I have drawn on before in my earlier works *Excessive Appetites* (Orford 2001) and *An Unsafe Bet?* (Orford 2011), and they are used again here. But they are now used to support the argument that addiction has the capacity to diminish personal agency; in other words, to disempower. The chapter moves beyond a strictly psychological understanding of addiction to include consideration of what some philosophers have had to say about addiction and loss of autonomy and what might be learnt from the way in which social theorists have dealt with powerlessness more generally.

The main point argued in Chapter 3 is that the powerlessness of those who experience addiction at first hand also undermines the control over their lives exercised by those who come into close contact with addiction at second-hand – notably close family members. To make this point, the chapter draws upon both the family research conducted by my colleagues and myself and on biographies of some famous names such as the wives of the poets Samuel Taylor Coleridge and Dylan Thomas. Illustrations are also given of the disempowering influence of addiction on close friends and work colleagues and groups. This material illustrates the impotence which is often felt in the face of addiction and the dilemmas people face in deciding how to respond. These are themes that colleagues and I have addressed previously, for example, in the books *Coping with Alcohol and Drug Problems* (Orford et al. 2005) and *Addiction Dilemmas* (Orford 2012). But in the context of the present book they are used to ask in what way these at-second-hand addiction experiences can be thought of as ones of oppression or bondage and might be likened to other experiences of subordination, such as colonisation or a lowly position in a socially stratified system. The question which social theorists have often asked – how can consent to oppression be explained – is brought to bear, as are relevant psychological theories such as social dominance theory and system justification theory.

A variety of sources, from the epidemiological to the anthropological, are drawn on in Chapter 4 to support the argument that addiction is unequally distributed among social groups, flourishing most where the power to resist is weakest. Amongst the evidence are findings of negative social class gradients and studies showing the vulnerability of minorities or groups who are socially excluded, including indigenous people and sexual minorities. Also highlighted are relevant studies of place, including those relating addiction to area deprivation, studies of the variation by area of alcohol and gambling sales outlets, and other studies which reveal the risks of harm in the way drugs are used in poor inner-city neighbourhoods. Attention is given to the work of those social scientists who have concluded that social and economic structures are largely responsible for addiction. Research on the harmful effects of addiction on neighbourhoods and communities is also considered. These various lines of theory and evidence raise the familiar structure versus agency debate which has been enjoined in community psychology and more generally in social theory, a discussion of which concludes this chapter.

The first half of Chapter 5 is devoted to considering the enormous size and power of the legal alcohol and gambling industries, including their capacity for influence via lobbying, advertising and other means. The subtle way in which they use their power to influence the policy agenda is described, with particular note taken of the various ways in which they attempt to influence research. More subtle still, it is argued here, is the way in which a number of pro-industry expansion discourses are deployed, such as the harmless amusement, ordinary business, freedom of choice, and responsible consumer discourses. The second half of the chapter considers the way in which power, often of a more directly coercive kind, is exercised in the course of trading in illegal drugs. Research from Myanmar and Britain is drawn upon to illustrate the many different roles played by people at different levels of the drug trade and the powerless position of people occupying many of those positions.

Chapter 6 draws upon evidence to suggest that successful addiction change involves social influence as well as individual cognitive change. Examples, such as company alcohol policies and family drug and alcohol courts, are given to support the theory that effectively standing up to addiction involves a combination of care and control, support and discipline. An element of coercion is often involved in the change process. Disempowered by their addictions, people submit to a process that allows others to exercise legitimate, expert or reward power. This thesis is supported with examples including Alcoholics Anonymous, change through religious means, contingency management and motivational interviewing.

Chapter 7, the concluding chapter, attempts to pull together the themes discussed in earlier chapters, arguing that power, and the various ways it is exercised at different points in the addiction story, have been neglected in the addictions studies field. A consequence has been an exclusive focus on the behaviour of those individuals who are themselves addicted and the assumption that the responsibility for addiction is principally theirs. Close family members also assimilate a sense of responsibility. The case for viewing responsibility and addiction more widely is made by discussing philosophical, psychological and legal views on addiction and diminished responsibility; the evidence that addiction is most disempowering where social resources to resist it are weakest; the ways in which the dominant discourses about addictive behaviour encourage the attributing of responsibility for addiction to individuals and divert attention from the powerful who benefit from addiction; and the ways in which the voices of those whose interests are least well served by addiction are silenced. The chapter concludes with a number of examples, from different parts of the world, of how the voices of those most disempowered by addiction have sometimes been heard. It is argued that addiction has largely been treated as a private, individual matter and that standing up to addiction collectively is now what is needed.

Acknowledgements

Although I have been actively working on this book for two or three years and thinking about it for a few years before that, it could not have been written without the background of many years in which I have worked with numerous colleagues from whom I have learned much and who have inspired me. They are far too many to list individually here. They include colleagues, particularly my early and lasting mentor Griffith Edwards, at the Addiction Research Unit (now the National Addiction Centre) at the Institute of Psychiatry in London; at the University of Exeter Psychology Department and Exeter NHS Clinical Psychology Department; at the Institute of Psychiatry in Mexico City; and latterly in the School of Psychology at Birmingham University and in the European Community Psychology Association.

CHAPTER ONE

Powerful connections
Three examples of addiction

David: a case of alcohol addiction

As my first illustration of the complex networks of power surrounding addiction, I have drawn on my research and reading on the subject to invent an early middle-aged man whom I shall call David[1]. His addiction to alcohol – lager and whisky are his preferred beverages – is now sufficiently strong that the ripples it has created within the social groups that David inhabits have become a maelstrom, drawing others in against their wishes. It has not always been that way, although he has been a regular and mostly heavy drinker since his mid-teens. As is not uncommon, the trajectory of his drinking since then has not been entirely smooth but has shown a number of ups and downs. His intake of alcohol was at its heaviest in his early to mid-twenties, before he settled down with his partner Marian, during a period of several months when he was working on a contract abroad and earning a lot of money, and, more recently, when he became unemployed and was finding it difficult to find new work. Consumption was at its lowest level when he and Marian first had a young family. It is now at its heaviest ever.

We could think of David's addiction to alcohol as a purely personal problem, one that he alone carries and is responsible for. Before accepting that prevailing conception, however, let us try and build up a picture of the people who are in some way connected with his excessive drinking. There turns out to be a lot of them. Most obviously there is David's family household consisting of he, Marian and their three children – two sons aged 21 and 16 and a daughter aged 19. The elder son is studying at university and is now only at home for part of the vacations, and the daughter has a steady boyfriend who has his own bedsit so she is dividing her time

---

[1] The three detailed illustrations of addiction in this chapter are hypothetical and do not correspond to any real people. On the other hand, each is very real in the sense that it is based on a digest of years of research and study of the subject carried out by the author and by countless others.

between his place and home. Each member of the household would have a story to tell about David's drinking, although the children try to escape from it and to avoid having to think about it too much of the time. Out of loyalty to David, Marian used to be very selective about how much she disclosed about the problem and to whom. But it is now gone beyond that point and she will now give her account more readily, provided she has a sympathetic and understanding listener who has the time.

Marian describes her life as having been turned upside down by David's drinking. She sees him as having become seriously dependent on drink, drinking large quantities every day, starting in the morning and spending most of his time in one of the local pubs or slouched in a chair at home with a drink beside him. She is worried that he is not eating properly, is sleeping badly and is now neglecting his appearance and hygiene. He has only worked sporadically in the last two years and they are now dependent on her modest income. There is no longer fun in their relationship and she feels she is losing the man she loves. Arguments have come to blows on more than one occasion, which is out of character for them both. Her biggest concern is for the children who she believes are distancing themselves from the family in ways that may not be in their best interests. She senses that their elder son is finding excuses not to come home in the holidays. She thinks the situation at home is driving their daughter into the arms of her boyfriend who would not be their choice as a partner for her. Their younger son is the one who gives her most concern: he is mixing with a roughish crowd, did not do as well as expected in his exams, has certainly been drinking heavily and smoking cannabis and, she imagines, experimenting with other drugs besides. She has tried pointing out to David that the children need his attention and guidance but that has only created more arguments and he appears now to have completely opted out of his paternal role. Marian has tried all sorts of ways of dealing with the problem: coaxing and cajoling, firmly challenging, a tender, 'softly, softly' approach, and trying to ignore it, even accompanying David to the pub, which was a disaster. Nothing seems to have worked. Like so many people in her situation she wonders if she is to blame in some way. Has she not appreciated him enough over the years? Has she ignored his needs? Should she have agreed to go with him when he was working abroad? He certainly seemed to acquire a taste for whisky on that trip. Is their marriage a failure? Has she failed as a wife and mother? Whatever the answer to those questions which go round and round in her mind, it certainly seems that her health is suffering. She too is sleeping very badly and she is often tearful. Her doctor has given her a prescription for anti-depressants, something that she never thought would happen to her. She hasn't yet decided whether to take them or not. She is confused, sad, angry, but her own overwhelming sense is one of powerlessness.

Close family members like Marian and their three children are in the frontline of addiction connections but there are many others who share some of Marian's feelings of impotence. In David's case, the work group of which, until two years ago, he had been an essential part for more than a decade was an important social group intimately connected with his drinking in a number of ways. He worked as a senior contract manager for a branch of a large, international civil engineering construction company. He had been a high flyer marked out for further promotions. He was widely known to be a keen drinker but in the fast lane of wheeling and dealing there was no harm in that, indeed it was generally seen as an advantage. But there had come a point when his colleagues began to question – mostly in their private thoughts to start with but increasingly in confidential discussions with others – whether David's drinking was altogether a good thing. There had been one or two complaints by junior staff and a hint from more than one representative of a client organisation that his drinking might be adversely affecting his work. His immediate senior, a close colleague of a number of years who had become something of a friend as well, was particularly upset and uncertain about what to do. The matter increasingly became a talking point in the office and opinions were divided: some thought that tough disciplinary action should be taken, others favored a more supportive, sympathetic approach, whilst another faction thought it was being blown out of all proportion and should be ignored. In the end, David's continued employment was in jeopardy and he was referred to the company's Employee Assistance Programme (EAP), which covered cases like David's. Staying with the company was made contingent upon entering treatment, which did happen, and upon continuing to make progress so that the drinking-related performance deficits would cease to be a problem. After what looked like a good start, the latter, unfortunately, did not happen, and the company 'let him go'. Notice how complex and far-reaching those connections were. Not only was the work of David's unit affected, but a number of his colleagues were caught up in fraught and sometimes quite acrimonious disagreements about what should be the appropriate course of action. While that was going on they felt some measure of the powerlessness which Marian had been experiencing.

Although the problem did not materially affect the health of most of his colleagues, this could probably not have been said for his immediate senior. The latter was very troubled by the whole affair and – as his own family could attest – his work satisfaction was certainly diminished while it remained unresolved. His position, already difficult because of the friendship that had developed between he and David, became more complicated when Marian, whom he had met socially, phoned him in desperation to find out what was going on. After that he and Marian spoke on a number of occasions, each feeling somewhat guilty that they were talking about David behind his back. When it became clear that David was going to lose his job, his senior felt wretched about it and believed, which was not the case, that Marian blamed him for not being able to do more for David. Since then his friendship with David has not been renewed but he has continued to keep in touch by periodically phoning Marian to see how David is faring. The thin and fragile connections between a person's home and his or her place of work – two systems, each so important but often so disconnected – are usually much more important than they appear to be. In the case of addiction, home–work connections are often affected in some way, either by becoming even more distant than usual or by providing new opportunities for solidarity in the face of something which appears to threaten both. New channels of communication may open up or, on the other hand, communication may become more difficult. Often it is the case that the two networks struggle alone, only later, or perhaps never at all, discovering that their concerns were shared by people in the other place.

The connections between David's addiction and his place of work extended well beyond his immediate colleagues. The company's human resources team were responsible for administering the EAP, and the company had its own team of health professionals to assess David and recommend treatment. A small cadre of fellow employees was therefore busy on David's case. The final decision to sack him was made at a higher level. The EAP, which proved helpful for a while, was devised at the company's headquarters in another country, although its adaptation to the country in which David lived, and in particular its use with cases of alcohol dependence, had been matters of lengthy discussion more locally. Notice how all these addiction connections, involving people with power over the lives of others, are ones that are likely to have been beyond the full awareness of David's family. How much, I wonder, would his younger son, whose life, according to his mother, was so affected by his father's drinking problem, know about his father's employer's deliberations about how to deal with employees addicted to alcohol or their particular deliberations about his own father? And, if he did know anything of this, what would he make of it?

Before we leave David's main place of work there is another important kind of connection to consider. Humane and well-intentioned though the company's policy may have been, Marian could be forgiven for thinking that it was the company's way of conveniently mopping up a problem that was, in large part, a problem of its own making. In fact, there had been times when she was quite critical of the conditions under which David worked, which often seemed to combine a heavy and stressful work schedule with an encouragement, or at least tolerance, of heavy drinking. This 'culture of heavy drinking', as it might be called, imposed itself most strongly in the contract side of the business in which David worked. He was not the only heavy drinker in the division and there was a feeling in some quarters that he had been made a scapegoat. Unlike most of the connections we have been discussing up to now this cannot be pinned down to a link with one or two specific people; it is, rather, a question of the attitudes and behaviours of a whole collective of people and the norms governing behaviour in the places where they meet and partake of potentially addictive substances and activities. Where power and responsibility reside is even less clear.

The two worlds of home and work are only the beginning of a full account of the myriad bonds that exist between David's alcohol addiction and other individuals and groups. It turns out, but only after careful enquiry, that there exists a substantial network of family members and friends each of whom knows something of the problem and has adopted his or her own position towards it. David has two brothers who have reacted in very different ways. His elder brother, previously close to David, has now all but broken off contact, encouraged, Marian thinks, by his wife, who has always been very critical of David and his drinking. David's younger unmarried brother, on the other hand, has always been a heavy drinker himself and his relationship with David seems to have got closer if anything. Marian now dreads his visits, which seem to provide an excuse for even heavier drinking than usual. Marian has a sister to whom she has always been very close. They can talk about most things but Marian has learned not to talk about David's drinking because if she does her sister 'gets on her high horse', as Marian puts it, and tells Marian that she should consider leaving David. Since leaving David is not on her agenda, Marian finds that unhelpful and surprisingly thoughtless of her normally very understanding sister. At least two of David's and Marian's siblings are, therefore, aware of the problem and have been required to respond in some way, albeit ways that have not been particularly helpful to David or Marian. Members of the previous generation have their own ways of worrying but mostly they keep their worries to themselves. David's and

Marian's mothers, both widowed, visit occasionally and, alarmed at what they have seen, try to find out more and be as helpful as they can by trying to keep in regular telephone contact with their respective offspring. Both feel downhearted, fearful for the family and – such a common feeling in the face of addiction – impotent to do anything.

David and his family also have a wide circle of friends, quite a number of whom know about David's drinking problem and are concerned about it. For some, those who are less close, it has led to discussions, nearly always inconclusive, about what help might be given, and sometimes those discussions have extended to debate about whether there is too much drinking in today's society, whether David is an 'alcoholic' and whether that is similar to or different from drug addiction. In some households it has even led to discussion about how to deal with household members' own possibly addictive habits such as a father's repeated attempts to give up smoking, a mother's unrealised wish to lose weight, and a son's current absorption with the internet which is worrying his parents – is this is the 'internet addiction' that they are increasingly seeing reference to in the news media? Some other friends and their families have made adjustments to the ways in which they interact with David and his family; in some cases they have let their occasional meetings lapse, whilst others have found ways of maintaining contact which do not involve staying over in each other's homes. A number have expressed sympathetic concern to Marian and one or two have made positive attempts to be helpful. An old friend of David's, who has known him since university days, broached the subject directly with David but only after much agonising about how he should do it and after seeking the advice of a number of his own friends, more than one of whom had experienced drinking or drug problems themselves or amongst close relatives. He was afraid that David would be angry with him for raising his concerns but in the event David was charming about it and thanked his friend for taking the trouble. His friend came away from the encounter, however, with a distinct feeling that his worries had been deflected, almost dismissed, as kind but unwarranted. He was left feeling deflated and uncertain what to do next. Marian works for a small business which provides massage and beauty treatments with a small shop and restaurant attached. It is run by a close-knit group of women from whom it is difficult to hide personal problems. There have been times when Marian's mind has obviously not been on the job and other times when she seems to have become over-committed to her work, spending as much time there as possible. Most of her colleagues now know that there are problems at home and her closest colleagues know what the problem is. One colleague in particular has been very supportive, letting Marian talk at some length, encouraging her to think through what to do but without imposing her own opinions. But Marian has often thought that she is taking up too much of her colleague's time and that the support had become a bit one-way, almost as if her colleague has become a counsellor.

Talking of counsellors, there is another whole system of links with people and organisations who promise to be less impotent in the face of David's addiction and who might help reduce David's and Marian's powerlessness. These are the people we might refer to, not entirely aptly, as the 'formal helpers'. Their power lies in their expertise and their official positions as sanctioned experts. Considering that David has had little formal treatment for an alcohol problem, there is a surprising number of such people. The link with the primary care health centre where both David and Marian are patients is a principal one. David's GP, who has been looking after his health for some years, is good at asking her patients about their drinking when the opportunity arises and has noted for some time that David's alcohol consumption is probably unhealthy. Her concerns were strengthened a year or two ago when he was admitted to hospital for a week with symptoms that were never satisfactorily explained. She has advised him on more than one occasion about recommended maximum levels of sensible drinking and has recommended that he cut down his intake. Marian sees a different GP at the same practice. He explored possible reasons for her poor sleeping and depressed mood and is now aware of what she is coping with at home, although prescribing anti-depressants was the only action he felt able to take. Although he and David's GP work in the same practice, the family records are not coordinated so a fruitful connection which might have taken place if the two GPs had communicated about the family has not been made. Nor was the connection with David's drinking recognised by medical and nursing staff at the hospital where David was admitted. That was despite the fact that excessive alcohol consumption is a known risk factor for a wide range of medical conditions and ward staff might have noticed the bottle of whisky that David kept in his bedside locker whilst he was there. A whole set of other connections with state and 'third sector' agencies have come about because of David's drinking and driving. Within an 18-month period he was picked up by the police three times and found to be driving over the legal blood alcohol limit. On the last occasion he was given the option of losing his driving licence for a period of time or attending an 'alcohol awareness' course run by a local non-statutory organisation with many years' experience of providing services for people with alcohol problems in the region. Embarrassing though he found it, David chose the latter and thereby came into contact with a knowledgeable group of people in charge of the course and a number of fellow drink-driving offenders.

When alcohol dependence or alcohol misuse are discussed in health circles, some mention may be made of home, workplace and the many other parts of informal and formal social systems, such as those we have been discussing relevant to David's case, but mostly they are hidden from view and are rarely discussed at all thoroughly. But beyond those little explored connections always lies a set of power linkages of which the Davids and Marians of this world, their family members, colleagues, friends and their GPs and other helpers, are mostly only dimly aware. Someone – or many people as is almost always the case – is supplying the dangerous substance or activity which carries the potential for addiction. In fact, the relatively hidden-from-view network of suppliers, along with the structures that support them, constitutes the most extensive nexus of addiction power connections. In the case of a legally provided substance like alcohol, the local part of that system, at least, is in fairly plain view. The local pub is a prominent feature of the village in which David and his family live. Unlike some pubs in other areas it makes a positive contribution to an area which local estate agents describe as 'sought after'. David knows it well, having spent much time and money there. He is on good terms with the landlord and landlady and is on first name terms with a dozen or more fellow regulars and perhaps another dozen whom he sees there less regularly. If you were to ask David about his intentions regarding his future drinking he would tell you that he ought to cut back a bit and intends to do so but that without the social life of the pub, of which drinking is an integral part, his quality of life would be seriously diminished. Whether one should cut back on drinking as one gets older is a regular topic of conversation in the pub and David is one of a group who are generally considered prime candidates for cutting back although such discussions are mostly light hearted and not followed up. Marian sees the influence of the pub on their home in a very different light. She can't help seeing it as a major source of danger to David's health and well-being and her own and her family's unhappiness. Although she does not think of herself as blameless, she believes the other pub regulars have some responsibility for encouraging her husband's dependency. She believes the pub landlord and landlady to be irresponsible in continuing to feed an addiction which to her seems so obvious. She is acutely conscious of holding a view of the village pub and those who work and drink there which is at odds with the generally held one, and that only makes her feel more uncomfortable and less like expressing her views to others. She herself goes to the pub rarely and feels uncomfortable when she does. Their elder son is another who now feels uncomfortable there. Having done some of his early drinking with friends in the village pub, once he became more aware of his father's excessive drinking and was becoming more distant from the village through his studies elsewhere, he plucked up courage on one occasion and 'had a quiet word' with the landlord, asking him if he couldn't discourage his father's drinking, perhaps by refusing to serve him when he had had too much. His intervention, about which he had felt extremely nervous, was met with surprise and an explanation that such a thing could only be done if his father made such a request in person.

The village pub is a 'tied house', owned by a well-known local county brewery and then taken over some years ago by a large international alcoholic drinks company. The pub landlord and landlady are just the local face of what is now a colossal corporate enterprise. Its network of international, national and area offices is extensive. In David's own country alone it employs, directly or indirectly under franchise, an army of people which runs into six figures in number. On the promotion and advertising of the drinks which David consumes it spends sums of money which make the local hospital and health centre budgets look miniscule by comparison. The company is a member of several 'social aspects organisations' and makes much of its corporate social responsibility policies. For example, it has championed and financially supported educational initiatives in schools for teaching about 'sensible drinking'. There are those, however, who are very critical of the corporate social responsibility policies of drinks companies. They are, the critics argue, simply a relatively cheap way of buying public and government approval, and hence avoiding heavier regulation, whilst continuing to make vast profits and do nothing effective to prevent new cases such as David's from arising. The critics would point, for example, to the fact that the company that ultimately owns David's local pub has put a lot of time and money into opposing leading recommendations by public health experts, including the nation's Chief Medical Officer of Health, that there should be a minimum price for the sale of all alcoholic drinks based upon the number of standard units of alcohol contained, thus outlawing such practices as cost cutting of alcoholic drinks by supermarkets. One of the company's subsidiaries has even tried to buy the services of an academic prominent in the field – working, as chance would have it, at the same university where David's son is studying – to provide a critique of a leading report which concluded that minimum pricing would have considerable preventive potential, including the saving of several thousand lives over the course of a decade.

None of this is known to David, Marian or any of their family or friends, although Marian caught something on the radio about minimum pricing and thought it no bad idea. What she does not fully appreciate, although none of it is secret, is how extensive and well-connected are the networks which supply the substance to which David had become addicted. She realises that the pub is an excellent source of temporary employment for village youngsters, including her own daughter at one stage and many of her children's friends. What she does not know is that the drinks company regional offices are not many miles away, providing further employment opportunities in the area, and that the regional manager lives in the next village. Nor does she know that their local member of parliament is on the company board. She is also unaware that she is not alone as a wife who believes that pub managers are failing to act responsibly, and she knows nothing about the local authority system of public house licensing and the fact that there is a procedure for making complaints when licenses are due for renewal. Like most people Marian is also only dimly aware of the role played by government – a complicit role the critics would argue – in supporting an ever expanding, innovating drinks industry. The company that controls the local pub is sufficiently large to be part of the FTSE-100 share index and if anything disastrous were to happen to it, it would have a significant effect on the national economy. The drinks industry in general is a major contributor to the economy. The local MP is only one of a score or more of parliamentarians on the government's side who sit on the boards of drinks companies. The Government Minister for Culture, Media and Sport, which leads on alcohol regulation, has refused to accept the Chief Medical Officer's recommendation about pricing. Not irrelevant is the recent national furore over the Home Secretary's refusal to accept the advice of his expert committee who have told him that alcohol dependence and misuse is probably the nation's biggest drug problem, far greater than the problem posed to the nation by the use of some banned drugs such as cannabis and ecstasy.

When Marian hears of such things in the news she senses that she is one of the few people who understands what some of the experts are on about. Otherwise she feels very alone in a world that she judges to be irresponsible and uncaring when it comes to booze and its effects on ordinary people and their families. She sees friends drinking amounts of wine which seem to her excessive. She knows the police are worried about late night weekend city centre drunkenness but she hears all around her the expectation being expressed that anniversaries, celebrations and festivities will all be associated with drunkenness. She wonders if she is becoming a prude, a killjoy when it comes to drinking. David has certainly accused her of that.

Amanda: addicted to drugs

Unlike David, whose preferred substance is perfectly legal, above board, and one that constitutes a significant part of the official economy of many countries, Amanda's drug consumption is illicit. Now in her early twenties, she first experimented with drugs, in the form of a surreptitious marijuana smoke with friends, when she was 13. By the age of 15 she was smoking skunk regularly at weekends and had tried a variety of pills, including ecstasy and speed. She was rebellious at home and at school at that age and sometimes played truant from school. But she was a bright girl and did moderately well in her exams and went on to study some of her favourite subjects at the local sixth-form college. Her drug-taking increased in both scope and frequency when she went to college; by 17 she was struggling with her studies and eventually dropped out before taking further exams. She had no clear idea what she wanted to do, and work at a time of rising unemployment was not easy to find. Drugs, on the other hand, were easy for Amanda to find and it was then that her drug consumption started to get more seriously out of hand. Although she maintained contact with a number of school and college friends, she was now having more contact with other young people in her town who had also left education but who were not in regular work or training, amongst whom excessive patterns of drug-taking were not uncommon. By the time she was 18 Amanda was a daily smoker of marijuana and a regular user of other drugs, including cocaine. In the next couple of years, as re-entering the mainstream world of further education and employment inhabited by most of her old friends seemed an increasingly remote prospect, Amanda tried inhaling heroin – 'chasing the dragon' – and some time later was shown how to inject herself with heroin. By her twenty-first birthday she was injecting regularly and had become an official IDU – injecting drug user – registered with the local drug treatment services. She is now being prescribed the substitute, longer acting opiate methadone, but has not got over her habit of sometimes using heroin and regularly smoking cannabis. Her alcohol consumption, heavy off and on since her mid-teens, has increased somewhat since she has been under treatment for her drug misuse.

It is not hard to imagine the ripples that Amanda's drug-taking and associated lifestyle have created within her family. The people most directly involved are her mother, Mercy, and her father, Gilbert. They separated a year or two ago partly due, Mercy believes, to conflict over how to deal with Amanda's behaviour and its ramifications, the chief of which was the birth of Amanda's baby son whom Mercy now cares for much of the time. Looking back, Mercy feels that she has been living with this problem for nearly ten years although for the first few of those years it was not clear what the problem was. Amanda was increasingly difficult to control at home and there were some terrible rows and scenes. Amanda had raised her hand to her mother on a number of occasions and Gilbert had given her a couple of severe beltings. The atmosphere at home was extremely tense: when Amanda was home Mercy was fearful of Amanda's anger towards her and of Gilbert's anger towards Amanda, and when Amanda was out her parents were in agony about where she was, what she was doing and when she would be home.

Mercy and Gilbert had both been occasional smokers of cannabis in the past, and Gilbert still occasionally indulged, so that did not worry them. But they started to suspect that it had gone well beyond that when stories started to circulate about the drugs on offer in some local pubs and clubs and when they met some of Amanda's new friends, who were outside the circles the family normally moved in. There were a few occasions when unknown people called at the door or telephoned asking for Amanda in rather demanding tones, and one unnerving experience when a policeman and policewoman called to see Amanda in the course of making investigations after a high profile raid on one of the local night clubs. Amanda denied for a long time that she was using anything other than cannabis but the truth came out slowly and surely, often in the middle of arguments. Even then, Amanda denied for a long time that she was taking heroin or cocaine. Mercy felt guilty for harbouring suspicions and it was some time before she accepted Gilbert's plan that they should put to one side their principle of respecting Amanda's personal space and should give her bedroom a thorough search. They discovered, at the back of a bottom drawer, white powder, foil, papers and matches. Mercy describes that as one of the most traumatic moments of her life, when her worst fears were realised and the seriousness of Amanda's drug-taking became clear. When they confronted Amanda she expressed rage that they had searched her room and she marched out. On that occasion she stayed with a friend for a few days and from then on she slept as much away from home as she did in her parents' home.

Like Mercy, Gilbert has felt a range of strong emotions about Amanda and her problems, anger and utter frustration being prominent ones in his case. He and Mercy are both second-generation immigrants, born in this country shortly after their respective parents came here. They were well aware of the hardship that their parents had faced in a new country and the prejudice which they had been exposed to. Their parents had taught them not to make a fuss but to show their strength by studying and working hard and conforming to a system that they believed allowed people who did that to show their potential. That is what they had done and what they hoped their children would do. It was what Amanda's older brother and older sister appeared to be doing, having done well at school and college and now doing well in reasonably stable employment. Amanda's parents, particularly Gilbert, had found it very hard to accept Amanda's deviance. Both felt they had 'lost the daughter they knew and loved' as her problems worsened. But, difficult though it was, Mercy always tried to cling on to her caring role towards Amanda, extended latterly to include caring for Amanda's infant. Gilbert, on the other hand, had not known what to do and had 'taken it particularly hard', according to Mercy. In fact, she felt that Gilbert had been near to a breakdown over it: it had certainly affected his concentration and productivity at work, and his general state of mind was affected. Difficulty sleeping, poor appetite and increased alcohol consumption were all signs. Mercy's worry level had come out in the form of a nasty skin rash and high blood pressure.

The different ways in which Mercy and Gilbert tried to deal with the problem illustrates well the capacity of addiction to drive wedges between the people to whom addiction is connected. In this case, Mercy showed her tender, caring side by such actions as going out on what she called 'rescue missions' whenever she had news of where Amanda was and what trouble she was in; buying food, clothes and other necessities for her when she was in need; cleaning up Amanda's place for her if she got the chance; and welcoming her back home without recriminations whenever Amanda asked. Gilbert was for a tougher approach: he favoured reducing contact with Amanda to a minimum until she came to her senses. That, he felt, would be more motivating for her than running after her in the way that he thought his wife was doing. The latter he found disruptive of his relationship with Mercy, which had been deteriorating for some time. Mercy's heavy involvement with Amanda's new baby and her decision to have the child live with them whenever Amanda was unable to provide the necessary care had been the final straw. Gilbert moved out to go and live in his own place in the next street.

It is not that Mercy has always been certain that she was doing the right thing; far from it in fact. Several people besides her husband have suggested that she should 'let go' a bit more and let Amanda sort out her own problems. There have certainly been times when Amanda was demanding and Mercy was left feeling that she was being taking advantage of and might not be doing what was best for her daughter. One occasion particularly sticks in her mind. Amanda was at home and, as she put it, 'strung out' and badly in need of heroin. Amanda was in such a state that Mercy was worried what she might do. After much hassling and pleading, Amanda had persuaded her mother to give her a lift to near the point in town where she had arranged to buy some of the drug and to 'lend' her the money for the purchase. Feeling all the while anxious, guilty and criminal, and telling Amanda that this would never happen again, Mercy complied with Amanda's request.

Amanda's pregnancy and the birth of her baby had changed everything. Now there was no longer just Amanda and the family and other connections with her addiction to consider but also a new innocent life which needed care and protection. Amanda spent more time at home during her pregnancy, which only served to increase the tension since her parents could not understand how she could endanger the baby's life by continuing to use dangerous drugs. Amanda countered that it was much harder than they realised to kick such a habit just like that and that, in fact, she was having success in reducing her drug intake. Amanda went into hospital early and after the birth the baby remained under close observation because of the concern that the opiates Amanda was taking would have been transmitted to the baby. In fact, the baby thrived and was discharged to Amanda's care in Amanda's own local authority provided accommodation. Mercy, in her new role as grandmother, was beside herself with worry which her regular visits to see Amanda and the baby did nothing to diminish. At first, Amanda seemed to be coping well but it was not long before Mercy noted what she interpreted as signs that Amanda's accommodation was not being cleaned and tidied properly and that the baby was being neglected. On more than one occasion there were other people present who were not known to Mercy and to whom she was not properly introduced. A young woman acquaintance of Amanda's appeared on one of her visits to be doing as much caring for the baby as Amanda was and on another occasion there were several young people present and Mercy thought she detected signs that they had quickly covered up their drug-taking once she had arrived. Mercy had suggested that Amanda should come home with the baby or should let her mother get more involved in caring for her grandson. That had led to stormy scenes and Amanda refusing to let her mother in. Very reluctantly Mercy had agreed with Gilbert that they should contact the local authority social services department to enquire what was going on and to express their concern. This led to a highly stressful and unhappy period for them all which was finally resolved with an order being made that Mercy would be the baby's main carer for the time being, with Amanda contributing to the care as much as she was able. One side effect of this difficult period was the reconnecting of Mercy and Gilbert. Gilbert was encouraged by Amanda's new resolve and Mercy had found Gilbert more supportive. She had been moved to find him sobbing his heart out at one point and, although they were still living apart, they had become closer again.

Although in nearly all cases it is the closest family which is most affected by another person's addiction, in Amanda's case, as in most others, there exists a legion of other people, near and far, whose lives are touched by it and who experience some of the same feelings of powerlessness. Her brother is several years older and has his own new family and his own busy life to lead. Their parents have used him as a sounding board on occasions and have found his calm, unruffled attitude reassuring. Other than that, however, he has been sympathetic but not much involved directly with Amanda, who has mostly tried to avoid him. Her older sister has been in a different position. Closer in age to Amanda, and always close emotionally since being young children, she has been much more involved. While Amanda's drug-taking was more contained, she played a role as advocate for Amanda in discussions about Amanda with their parents. She shared in her sister's social life and many of Amanda's friends were hers also. She was familiar with the kinds of drug-taking that went on in their part of the world when they were teenagers and, like many of their friends, she had experimented with some of the same drugs. She was open with their parents and took it upon herself to educate them about the current drugs scene. Although appreciative of her efforts, Mercy and Gilbert were not entirely reassured. It was when Amanda started to drop out of college that her sister realised that their lives were heading in different directions and that the position of drug-taking in their lives had diverged. She had never felt easy about some of the people they obtained drugs from and she was more and more alarmed at some of the people that Amanda was beginning to mix with. Although she continues to feel that they are basically very alike, sharing a sense of humour and always able to talk freely with one another, as Amanda's drug-taking has become a bigger part of her life she has been on the receiving end of some very inconsiderate behaviour on Amanda's part. Since then she has increasingly come to the view that there is not a lot she can do for her sister. She has, on the other hand, been as supportive as she can to her parents and has recently taken a lot of interest in her new nephew.

At slightly greater remove are those related to Amanda's addiction because they are part of a quite extensive network of family members and close friends, mostly living close by in the same part of town in an area settled by many immigrant families 30–40 years earlier. News travels fast in this community and Mercy's and Gilbert's problems with Amanda are well known. It would take Mercy some time to talk you through all the people she has spoken to, the different stances they have each taken, the advice they have given her and how she has received it. There are those whose opinion is that Amanda should be locked up without recourse to drugs and others who think that she needs a good thrashing. Others think that Mercy should cut her ties with her daughter. None of these does Mercy find very helpful. She is upset to learn how many people there are who, when talking about Amanda, seem to 'write her off'. There are others who appear much more understanding: they let her talk, seem interested, show concern for Amanda as well as for Mercy and Gilbert and help her talk through options rather than confidently offering advice. Notable are two other mothers, both of whom have sons with drug problems. A particular aunt and uncle of hers, and also Gilbert's mother and father, have surprised her with their kindness and understanding. A number of people have been forthcoming with practical support; for example, helping them find out information about health and social services or simply by giving them lifts to the hospital or elsewhere.

All the family have been regular attenders at their local Episcopalian church, although Amanda's attendance has been sporadic in recent years. The rest of the family have found the church group, and especially the minister, who is a longstanding friend of the family, to be a source of great support. Mercy has found her religious faith to have been of great comfort. She believes in the power of prayer and is comforted knowing that other members of their church community are praying for Amanda and for the family.

There is another group of informal connections at yet one further remove. This group of connected others comprises neighbours, shopkeepers, landlords and landladies and others whose contacts with Amanda are complicated by virtue of drug addiction, about which they may or may not know anything. There has been credit extended, bills unpaid, possessions sold or pawned, rent in arrears. All have involved uncomfortable transactions. In some instances those involved have approached Amanda's parents, either thinking they were being helpful in letting them know what was going on or in the expectation that they would settle Amanda's debts.

At one particularly low point Amanda was briefly 'on the streets', thus entailing further connections with clients and the police.

Besides all the family, friends and other informal connections, there are, in Amanda's case, a whole host of links with people and organisations that have been drawn in to trying to help Amanda. They include the teacher responsible for final-year pastoral care at Amanda's school. She became involved because of Amanda's increasing truancy rate and the possibility that a procedure for suspending a pupil from school might need to be brought into play. She had met on one occasion with Amanda's parents and was, therefore, aware that her behaviour was causing problems at home as well. This teacher had tried to form a relationship in which Amanda would feel free to talk about what was going on, but Amanda was not forthcoming and that did not happen. That early, abortive, helping relationship with its twin themes of counselling and control, which is so familiar in professional addiction encounters, was to be repeated many times over in one way or another in the years that followed. What happened when Amanda went to college was not dissimilar. Since then there has been an escalation in the number of professional helpers with whom Amanda has come into contact. Most, broadly speaking, fall into one or other of two arms of the state: health and social services. The, by now, dense network of health connections comprises both primary and specialist care. There are several parts of the local national health services with which Amanda is now very familiar. One is the local general hospital where she has visited the accident and emergency (A&E) department on several occasions and one of the wards to which she was admitted for two nights following an overdose. The latter she found a traumatic experience involving brief contacts with a large number of hospital staff, all playing their parts but none apparently in a position to make any constructive comment on the underlying reason for her being there. Most treated her professionally but unsympathetically and sometimes with a degree of open hostility. The A&E department, on the other hand, is now familiar and not entirely unpleasant. Although Amanda's attendance there is always associated with pain and discomfort of some kind, in some ways it is like a haven, warm and dry in winter, staffed by people who seem efficient at their jobs and, mostly, remarkably pleasant and welcoming considering the nature of their work. She now recognises and is recognised by some of the staff: one of the receptionists and a triage nurse, for example (although she has never quite fathomed what 'triage' means).

Located elsewhere in the town, and, as far as she can tell, unconnected to the hospital – although she supposes that there is some link behind the scenes – is the substance misuse treatment service. This is where she was referred for treatment by her primary care general medical practitioner (GP) and where she has now been attending for almost two years. It is here that she has seen a number of consultant and junior psychiatrists and a clinical psychologist and community psychiatric nurses (CPNs) for assessment and at intervals for monitoring and follow-up. It is here that methadone was first prescribed. Most of her meetings here have been quite formal, involving many questions and tests, plus discussions about her current level of drug use, what amount of methadone she should be prescribed and how continued monitoring should be arranged. Some of the professional people she has met she has liked more than others but the one that sticks in her mind is the series of sessions she had with a trainee clinical psychologist: a young woman, not very different from Amanda in age, who seemed to understand Amanda and with whom she got on well. But she was in training and her placement with the drug team came to an end. After a while responsibility for her repeat prescriptions moved to her primary care surgery. There Amanda saw her own GP, and occasionally other doctors when hers was away or unavailable, and from time to time, a CPN who specialised in drug misuse and who took a clinic at the surgery every other week. Amanda found this team of professionals supportive, as did her parents. Mercy and Gilbert had been to see one of the practice doctors whom they found very sympathetic. This particular doctor, perhaps because of her own family experience of a serious drinking problem, took a special interest in family members trying to cope with a close relative's drug or drink problem. They were also impressed that the specialist CPN had taken the trouble to visit them at home to explain the rationale for methadone treatment and to try to reassure them that Amanda was making progress despite the continued use of heroin from time to time. One member of the team with whom Amanda struck up a warm relationship was the pharmacist, who ran the small pharmacy attached to the surgery and from whom Amanda collected her prescribed medication. This he did with a smile, without the least hint of disapproval, but sometimes with a brief piece of helpful advice and always with time for a bit of chat – something that seemed to be lacking in the case of all the other professionals that Amanda met.

Professional connections and controls multiplied once it became known that Amanda was pregnant. As well as adding the maternity hospital to the list of health service facilities with which she was familiar, and midwives and other antenatal staff added to her list of professional contacts, there was now added the other major arm of the statutory services, the social services department of the local government authority. Unlike in the various health services she had contact with where care was more in evidence than control – although even there Amanda had felt that the threat of coercion was never far below the surface – now, in her dealings with social workers, she felt it was the coercive element that held sway. Although she liked several of the social workers she met and had appreciated the difficult job they were trying to do, their suspicions about her adequacy as a mother were obvious to her and she felt that her capacity to be a good parent was under-estimated and not properly acknowledged. In the end, the question of arrangements for her son's care was to be decided by a family drug court, a new service that was being trialled in Amanda's area at that time. This brought Amanda into relations with a large number of other professionals who played the roles of case assessors for the court, advocates for the child's interests, those who could provide support for Amanda, including further treatment for her drug misuse during the nine months of regular contact with the court, a parent mentor, and, finally, the judge who would be responsible for the final decision. Taking part was voluntary, but Amanda cooperated on the grounds that the chances of retaining custody would be greater if she did. She was impressed by the care with which the whole procedure was explained to her and the options laid out before her. Amanda was most impressed with her judge – having the same judge throughout was considered to be one of the great merits of the scheme – who was a charismatic and authoritative figure who seemed to take a genuine interest in her and her young son, even asking on one occasion if he might see a photograph of the boy.

Thus Amanda had direct dealings with a quite extraordinarily large number of professional people who formed the care and control system. But what of the systems beyond Amanda's and her family's immediate experience? How many meetings must there have been, involving how many different people – largely professional people and therefore of a different 'class' than Amanda and her family – to set up and maintain health and social service systems for the care and control of drug-addicted people in Amanda's area? How many 'drug action teams' or other 'joint planning committees' had there been? How much effort, on the part of how many people, must have been involved in working out the details of the new primary health responsibilities for the treatment of drug misuse or the new family drug court? 'Behind the scenes' though it may be, this complex of overlapping sub-systems has a direct bearing on how the drug problems of Amanda and others like her are dealt with. And that is just on the local level. At the national level there are civil servants in the health and interior ministries who have been dealing with drug misuse as a major responsibility. The health department works closely with an agency it set up specially to advise services on what is currently considered to be best practice in the treatment of drug misuse. In the last few years, while Amanda's drug problem was becoming more serious and her involvement in local services deeper, a sizeable number of experts in the field had sat on or given advice to relevant committees, working parties and commissions. Amongst their products were a major update of the government's strategy for the management of drug misuse, a report from the national treatment advisory body on the involvement in treatment of affected family members like Mercy and Gilbert – 'carers' as the report preferred to call them – and the help they needed for themselves and a report on the whole issue prepared by a special committee of a long-established and much-respected independent national society. Of course, Amanda knew that drugs and drug addiction were matters of national debate and concern but she might have been surprised to know how many people nationally, the great and the good amongst them, were directly concerned with problems of a kind she had been experiencing and who were therefore, indirectly, concerned about her personal case.

What of the government itself? Its position on 'drugs' is about as different from its stance on David's preferred drug – alcohol – as it is possible to be. Heroin, cocaine and ecstasy are all in the highest 'A' category of drugs, which are judged to carry the greatest danger of misuse. Their production, supply and use are illegal and carry quite severe maximum penalties. The outlawing, some would say demonising even, of a range of different drugs in this way, so different from government encouragement of the commercial supply of alcohol, is highly controversial. Many experts, and more than one national campaign group, believe it is crazy and counterproductive, amplifying any deviance which can be attributed to the drugs themselves. The recent sacking by the government of the chairman of its committee of advisors on drugs policy was media headline news in Amanda's country for several weeks. He and his committee had dared to suggest that alcohol and tobacco were far more dangerous than some of the supposedly most 'dangerous' drugs: ecstasy, for example, was in their view less dangerous than a number of sporting activities. The government appears intransigent in its refusal to openly debate the possibility of a major change of policy in this area. For one thing, its hands are tied by international policies; for example, those enshrined in the United Nation's Single Convention, driven, some would say, by policies insisted upon by successive US administrations and their commitment to a 'war on drugs'. Furthermore, it is generally considered by politicians in Amanda's country to be political suicide to be seen even to suggest that the tough approach on drugs might be softened.

Although all this activity takes place in locations remote from Amanda's town, she would surely have been affected by the rhetoric which surrounds illicit drug use emanating from high places in her own country and abroad. Drug use and misuse is so controversial, patterns of drug use changing so much – for example, cocaine use was nothing like so widespread when Amanda was a small child as it was a decade or so later – and the problem of tackling drug misuse so difficult and uncertain that the official discourses on the subject have changed markedly in Amanda's lifetime. Not very long ago, before Amanda was born, when drug dependence had been accepted as a form of disease, the dominant discourse was one of need to make treatment available, largely on a voluntary basis. The rise of HIV/AIDS ushered in a new era dominated by the discourse of 'harm reduction', aimed not so much at curing drug dependence but rather the minimisation of the harm associated with drug 'misuse'. As Amanda has got older the wheel is turning again. Although it is not clear where this is leading, some detect a hardening of attitude towards 'drug misusers'. No longer are they seen principally as victims of an insidious disease process which takes them unawares and for which they deserve treatment in the same way that other ill citizens merit treatment – although the vestiges of that position remain. More dominant than before, according to some commentators, is the view of drug misusers as people who are a major source of harm to others, including their families but more generally to society at large. If there is any truth in these observations, then drug misusing mothers like Amanda are likely to feel the ripples as much as anyone. If members of society need protecting from drug misusers, then the young children of drug-misusing mothers are likely to be highest on the list of those who need protection. Amanda's world may be far from the forums where drug policy is made but the ties that bind them together are very real ones.

There exists, of course, another extensive set of power connections which supports Amanda's drug use by giving her access to the drugs she consumes and to the culture which encourages drug use. Like the state-supported systems of relations around the treatment and control of drug misuse, the connections which support or encourage drug use extend from the very local to the utterly remote: in Amanda's case from her street to some of the most remote, rural parts of countries on other continents. Not unlike David and his wife's limited knowledge of the drinks trade, other than its local outlets in their village or nearby, Amanda's knowledge of how her drugs of consumption are supplied is also confined to the local, and her parents' knowledge is even hazier. Amanda's mother and sister have had fleeting contact with people from whom Amanda purchases Class A drugs. In fact, for some time there has been a thriving market for such drugs in the town and a number of people are making money from their sale. These are all local people, many under the age of 21. Some are not users of the kinds of drugs they are selling, whereas others are selling in order to fund their own drug use, sometimes making a small profit in addition. Most of this group are what are sometimes referred to as 'runners', getting by through selling relatively small quantities for the more serious 'sellers' who are in effect running small, illegal drugs supply businesses. Not all local illicit drug markets are so locally integrated, but in Amanda's town quite a large number of people were making a living out of supplying dangerous drugs and it could be argued that the local community was benefiting in some ways. Some played very minor roles; for example, earning small amounts of cash by stashing drugs or driving vehicles. Some families benefited from the income, and a number of local businesses benefited from the circulation of money from drug sales.

Amanda's experience of the drug market has been a very mixed one. She is constantly on the alert in order to protect herself from being cheated and abused. There have been times when she has dealt with the same trustworthy supplier for months. At other times she has dealt with a succession of dealers who have 'ripped me off' or who have made her feel very unsafe. She says that, although you cannot generalise, when you take the kinds of drugs she is taking you are bound to come into contact with 'some quite nasty people'. She has had some very unpleasant experiences with men in the course of obtaining and using drugs: although not all are sexually predatory or interested in having a relationship in which the man is very much in control, including in control of their mutual drug use, Amanda has found that many are. For someone as involved in the local street illicit drug scene as Amanda is, life is dangerous and demeaning in other ways as well. She is always vigilant about the presence of the police, who she views as constantly harassing her and other drug users, very often making things worse by disrupting a safe and reliable drug sales network which had been getting established. To other drug users, dealers and the police can be added a procession of passers-by, shopkeepers and others who at best ignore her but who are regularly rude and abusive.

At earlier stages of her drug using career her 'supply' connections were of a different kind. It is a common observation that some forms of illicit drug-taking had become 'normalised' by the time Amanda was a teenager. Most young people of her era had at least been offered some illicit drug or another and most said that it was relatively easy to obtain drugs such as cannabis, amphetamines or ecstasy. The 'rave scene' was in full swing. Officially illegal though they were, the taking of a number of the kinds of drugs that Amanda had taken was supported by a relatively tolerant youth culture in much the same way as David's drinking was supported by a culture highly tolerant of alcohol consumption, albeit in his case one that was legal and historically of long standing. Besides the general youth culture and the large numbers of Amanda's friends and acquaintances who were part of it, there were a number of individuals whose connections were important ones because they played a significant role in the development of Amanda's drug use. A close school friend, like Amanda, had been more than averagely keen to experiment and they had done so together. Amanda and three college friends took their experimentation further, deviating from the general norm by starting to use cocaine on a weekly basis. The subsequent paths of members of that friendship group diverged markedly thereafter. One quickly tired of the group's drug-taking activities, parted company with the others, went on to do well scholastically, left the area and was last heard of in a high-flying job in the financial sector. The remaining two, like Amanda, became further involved in drug-taking. One of those two drew the line at injecting drugs and has subsequently cut back on the numbers of different kinds of drug she is taking and the frequency of use. In fact, she has since played a significant role in Amanda's helping network. She has made it her business to keep in touch with Amanda and at times has played an important linking role between Amanda and her family; for example, she has been to see Amanda's mother and sister, reassuring them that Amanda was safe and encouraging Amanda to let her family know where she is and how she was faring. The fourth member of her college group went on to become an injecting drug user: it was her, in fact, who initiated Amanda into injecting, showing her how to do it cleanly and safely. Mention should also be made of the father of Amanda's baby. Like a number of Amanda's boyfriends of recent years, he is what Mercy and Gilbert describe as a 'thoroughly bad influence' – also a college drop-out with only occasional employment and a regular drug user, although not an injector or user of heroin.

Like the drinks trade, the illegal trade in drugs with addiction potential is international. Its illegality and its lack of regulation renders supply unstable. New, more powerful forms of drug, such as crack cocaine or the skunk variety of marijuana, become available without regulation; purity and price fluctuate, taking consumers unawares; and supply routes and methods of transportation vary in response to official efforts at interception. For example, recently Amanda's cocaine, which started its journey to her town in Colombia, came via a circuitous route through Mexico and the Caribbean. The effects of the illicit drug trade on producing and transporting countries like Colombia and Mexico could hardly be greater. All along the supply route the attractions of dealing in a commodity which is of such high demand and for which those in richer countries will pay so much are obvious. Sometimes unscrupulous and violent criminals are prepared to take great risks for enormous profits. Sometimes it is a case of ordinary, poor people playing a small role because there are few or no alternatives for making a living. Very often, by all accounts, the system is maintained by virtue of the purchase of the connivance of so many people – police and politicians included. All this may seem a long way away from Amanda's drug use and her parents' and helpers' concerns about her. But the links are clear: the drugs she buys on the streets of her town have come to her through a number of hands and livelihoods and profits are being made. The nature of those links is also a matter of the utmost controversy on a political and policy-making level. Western countries, particularly the USA in relation to countries in Latin America, have been inclined to put the blame on supply countries such as Colombia. Pressure has been put on the latter to act more firmly to curtail supply. Sometimes more active steps have been taken; for example, spraying of crops that provide the raw materials for drugs such as Amanda's cocaine or providing military support if it is believed that armed anti-government groups are heavily involved in the drugs trade. Governments and others in countries such as Colombia have been arguing back, pointing out that the demand for drugs such as cocaine in richer countries is having a devastating effect on crime in their countries and even on the prospects of achieving democracy free of widespread corruption. What is the relationship, then, between Amanda's drug addiction and police corruption in a distant country which she has never visited? Can she, and others who share her problems, be held accountable for the surge in the homicide rate in Mexico? Or is she a victim of the greed and thoughtlessness of all the people along the routes via which her drugs have reached her, including the peasant farmer, the bent policeman, the drivers, ship owners and individual 'mules', the big-time crooks, and small-time 'runners' in her own town? There are probably no simple answers to those questions but the connections, involving organisations and individuals – powerful and powerless – are certainly there.

Caroline: a case of gambling addiction

Caroline is addicted to playing gambling machines. She first came across 'fruit machines' as a 14 year-old in the 1970s when the dangers of playing such machines were less recognised and control on young people's access to high-street gambling arcades was very lax. Although regulations have been tightened since then, Caroline still sees young people playing in the arcades who look well under the 18 year old age limit. She didn't play the machines much herself at first; it was mainly the boys who played and the girls who watched them, but at that age she found the local arcades exciting. They were places in which to hang out with friends of both sexes, free of adult supervision, in a place that parents would have disapproved of had they known. Some of the boys were older and appeared very knowledgeable and confident about playing the machines. They seemed to her sophisticated. They played fast and were constantly either cursing the machines when they lost or sharing with those around them their joy at winning – mostly small amounts but quite often sums which seemed large in Caroline's eyes. It was hard not to participate in the ups and downs of fortune and the accompanying roller coaster of emotions. She sensed that she should be disapproving of it all but she was caught up in the excitement. Sometimes the boys let the girls play and a few times she won small amounts. But an event occurred which, looking back, Caroline believes was significant, when her grandfather took her to his local cricket club where there was a machine that offered larger jackpot prizes than the ones she had seen in the arcades. Her grandfather let her have a go and no one at the club stopped her. As luck would have it she won the jackpot, £25, a huge amount at that time for someone of her age. She remembers being the centre of attention as club members gathered round and congratulated her and her grandfather. Her parents, when she got home, were not altogether pleased but kept their reservations to themselves, reassured that Caroline would put the money towards her savings. That she did, but she now believes that the damage was done. She subscribes to the theory which she has read about; that a big early win is an important factor in the development of a gambling habit.

Caroline believes that her potential addiction to gambling machines was in a kind of limbo state for the rest of her teenage and young adult life, held in check by the demands of everyday life, particularly having a family. She was happy at home and school, taking a secretarial course after leaving school at 16, enjoying the world of work and boyfriends, marrying her husband in her early twenties. Throughout her twenties gambling was mostly far from her mind, taken up as she was with making a home, caring for her daughter Karen and, as time went on, getting back into work via a number of part-time office, factory or cleaning jobs. But the attraction of the machines must have been lodged somewhere in her subconscious and from time to time would come to the surface on the frequent occasions when the family were at the seaside or passing through a motorway service or railway station where machines were easily accessed. All her family – parents, brother, husband and daughter Karen as she grew up – joked that Caroline had 'a thing' about fruit machines. Their attraction for her, which no one else in the family shared, was obvious. But the role of gambling in her life was strictly circumscribed. Caroline was in her late thirties before that started to change. For the first time that she could remember, her life had been taking a turn for the worse. In particular, her relationship with her husband had cooled and finally collapsed when she discovered he had been having an affair – probably not the first – and things between them turned nasty. After her husband had hit her on a number of occasions, and Caroline had agonised about whether to leave him, the latter was resolved when he announced that he was leaving to live with 'the other woman'. There were few compensations in other areas of her life at that time since Karen was now in her late teens with a serious boyfriend of her own and requiring much less of her mother's attention and Caroline had only one part-time job which was not particularly fulfilling. She had tried to keep what had been going on in her marriage as secret as possible and therefore had little support from other family or friends. It was around that time that she started to spend more time in an arcade in the local town, a mere five minutes from home by bus – and a 30-minute walk back if all her money had gone into the machines as was often the case.

Caroline's addiction developed quickly from then on. From an activity which had been limited in terms of frequency of occurrence, time devoted to it, and proportion of income spent on it, her habit rapidly escalated to the point at which she was playing machines virtually every day, often spending several hours playing, and in the process losing in the region of 20–50 per cent of her now quite-limited income. It was not long before she gave up her part-time work which only worsened the impact of gambling on her finances.

Caroline's feelings towards gambling machines and the arcades in which they were to be found also changed completely. From being a source of positive excitement, her gambling was now driven by a mix of escapism and sheer habit. From the moment she put her coat on to go for the bus into town, her mind was on the prospect of playing. The nearer she got to the arcade the more focused her attention became, a focus that was heightened further once she was surrounded by the atmosphere of the arcade with its insistent and familiar sights and sounds. Once she was playing her attention was almost total. If you had seen Caroline playing a machine, as Caroline's brother John did later on when attempting to rescue her, you might be excused for thinking that she had entered a different state of consciousness, so concentrated was her attention on playing and so irritable would she become if any attempt were made to interrupt her. Indeed, in more reflective mode, well away from the machines, Caroline herself described her state when playing as a 'hypnotic' one, as if she was in some kind of 'trance'. Although it might be said that she was now greatly 'attracted' to her favourite arcade, she would not now describe it as an attractive place. In fact, her feelings about it were predominantly those of anger and dislike. She despised the arcade attendants and directed her anger at the machines, often swearing at them and sometimes hitting or kicking them which provoked a telling off from the attendant. She was even temporarily barred from the arcade after one such incident. She sought out other locations where gambling machines could be played, finding such places without difficulty. There were three arcades in the small town and she also found several pubs, a bingo club and the railway station, all of which had machines. It was a bit later on that she discovered that the three local betting shops – places that had never interested her in the past and which she had never imagined that, as a woman on her own, she would enter – also housed gambling machines, including a new type on which you could play casino type games such as roulette. Even the 'fruit' machines had changed since Caroline was a teenager. The machines she remembers from that era now seemed incredibly slow and simple. The boys whom she looked up to in those days were convinced that they had the skill to 'beat the machines' although it was really evident to everyone that they couldn't. Developments in machine technology since then had encouraged this illusion of control. Long gone were the days when all you could do was pull a lever – hence the term 'one-armed bandit' – and wait for the fruit symbols to come to rest. Now Caroline found there was a variety of knobs that could be pressed, options that could be taken, routes that could be followed, all giving her the spurious sense that she was on the verge of a big pay out and that her choices made a material difference. The stimulating noises the machines made, the colourful fairground appearance of the machines, and the alluring signs in the arcade window all played their part in keeping her hooked.

Members of Caroline's immediate family eventually realised what was going on and became seriously concerned about her machine gambling. But it had taken many months before they reached that position. Brother John, who lived an hour's drive away, and daughter Karen, living nearby but with her own life to lead, both started to notice a change in Caroline. But for a long time they were uncertain about what they thought they were noticing, did not share their mounting worries with each other, and certainly did not attribute the changes to gambling. The first thing they were both aware of was an uncharacteristic elusiveness. Sometimes the phone was not answered at a time of day when they would have expected her to be at home. On occasions she turned down invitations without explanation and at other times she was late for meetings and once or twice failed to appear, all of which was very unlike the sister and mother they had known all their lives. They started to share their worries when they were all meeting together for a meal in a local pub – Caroline, John and his family, Karen and her partner, Ian – and Caroline got up before the meal was over, making a flimsy excuse that she had an appointment elsewhere. It was then that the family realised that they had all been worried about Caroline and all had rather similar experiences to share. From then on Karen and her uncle kept a closer eye on Caroline and regularly shared their thoughts. They realised that their anxieties went beyond surprise at her odd behaviour. They both thought she had changed in ways that were difficult to be sure about. Were they right in thinking that she had lost weight? From being someone who had always been very careful about her appearance, had they noticed that she was letting her standards slip? Wasn't she more irritable than usual, smiling less, frowning more? She seemed often to be on edge, distracted. Could she be depressed? Karen tried to spend more time with her mother, offering her support and trying to find out if anything was the matter. She and Ian, who were planning their wedding, discussed it together and concluded that Caroline had not got over the failure of her marriage, was finding it difficult to get back into work, and was therefore going through a low point in her life from which she would soon recover. That theory was quickly shattered by a number of events. First, Karen by chance saw her mother going into the local arcade. Later that day, after several unsuccessful attempts to reach her at home, Karen mentioned to her mother that she had seen her and was surprised to get an evasive response delivered in an almost aggressive tone. Not long after, when visiting her mother, Karen was stopped by Caroline's next door neighbour, who asked Karen if her mother was alright. She had also noticed changes in Caroline's behaviour, mood and appearance and had been very surprised that Caroline had asked to borrow some money from her and, despite promises, had not paid it back. When Karen told Ian about this, she was alarmed and somewhat annoyed to learn that, without telling her, Ian had also lent his future mother-in-law some money and had not had it back. Things escalated rapidly from then on. Caroline's guilty secret about the time and money she was spending playing gambling machines was now out in the open. Things turned out to be much worse than had been feared. Karen and John confronted Caroline together. The extent of her gambling losses became clear – amounts now totalling several thousand pounds. She had lost weight, and no wonder, since she was regularly skipping meals. She had tried to stop the gambling but without success and was now clearly depressed, admitting tearfully that she had entertained thoughts of suicide. By chance Karen found out that her mother had been dismissed from her last two jobs because of bad time-keeping. At her last place of work there had also been the suspicion that she was responsible for money that had gone missing although it was impossible to prove that Caroline was to blame. The family urged Caroline to go and see her GP and to contact Gamblers Anonymous. She accepted the former suggestion, and was prescribed anti-depressants, but the family was not convinced that she had talked to her GP about her gambling. The latter continued but, the problem having been identified, discussing it with Caroline became no easier. She became, if anything, more defensive and elusive about it and the family was left uncertain from week to week whether Caroline was trying to overcome the problem and, if so, to what extent she was being successful. Meanwhile, they felt awkward and embarrassed about mentioning the subject and Caroline offered them no encouragement to do so.

What help was available for Caroline and others like her with the problem of gambling addiction? Very little, as it turns out. Although the extent of services for drug or alcohol addiction in Caroline's country is often criticised, the number of specialist helpers dedicated to Caroline's problem is negligible compared to the numbers potentially available to David or Amanda. This is despite the fact that the figures for the prevalence of illicit drug and gambling problems in Caroline's country are quite similar (the prevalence of alcohol problems is significantly higher). Caroline's brother John made it his business to search for sources of help for his sister. He found a national charitable organisation which provided a telephone helpline for people with gambling problems and for family and others who were concerned. Through using that helpline he discovered that the same organisation was promoting a counselling service in different parts of the country, offering training and support to organisations – mostly those already helping people with alcohol or drug problems – to add a component of gambling counselling to their existing work. Unfortunately, their part of the country was one not yet covered by that scheme. He was also told about two residential rehabilitation houses for people with gambling problems but neither was anywhere near where Caroline lived and, in any case, residential care did not seem appropriate. Under the umbrella of the state health service, a new treatment centre had recently opened in the capital, but this was far away and not practically very helpful. He found a self-help website operated from a centre in another country and a local university that was planning to develop such a website but could give no assurance about when it would be up and running. John at one point screwed up his courage and phoned the government health department directly. His inquiry was treated with great courtesy but he was passed around from person to person, eventually to be told that gambling addiction was not something that was currently a priority for the department. There had been some moves by one or two people to change that situation but they had since been moved on to other parts of the department and, since there had recently been a change of government, everyone was now waiting to see what their political masters' priorities would be before making any further moves on this subject. John felt he had learnt something in the process about how the world works which he had not previously been aware of but was aware that his call to the department had not helped Caroline. His call to Gamblers Anonymous – after some difficulty tracking down someone locally he could speak to – was much more productive. Yes, Caroline's problem was one with which they were very familiar and she would be most welcome at any GA meeting. A meeting was held regularly in Caroline's county town, not difficult for her to access by public transport. Indeed someone from GA would come to Caroline's home, if she would like that, to tell her about GA and invite her personally.

With Karen's support, John put the options to Caroline. At first her view was that she could conquer the problem on her own, indeed that she was already doing so. This threw her family into indecision, already uncertain whether they were doing the right thing, perhaps making a mountain out of a mole hill, perhaps interfering in a way that might be unhelpful in the long run. Perhaps Caroline was right and she was getting the problem under control herself, and perhaps that was the best way. She did agree to go and see her GP but, like most hard-pressed GPs, Caroline's had not knowingly come face-to-face with a patient's gambling problem before and was not aware of any treatment for it. In any case, Caroline was ambivalent about openly talking to her GP about it. Quite apart from her embarrassment about it, she wondered whether, if her GP knew she was a compulsive gambler, it would affect her doctor's view of her as a person and whether she would forever after be in disgrace in the eyes of the medical profession. She was, therefore, relieved when her tentative aside about her gambling was not followed-up and the rest of the 15 minutes she spent with her GP – she thought she had probably taken up too much of his time – focused on her mental state and whether she was finding anti-depressant medication useful.

When it became clear that Caroline was still struggling to control her gambling, the family kept up their encouragement of the idea that she should take up the GA offer. She did not fancy the idea of a home visit but, much to the family's relief, she did go along to a number of GA meetings. Reluctant to probe too much but increasingly concerned that she get help, Karen and John tried to keep abreast of whether she was continuing to attend and with what effect. At first the signs were good but it was not long before they felt disappointed and let down when they realised that Caroline had only attended two or three meetings. When they finally pinned her down about it she told them that the attenders at the meetings were nearly all men and that she had found it difficult to identify with them and their problems. Amongst them had been big sports betters, casino gamblers or, even in one case, someone who gambled on financial markets. Several had debts which seemed to her colossal and she felt she was not in their league. No one ever said so directly but she felt most of them thought her gambling was stupid and trivial.

Caroline, like tens of thousands of other people, was experiencing a loss of control over her life with very little understanding on the part of those services which might have been expected to be able to help, about the nature of her powerlessness. Yet, as was the case for Amanda and for David, the number of people with whom she came into contact and who were touched in some way by her gambling addiction added up to a considerable total. To members of her family, her next door neighbour, several employers and fellow workers, her GP and members of GA could be added those who dealt with her in the course of her application for and receipt of social welfare benefits and, later on after a period of homelessness, a range of people in the local authority housing department and at the housing association through which she obtained a small flat.

But what of the broader picture? John has certainly wondered about this. The little he has heard from Caroline about the places in which she plays gambling machines, plus his frustrating experience with the health department, has left him angry. It appears to him that money is being taken off his sister in an exploitative and uncaring way, destroying her health and happiness and upsetting the family in the process, without anyone in any authority caring that this is happening. He was further angered when he read in the paper about the dispute caused by the promotion to the upper house of parliament of a prominent donor to one of the country's main political parties, widely accused of living abroad as a tax exile, and who, it turned out, had made much of his money in the gambling machine business. The latter aspect had not been one that had been brought out in the newspaper articles that John read, which just fuelled his conclusion that 'no one cares' when it came to his sister and others with her problem. Caroline has told him that she recognises a number of people, some of them youngsters, who are regularly to be found in the arcades and who are clearly spending a lot of their money there. Her brother has spent time searching for information on the internet, has written several letters to local papers, one of which was published, and has wondered whether he is getting too obsessed with the subject.

John has started to find out a number of interesting things about the broader picture. For one thing, he has discovered something about changes that have taken place in the provision of gambling and its regulation. It seems to him that the government has been 'hell bent on helping to promote more gambling', has given into the gambling providing industry all the way along the line, has thrown caution to the wind and left people vulnerable to exploitation and without any help. He discovered, for example, that a government commission of the 1950s had actually recommended that gambling machines should be illegal, but the government of the day had not heeded that advice. An Act of 1960 allowed machines, poorly regulated, to proliferate in arcades, pubs, private clubs, bingo halls, fish-and-chip shops and elsewhere. He has read how the government got involved in the 1990s, not just in encouraging regulated gambling but also in promoting it themselves when it set up the country's national lottery. He has then read a lot about the gambling review that was set up by the government at the turn of the millennium and how it was instructed by government to suggest ways in which impediments to the expansion of commercial gambling should be relieved, how it was chaired by an ex-top civil servant whose pro-market views were well-known, and how while the committee was deliberating the lead government department for gambling was changed from the interior ministry, concerned with national order and justice, to the culture and sport department. He has learned that the gambling machines which his sister came across in betting offices – on which casino type games can be played – were a source of controversy for some time but had now been legalised. He has learned something about how complicated is the regulation of gambling machines and how many different categories of machines there are, varying in maximum stakes and prizes and in terms of how many are permitted in what types of location. He wonders how a member of the public can be expected to understand the differences. He has learned that his country is about the only one which permits children to play on gambling machines, albeit of the type where the maximum stakes and prizes are low. He remembers that Caroline started playing machines when she was a young teenager and again he thinks 'who cares?' when it comes to the new generation of youngsters. He has seen evidence of how the association of machine manufacturers has lobbied to have this national anomaly maintained, how arcade proprietors are already campaigning to have the permitted numbers of machines increased from those laid down in the present regulations, that gambling premises licence holders are finding ways of getting round the regulations, for example, by splitting their premises into two, and that machine designers and manu-facturers are all the time developing new, more attractive machines. He has come to appreciate how colossal and global is the gambling industry. He has read of the aggressive tactics used in other countries; for example, by those who manufacture the 'poker machines' or 'pokies' in Australia. It has made his blood boil to read some of the statements they have put out to support the argument that the number of people with gambling problems is tiny and that those with such problems are, in any case, a group of already very disturbed people who, if it were not for their gambling, would be doing something worse. As a supporter of the European Union, he has been dis-mayed to realise how the gambling industry sees the European market as a potential goldmine and how determined they are to undermine existing policies which individual member countries had in place and which serve to protect their citizens from exposure to forms of gambling which had not previously existed to any great extent or at all in their countries.

Caroline's brother, John, is perhaps unusual in having found out so much about the connections of power which bear on his sister's addiction problem. But he has, of course, only scratched the surface. There is much he does not know about the international reach of the gambling industries, about technological innovations in the planning which will increase the exposure to gambling of people like himself and his sister and the next generation, about the intense industry lobbying to which parliamentarians in his county are exposed or about policy discussions which civil servants and advisors are having which will affect the dangers which ordinary people face. In any case, like all affected family members, his prime focus is the relative whose addiction he is concerned about, not the wider picture about which he has discovered a little. That is even more the case for Caroline. When John tells her about something of the way power is exercised in the world of gambling, she briefly shares his anger and agrees 'something should be done about it'. But her attention and her family's, too, is on her behaviour. They may have glimpsed part of the truth about where power lies and how it works, but it is hard for them and millions like them not to quickly return to the default assumption that when it comes to apportioning responsibility for addiction, it is the Carolines, and the Davids and Amandas who carry the can.

CHAPTER TWO

How addiction erodes free agency

Power and its distortion as the book's main theme

It is in this chapter that I want to begin to develop the idea central to the book: that addiction, with all its social connections, may be understood as a phenomenon associated with serious distortions of the relationships of power between people. That idea may, on first hearing, seem a mysterious one. The term 'power' is mostly familiar in the context of politics, social movements or matters military. But, of course, it is a term used much more widely than that and one that has a long history of usage in philosophy and the social sciences. Throughout the rest of the book I shall draw on ideas about power borrowed from a number of different disciplines. From political science comes the idea of the concentration of power and the question, hotly debated in the 1960s, of whether power (principally in the USA) was largely wielded by relatively small numbers of people – the elites – or whether society was more pluralistic and power more widely dispersed (Dahl 1961). Since then political and social theorists have shown us how complex the concept of power is (Clegg 1989; Lukes 2005). For one thing, power's scope is variable, some power-holders compared to others exercise power over far larger numbers of other people and/or over a greater number of domains of other people's lives (Wrong 1979). Power is sometimes viewed as legitimate, accepted as functional for the social group, thought of as serving collective interests, and often referred to using terms such as authority, leadership or expertise. But power can also be exercised coercively or manipulatively, more obviously serving the interests of the power-holder and contrary to the interests of the powerless.

A leading theme has been the way in which power, to be most effective and least resisted, is masked in one way or another. Power theorists have written about several different types or faces of power – three or even four in number – varying from the power to control outcomes in situations of overt conflict (the first type) to other, more subtle ways in which power is exercised (Servian 1996; Lukes 2005). The latter include exercising power by keeping 'off the agenda' any questions or issues which would expose or challenge positions of power (this is the second type). The third face of power, more subtle still, involves the shaping of people's attitudes and preferences in such a way that the powerless accept things as they are and the true state of power is hidden behind an ideology to which most subscribe most of the time without question. Some theorists wish to distinguish a fourth form of power, more covert still, which turns the powerless into their own agents of control. This is the power from within, rather than power from above, which Foucault and other post-modern social theorists have written so much about.

Power has been surprisingly neglected in my own discipline, psychology, but there are encouraging signs suggesting that is changing. Social psychologists have studied the effects of power differences on perception and action and have sought to apply ideas drawn from the theories of social dominance, social identity, and system justification (Guinote and Vescio 2010). Power is, of course, central to both feminist and post-colonial theory, research and action, and ideas of power and powerlessness are now key to the growing field of community psychology (Orford 2008a). The comparatively recently developed concept of human capabilities – promoted by the economist Amartya Sen (1985) and the philosopher Martha Nussbaum (2000) – is also attractive from a psychological point of view because it deals with the way in which people's circumstances, particularly their positions of power or powerlessness, affect their capabilities to lead a full life of their own choosing.

There is no one agreed definition of power. It has often been defined in something like the following terms: A has power over B if A can influence B's behaviour more than vice versa; or, to put it another way, if A has the greater influence on the outcome of their interaction; or if B is more dependent on A than the other way around, or, expressed in yet another way, if their encounter serves A's interests more than those of B. But any such definition is immediately open to criticism, not least because it seems not to do sufficient justice to the dynamic, ever-changing picture of relative power, nor to the way in which the exercise of power is constantly contested and resisted. Such definitions do not sufficiently reflect the social context of power. Furthermore, whenever people's interests are invoked, we stumble into the endless but always intriguing arguments about what people's interests really are, whether people know where their true interests lie, and debates about consciousness-raising and false consciousness. These are all ideas and controversies upon which I shall draw in this and later chapters. What is never in doubt, however, is the importance of power. The English word derives from the Latin *potere*, 'to be able'. There are obvious areas of overlap with other social science concepts such as status and domination, and with concepts that have been much more prominent in psychology, such as control and efficacy. Those who write about power are fond of referring to the philosopher Bertrand Russell, who famously opined that power was *the* central concept in the social sciences, akin to energy in physics.

Addiction undermines personal agency

But why try to use power as a central organising idea for understanding addiction? Perhaps it is because addiction as a concept and as a subject for study and treatment has been appropriated by the biological and medical sciences, at least from the mid twentieth century, if not earlier, that the invocation of power as a core theme may seem novel. In my effort to persuade the reader how apposite it is, I shall begin in this chapter at the centre of the complex networks of addiction connections – with the experiences of those who themselves are addicted.

The argument of this chapter will be that people who experience addiction at first hand, like Amanda, David and Caroline, who we met in Chapter 1, are disempowered by it. That idea, simple though it may sound, is by no means uncontroversial and it will be necessary for me to defend it as I go along against the criticisms of those who may see it as a way of smuggling back into the addiction debate some old and largely discredited notions of, for example, 'enslavement' to drugs or inherent character weakness. There are many definitions of addiction; most of them are unnecessarily complicated or make unwarranted assumptions about causes of addiction. As I argued in my earlier book, *Excessive Appetites* (Orford 2001), addiction, broken down to its essentials, is a strong attachment that has formed to a particular class of object of consumption – an attachment sufficiently strong that the person concerned now finds it difficult to curtail consumption despite the fact that it is causing harm. Most of us like to think that we are our own masters when it comes to consumption choices. We may of course over-estimate the extent to which we are free agents in these matters, but it is reasonable to say that those of us who are lucky enough to have much choice at all are able to micro-manage our own consumption habits. I like a cup of coffee at 11:00 a.m. each day and a glass of wine at 6:00 p.m. – edging towards 5:30 as I get older. Obsessive though some of my friends find this, I believe I would have no difficulty in modifying or completely giving up either of those habits in the face of a relatively minor incentive to do so. That is not the case for David and his alcohol consumption, for Amanda and her drug-taking, or Caroline and her gambling. Their ability to govern their own behaviour has been compromised (some will immediately charge me with adopting a superior tone here, assuming a power position as someone who is in control of himself whilst some others are not, but I hope it will become clear that that is not my view).

The largest group of people who know about that at first hand are not addicted drinkers, drug users or gamblers but rather those who were unlucky enough to begin tobacco smoking as adolescents. One of the best illustrations of that is contained in the findings of a UK Government Social Survey carried out in the 1960s. Amongst other questions, smokers were asked two key ones: *Would you like to give up smoking if you could do so easily?* and *Have you ever tried to give up smoking altogether?* If the answer to either question was positive, the respondent was said to be a 'dissonant smoker'; in other words, someone who was continuing to consume in a way that was not consonant with wishes or intentions. In fact, almost half of both the adult and the adolescent smokers surveyed were currently dissonant smokers according to that definition. As the authors of the report put it at the time, 'Dissonant smokers appear to be people who are trapped by the smoking habit, somewhat against their will. The majority of them have in fact tried several times to give up smoking' (McKennell and Thomas 1967, p. 90). Although since then there has been a sea change in public policy regarding smoking in many countries, half a century later tobacco smoking continues to kill people around the world on a massive scale and the erosion of the will to stop smoking once trapped in the habit remains at the heart of the problem.

Another angle on this erosion of power over an aspect of one's own consumption is offered by the strange phenomenon of asking for some external power to bolster or supplement one's own weakened willpower. Let me explain what I mean. When I was a new, young researcher in the addiction field I met a woman who was receiving treatment for her alcohol addiction at the psychiatric hospital I was attached to. She explained to me that she had got off the bus at Camberwell Green, perhaps a quarter to half a mile distant from the hospital. Because she was required to pass at least two public houses on the way, and being lunchtime, the pubs would be open for custom (this was long before legislation permitting much longer opening hours), she had asked a kind policeman to accompany her to the hospital (this was in the days when, wherever you were in London, you could easily find a policeman on the street). Maybe that was a tall story, or at least exaggerated, but I accepted it at the time because it fitted in with ideas that I was beginning to develop about the nature of excessive consumption problems. But we do not need to rely on my early informant. In the world of gambling – now recognised to be potentially addictive – there is the extraordinary case of what has come to be called 'self-exclusion'. This seems to have originated in methods that casino operators have long used for evicting unruly or unwanted players. But it is well known that gamblers sometimes take the initiative *themselves* and ask to be excluded in order to help them resist temptation (Blaszczynski et al. 2007). This developed into formal self-exclusion programmes as part of gambling industry social responsibility policies. Such programmes are now to be found in many states and provinces in North America, Australia, New Zealand, South Africa and several European countries including the UK. The period of exclusion can vary from as little as six months to as much as five years. Sometimes it is family members or other concerned individuals who suggest that a gambler might be excluded, but it is more often the gambler him- or herself who makes the request. In the US state of Missouri, alone, there were over 7,000 such applications in 2004.

Extraordinary though self-exclusion may appear to be, it is just one of a whole variety of actions taken by addicted individuals in an effort to reassert power over their own behaviour. Another gambling example is what is now being termed 'pre-commitment'. Building on the idea that one way of controlling one's consumption behaviour is to set a limit beforehand on how much money or time will be spent, a punter is invited, before playing, to commit to a certain limit which, when reached, triggers some mechanism for preventing play to continue. This is likely to become more familiar to internet gamblers. In Australia, where electronic gambling machines (EGMs) – the so-called poker machines or *pokies* – have caused a lot of problems, the national government has proposed mandatory pre-commitment for EGMs, a move which has been strenuously resisted by proprietors of social clubs which make a lot of money from the machines (Xenophon 2012). Another, perhaps even better known, example of requesting the intervention of an outside power is the use of the anti-alcohol drug Antabuse (disulfiram) in the treatment of alcohol addiction. Not trusting themselves to withstand temptation in the heat of the moment, countless people who, like David, have found their power over the consumption of alcohol diminished have accepted the medical prescription of the drug, which helps them impose control on their drinking by producing very unpleasant psychophysiological symptoms should alcohol be consumed on top of it. Many other examples could be given. In fact, they are all part of a general class of actions which behaviour therapists recommend that people use when trying to reassert their power to manage forms of consumption that have become out of control. In behavioural terms, they are all forms of 'stimulus control': ways of organising the environment so that temptation is reduced. With effort and forethought, people who have lost power over consumption can often re-establish it in this way themselves; but the stronger the addiction, the more likely it is that others will be called upon to assist.

What we have here, then, with each of these examples, is a clear indication of what addiction is. It is a loss of the power, in one specific area of one's life, to make those decisions about consumption which most of us take effortlessly and without thought most of the time. Lest I be misunderstood, let me enter a caveat straightaway. Power is diminished, according to this view, but it is never completely lost. Addiction is, in any case, on a continuum: cases of mild or moderate addiction greatly outnumber those of severe addiction. So the disempowerment associated with addiction is by no means an all-or-none matter. Indeed, if it were, understanding and treatment of addiction might be more straightforward. As it is, the early signs of addiction are not easy to identify with certainty and the process of entrapment which addiction entails tends to take people unawares. The disempowerment associated with addiction is relative. It is important to be clear, therefore, that the view being put forward here is not that certain substances and activities automatically render their consumers utterly powerless, a view that has sometimes been taken in regard to substances like heroin or cocaine. But, misunderstood though addiction has often been in that way, central to the notion of addiction being developed here is the idea of personal agency undermined – the ability to manage one's own behaviour eroded.

Sceptics may ask whether applying the word 'addiction' to the excessive or irresponsible use of a substance such as ketamine – an amphetamine-like anaesthetic causing concern in the UK at the time of writing – or engagement in an activity like internet poker playing is simply to employ a linguistic device that exculpates the actor and at the same time stigmatises the activity. You might just as well say that playing golf is addictive or that I'm addicted to gardening, protests the sceptic. That requires an answer, which is what I shall now attempt to provide. The question is this: what gives certain substances and activities their power over people? Wherein lies their capacity to abrade people's power to govern their own behaviour?

The answer, I believe, is not in essence hard to grasp once a few fundamentals are understood. It boils down to the following three tenets.

1. Those objects of consumption which have the greatest addiction potential are those which have the capacity to bring about a rapid, rewarding change in a person's mood – using that word in a broad sense to mean 'state of mind or feeling'. They generally come in appetising 'pieces' (pints, fixes, bets) and the act of consumption can be repeated, with suitable 'rests', often and almost endlessly.
2. They therefore possess the capacity to create, under the right circumstances, habits of consumption which are strong and not easy to break. Addiction is essentially a disorder of habit.
3. Such habits change over time. Unless checked they entrain processes which serve to amplify and change the habit, rendering it yet more harmful and difficult to curtail.

Those are important points because they are not always appreciated and, as a consequence, there is misunderstanding about how it is that addiction can be so disempowering. For one thing the idea that addiction is a habit problem is one that some people find unconvincing. How can mere habits be so powerful? But, as one addiction expert put it many years ago, 'Never underestimate the strength of a habit' (Reinert 1968, pp. 37–8). William James (1891), often considered to be the father of modern psychology, was quite clear that acquiring positive habits and avoiding harmful ones was central to healthy human development. In fact, so important are habits believed to be that some go so far as to talk of human beings as essentially 'habit machines'.

Mood modification as a source of the power of dangerous forms of consumption

The following attempts to summarise the present argument about the process whereby addiction disempowers. Let me begin at the beginning: all potentially addictive forms of consumption are powerful mood modifiers. It is probably not necessary to labour that point in the case of some of the drugs, such as alcohol, heroin or cocaine, which act strongly on the central nervous system and which produce mood states that are often referred to as intoxication or euphoria. Hear, for example, what was said about injecting heroin by one young man in South Sulawesi in Indonesia:

> It's hard how to describe that rush. It's like a total explosion that blocks you out from your surroundings. You just instantly forget everything that

bothers you. You just feel a total peace with yourself... It's like nothing can put you in the troubles, no matter how difficult your problems are. (Nasir and Rosenthal 2009, p. 240)

One observation which might give pause for thought here is that the intoxicating effects of these substances are often experienced as making people feel more powerful, not less. Indeed, whole theories of alcohol consumption have been developed on the basis that drinking makes people feel, at least temporarily, more capable, more optimistic, stronger – in a word, empowered (McClelland et al. 1972). What an irony! A substance that seems to enhance power turns out for many to undermine even the power they started with. Power has generally been thought of as a capacity held by people, individually or collectively. But, as one power theorist put it, 'Not all agents are human actors. Agency may be vested in non-human entities as diverse as machines, germs, animals and natural disasters' (Clegg 1989, p. 188). Certain substances are powerful – something which we normally associate with powerful other people or with calamitous 'acts of God' – and can turn otherwise disciplined appetites into ones that are unruly and disordered.

But what of addictive activities which are not ingestible substances? Gambling is probably the best example and it has long been known to be dangerous. Along with alcohol it constituted one of the 'social evils' which worried late Victorians (Rowntree 1905). Psychiatrists of that era recognised 'gambling mania' alongside narcomania and dipsomania. Many addiction experts were slow to admit gambling to the class of the addictions, but 'problem' or 'pathological' gambling is now well accepted and modern addiction theory has no difficult embracing it (Orford 2011). So, in what way is gambling a powerful mood modifier? There is a view, widely held by experts, players and the general public, that in many respects gambling is 'like a drug' (Orford et al. 2009a). One of the relatively early studies concluded, that '*All* compulsive gamblers... talk of the action aspect of gambling. It is described in terms of "getting my rocks off" and "adrenalin flowing" and most often compared to sexual excitement' (Lesieur 1984). These are effects not unlike those of stimulant drugs such as amphetamines. Most people have experienced something of the excitement that mounts during the course of a horse or dog race or other sporting event on which a bet has been placed, a game of bingo as the card gets filled, the playing of a fruit machine as the symbols come to rest, or even the football pools or the lottery as the results come in. The changes in mood, which are easily observed in a person's demeanour, have been confirmed in a number of studies that show physiological arousal – increased heart rate, for example – when gamblers are playing in a casino, playing gambling machines or watching a horse race on which they have a stake (e.g. Griffiths 1995). Undoubtedly much of this mood change can be attributed to the fact that money is involved and to the tension created by the uncertainty of winning or losing. Money, after all, is foremost amongst what behavioural psychologists call 'generalised reinforcers': it is one of the most powerful shapers of behaviour by virtue of its commutability – it can serve so many different purposes that it is of value to everybody everywhere. That a gambler can get excited is hardly surprising. But, of course, there is much more to it than the money. The setting in which consumption is enacted is crucial in helping to create the spell that changes mood; for example, the dealing of the cards, the rolling of the dice, the parading of the horses and jockeys before the race, and the clinking of the coins when a machine player wins are all an integral part of the mood-altering setting (Parke and Griffiths 2007). There is yet more, though, to the experience than financial uncertainty and the accompanying sights and sounds. Just as alcohol is almost always consumed in a social setting, at least until dependence is becoming established, so, too, with gambling (e.g. Newman 1972; Fisher 1993).

Something which is often said about the most popular drugs, alcohol and tobacco – in terms of total harm, the most dangerous drugs – is that much of their power lies in their versatility as mood modifiers, and the same may be true for gambling. They can all do different things for different people and even for the same person on different occasions. One finding was that two different motives for involvement in gambling could be distinguished: 'action seeking', which corresponds to the stimulation-excitement kind of mood modification described earlier, and 'escape seeking'. The latter was found to be more common amongst women gamblers. Gambling, which was described as a means of escaping from problems at home, in their pasts or in relationships, was often described by women as an 'anaesthetic' or 'hypnotic'. That distinction is an ubiquitous one in writings about addiction, corresponding as it does to the distinction that behaviourists make between positive and negative reinforcement; the former reinforcing behaviour and building a habit by virtue of offering something new and positive (fun, excitement, euphoria), the latter the relief of an unwanted state of mind or feeling (pain relief, distraction from worries). An historical example is provided by nineteenth-century use of opium in England, which was widespread: discriminations were frequently made between medicinal use, or use as a pick-me-up by the under-privileged poor, on the one hand,

and hedonistic use as a stimulant or 'luxury' on the other (Berridge 1979).
A more recent example is provided by my own and colleagues' research
with untreated heavy drinkers, amongst whom the social rewards from
drinking were uppermost in conversation, but talk of escaping worries
never far from the surface (Orford et al. 2002). Although it is important to recognise how potentially addictive forms of consumption can
serve these two broad classes of purpose, in reality motives are usually
mixed and the distinction blurred. One important piece of research, which
involved lengthy interviews about their drinking with around a thousand
adults and a thousand adolescents, referred to the two classes as 'enhancement' and 'coping' motives. It was concluded that only a minority (11%
of adult drinkers and 14% of adolescents) could be classified as purely
coping drinkers, and another minority (13% adults and 16% adolescents)
as enhancement drinkers, leaving the majority whose rewards from drinking were mixed (Cooper et al. 1995). Amongst our heavy drinkers, also,
the benefits obtained from drinking were described as mixed; the word
'relaxation' was regularly invoked in a way that conflated the two types of
reward.

The literature on 'internet addiction' is so new that it is difficult to draw
confident conclusions but it is already clear that researchers are finding
evidence of varieties of mood modification in much the same way as they
have in the case of the better established addictions, and again distinctions
are made between using the internet excessively as a diversion from worries –
much of the research has been carried out with young people with worries
about school or college and family – and positive enhancement, particularly
to do with ease of access to forming online relationships. Once again,
in practice the distinction is fuzzy. One line of thought about internet
addiction is worth special mention. A number of writers on the subject
have identified what they call 'flow' as a critical factor (Thatcher et al.
2008). By that they mean a complete immersion in an enjoyable activity,
amounting almost to an altered state of consciousness. As well as being an
interesting observation in itself, this fits well with the idea that enhancement
and coping benefits are very often melded together, since such an altered
state of mind, as well as being experienced as positively enhancing, is also
likely to be an ideal way of distracting oneself from negative thoughts.
Interestingly enough, one of the suggestions about gambling has been that
it can be so absorbing that it produces a kind of dissociative state akin to a
memory blackout, trance or out-of-body experience, as it did for Caroline
(Chapter 1). In one study, over two-thirds of a group of compulsive gamblers
said that they 'felt like they were in a trance' and 'felt like a different

person' at least occasionally, and in many cases more often, and half had 'felt outside themselves watching themselves as in a dream' (Jacobs 1993). One historian of gambling unearthed many such anecdotal accounts of experiences when gambling, such as taking on a different identity, a feeling of timelessness, separation from the rest of life, disassociation, intense concentration, and even vertigo (Reith 1999). The worlds of gambling and the internet now overlap substantially since opportunities for online gambling have been added to more traditional forms. Indeed it could be said that the internet has made potentially addictive activities of a number of kinds, or at least information about the objects of addiction, more accessible and has, therefore, increased the potential for addiction generally (Griffiths 2011).

Tobacco smoking – which figures on quitting the habit suggest may be the most difficult addiction to give up – presents a challenge to the idea that mood modification is one of the central reasons why some forms of consumption are agency abrading. For a form of drug-taking which produces no obvious 'high', smoking is surprisingly popular. As already noted, it has been argued that smoking in fact provides a remarkably versatile resource for changing mood in a rewarding direction. Its very versatility might be its secret. When smokers are systematically asked why they smoke, as they often have been, some emphasise its stimulant effects – an effect supported by evidence that smoking increases blood pressure, heart rate and other indications of psychophysiological arousal – while others emphasise the relaxing or sedative effects of smoking (Russell et al. 1974). There may be many factors which contribute to an explanation for why smoking sometimes appears to have one effect and sometimes another; but the fact remains that, despite the evidence that smoking probably increases arousal, it is very common for smokers to agree with statements such as, 'I smoke more when I am worried about something' and 'I light up a cigarette when I feel angry about something', suggesting that they are using it to *reduce* arousal. Others who have studied smoking subscribe to the theory that the apparently beneficial mood-modifying effects of smoking are due to the early establishment of an addictive smoking habit and that the mood changes brought about by smoking, such as the soothing effects, are restorative of normal functioning in regular smokers whose mood is impaired, or in danger of becoming so if they do not smoke again soon, as time passes since the last cigarette (Parrott 1998). This still qualifies as a form of mood modification, but it is an artificial one created as a result of the quite rapid establishment of a regular consumption habit, in most cases at a stage of life when the consumers are young, immature and vulnerable.

Whatever the exact mechanisms may be, most of those who have carefully reviewed the evidence are left in no doubt of nicotine's power to produce many mood-changing effects, including contributing to sustained attention, giving the smoker sensory-motor pleasure (touch, smell, etc.), the control of pain, relief of anxiety and aggression, weight control and perhaps stimulation of basic reward centres in the brain. One review referred to the 'intricately woven patterns of motivation' involved in the use of nicotine which could simultaneously affect 'all the major functional systems governing behaviour' (Ashton and Golding 1989, pp. 42–3). Another referred to how smokers learnt to 'use' nicotine, 'to regulate or fine-tune the body's normal adaptive mechanisms' (Pomerleau and Pomerleau 1989, p. 74).

If the secret of nicotine's power, as well as the power of gambling and a range of other drugs and activities, lies in rewarding changes in mind or feeling, then we might expect to be able to pin this down by studying the effects of such substances and activities on the brain. Not long ago a simple reading of findings from the rapidly developing field of neuroscience and addiction gave cause for optimism that the answer lay in the ability of most, perhaps all, such powerful consumptions to promote the accumulation of one of the principal neurotransmitter chemicals, dopamine, in an area located quite deeply within the central, limbic, area of the brain (specifically in a pathway running between the ventral tegmental area and the nucleus accumbens) (West 2006). Not only do a number of powerful drugs, such as amphetamine, cocaine, nicotine, morphine and alcohol, increase dopamine concentration in that part of the brain, but a number of studies have now suggested that this same site may be involved in gambling. There is evidence, for example, that uncertainty about the receipt of a reward activates dopamine brain pathways and that the same brain area is activated by winning money on a gambling game and even by experiencing a 'near-miss' during such a game – a significant finding in view of what is believed to be the importance of near-misses in motivating continued gambling (Clark et al. 2009). The importance of this work lies in what is otherwise known about this sub-cortical, mesolimbic brain area. In evolutionary terms it is 'old' and there is much evidence to suggest that it plays an important role in basic functions to do with emotion and motivation; it has been found to play a role in eating and sexual behaviour, both of which can give rise to addiction-like excess – bulimia or binge eating disorder and hypersexuality (Orford 2001). It might even be seen as a part of the brain corresponding to relatively 'primitive' or 'impulsive' attractions and aversions and actions that occur without thought or reflection. It is possible, therefore, that what the various forms of consumption we are concerned with have in common is their ability to provoke stimulation in a key area of the central nervous system, experienced as rewarding changes of mood. If that were the case, and current thinking is that there is much truth in that idea, then it would constitute an important part of our understanding of how such activities have the potential to be so disempowering.

Although neuroscientists are sometimes guilty of over-simplifying what is in fact a scientific field full of competing theories and loose ends, and are not above making exaggerated claims about the relevance of their work for understanding social and psychological problems, they are amongst the first to point out that the matter is actually rather more complicated than the foregoing paragraph suggests. For one thing, attention has shifted recently towards the relevance for addiction of activity in the 'newer', neo-cortical, parts of the brain, and to the balance between activity in the neo-cortical and sub-cortical areas. Nor, it seems, does the answer lie just in dopamine transmission; other neurotransmitter systems may be just as important, including those involving serotonin, noradrenalin, endorphins and gamma-aminobutyric acid (GABA) – hardly surprising in view of the versatility of addictive activities to alter mood. In any case, the idea that the mesolimbic dopamine pathways constitute a basic brain 'pleasure centre' or 'reward centre' is now generally considered to be a gross over-simplification. One theory is that this brain system signals the importance or salience of stimuli, helping to render the objects with which those stimuli are associated especially attractive or 'wanted' – not necessarily the same as 'liking' or pleasure (Robinson and Berridge 1993). Other theories make proposals about what happens in the brain with repeated consumption, for example, that the dopamine system becomes *hypo*sensitive or 'down-regulated', so that with time it needs to be activated more strongly to produce the same effect (a form of tolerance), that the dopamine system becomes *hyper*sensitive, increasing the incentive to consume; or that the sub-cortical impulse system starts to overwhelm the more 'reflective' or 'executive' neo-cortical system, which becomes less capable of holding the impulsive system in check (Bickel et al. 2007) (incidentally, neuroscientists point to the increasing evidence that in adolescence the brain is still developing: the impulsive system may be working robustly but the executive remains immature – a neat, perhaps over-neat, explanation for why young people may be particularly vulnerable).

The foregoing are important ideas about the power of mood-modification derived from psychology and neuroscience. Taken alone, they privilege individualistic explanations and grossly underplay the importance of the social. Not only do they provide a very incomplete account of how agency-eroding habits are acquired but also, because they focus on the 'interiority' of people's minds and brain processes, they can be used – as we shall see in later chapters – to locate responsibility and blame onto individuals, in the process distracting attention from the social settings and social structures which provide the contexts for addiction. No account of how consumption habits are acquired would be complete without a lot of attention being given to the power of social influence; in the form, for example, of tutoring by parents, modelling of behaviour on that of others who are liked or admired, the contagion-like spread of behavioural fashions amongst friends, or simply the very human tendency to do as others are doing. The local pub and the people he met there were crucial factors in supporting David's habit, as were the places and people in Amanda's town where she obtained her drugs and the local amusement arcades for Caroline (Chapter 1).

Even the basics of mood modification cannot be divorced from the social setting. Many smokers say they enjoy smoking more when in company, and some smokers, particularly adolescents, admit that smoking contributes to social confidence; for example, helping them, 'feel more sure of themselves' or 'feeling that by smoking they looked more relaxed to others' (McKennell and Thomas 1967). Other research with teenagers has confirmed the importance of smoking as a means of promoting a desired self-image (Bynner 1969). Although the circumstances differ markedly, preserving one's reputation as a tough gang member worthy of respect has been identified in countries as different as Indonesia and the USA as an important set of factors contributing to risky drug use amongst males living in marginalised urban neighbourhoods (Bourgois 2003a; Nasir and Rosenthal 2009). Much the same is true of gambling. Irving Goffman (1967), one of the most famous of all sociologists, having worked as a blackjack dealer and croupier in the Nevada casinos, concluded that by engaging in the risk-taking associated with gambling, casino gamblers could demonstrate to others certain forms of character strength, such as courage, gameness, integrity and composure. There have been many other similar suggestions. One, based on observations of betting shops in London's East End, was that gambling provided opportunities to experience control, to exercise intelligent choice, to discuss gambling with others and to appear knowledgeable to them (Newman 1972). Another researcher worked for a time as an unpaid cashier in an English 'amusement arcade'. She believed she had identified a number of distinct, but overlapping, groups of young people for whom playing fruit machines was serving different social functions.

Amongst them were two groups she called the 'kings' and the 'apprentices'. The former were 'quasi professional' players, knowledgeable about the machines and how to play, believing that there were skills in playing which they had learned, and highly regarded by others including the apprentices, usually younger, who fulfilled the role of appreciative audience as well as fetching food and drink and performing other services for the kings (Fisher 1993).

In psychology, seemingly reluctant to interpret these matters in power terms, social influence has been embraced as part of social learning theory – an extension of individual learning theory with an emphasis on the way in which behaviour is modelled on that of influential others and is responsive to prevailing social norms. In social theory more generally, the concept of power is invoked more readily. For example, Bourdieu's idea of 'habitus' captures the idea that much behaviour is dominated by the 'natural', taken-for-granted ways things are within the social groups and places which a person inhabits. This form of domination may not be appreciated as such by those subordinated to it, but, almost as if by magic, the right ways of acting in the group become embodied as the dispositions of individual members. Because they are so deeply social embedded, such dispositions are very difficult to alter. Bourdieu (2000, p. 172, cited by Lukes 2005, p. 143) speaks of 'the extraordinary inertia which results from the inscription of social structure in bodies'. When such dispositions concern risky consumption habits then the subordination is potentially greater still. Not only are David's, Amanda's and Caroline's behaviours moulded, without them being fully aware of it, by the people and places that constitute their social worlds, but in their cases the habitus is a dangerous one, putting them at risk of falling into habits of consumption which wield their own power.

The power to create strong consumption habits

This takes us to my second key point: owing to their capacity to change feelings and alter states of mind, certain substances and activities hold particular danger of creating powerful habits that are difficult to break. How is that so? Even if alcohol is a powerful relaxant, why don't people quickly learn that it is also harmful, producing hangovers, making one belligerent with friends, and hurting one's family? Gambling may produce intense excitement, but surely everyone learns if they didn't know already, that gambling is a fool's game and everyone loses in the end? Heroin may produce a 'high', but isn't its reputation as a dangerous drug sufficient to deter? There are several quite basic ideas in psychology which together go a long way to answering those questions. They are conformity and restraint theory; learning theory, behavioural economics and the erosion of discrimination; and the part played by cognition. I shall say a little about each of these.

Restraint theory

The idea that our impulses are subject to restraint appears in a number of different forms in the behavioural and social sciences. One is the psychology of conformity to norms, laws and proscriptions (Allport 1934). Most people most of the time obey laws, religious dictates, moral teachings, widely accepted advice. Most drivers stop at red lights despite the temptation to do otherwise; most of us arrive more or less on time for meetings or social engagements despite the many other tempting things that we could be doing; most people never try the drugs that are believed to be most dangerous despite the attractions of having time off from our normal states of mind; most people have a quite small number of lifetime sexual partners despite the fantasised attractions of being more promiscuous. In criminology the same idea comes in the form of *deterrence* or *control theory* to help explain why most people are relatively law-abiding (Hirschi 1969). Control theory embraces the power of legal sanctions as well as the constraining influence of informal social bonds to groups and institutions, and the inhibitory control exercised by the time involved in, and attitudes associated with, practices inimical to greater involvement in dangerous consumption – including factors such as religious beliefs and attendance, family engagement and values, work, or all-consuming sports or leisure activities.

Social geographers refer to several types of what they call space–time constraints on people's actions (Marshall 2005). One category consists of 'capability constraints' which put sheer physical limitations on action; for example, the lack of a public house in the village, combined with lack of transport, places a capability constraint on a person's drinking. The second category, 'coupling constraints', refers to the need to interact with other people, places or materials: for example, if the preferred form of gambling is betting on horse races at the race track, then the programme of horse race meetings imposes severe constraints. 'Authority constraints', the third category, are those imposed by rules and regulations such as those which make the possession of certain drugs an indictable offence. Mundane and obvious as such constraints may appear to be, they are probably basic for understanding why not everyone succumbs to the power of mood-altering consumptions. So much effort has gone into trying to understand the vulnerability of those who do develop strong addictive habits – their personalities, family backgrounds, stresses and traumas experienced – whereas the restraints which hold most people back and protect people from addiction have been studied less.

Learning theory and behavioural economics

Restrained though most people mostly are, the numbers who develop at least one addictive habit to the point at which free choice over consumption is diminished is legion. A fundamental explanation for this is offered by the learning theory concept of the *gradient of reinforcement*. We sometimes go on repeating actions that appear to be counter-productive for us because of the greater power, when it comes to shaping our future behaviour, of the immediate consequences of action compared to consequences which are more delayed. The reinforcement of being caught up in the 'flow' of engagement in a multi-player online game has an immediacy about it. Feeling tired the next morning, missing breakfast and being late for school are punishing effects but they follow the game-playing actions only after a delay and are, therefore, less potent drivers of future conduct. Behavioural economists – practising a newer branch of psychology – have a particular way of looking at this which involves something they call temporal discounting or *delay discounting*. Almost everyone judges something of value to be worth more now than if its arrival is delayed (for example, preferring €100 now rather than €120 in a year's time). It has been shown that the value people put on delayed rewards diminishes quickly with increasing small delays (one week, two weeks, three weeks, etc.), with the fall-off in value slowing with further increases in delay according to a hyperbolic curve. Addiction is found to be associated with a greater degree of delay discounting, both for the preferred addictive object itself and for monetary reward which could be exchanged for the addictive object (Bickel et al. 2007).

A further, very important, piece of the jigsaw, again derived from learning theory, relates to the gradual way in which habits generally develop. There are two aspects to this. One is the surprising power of reinforcement which is 'partial' or inconsistent. Action does not need to be reinforced consistently and regularly for the habit of acting that way to develop. In fact, partially reinforced behaviours become habits that are particularly difficult to break. In the well-known early animal experiments carried out by B.F. Skinner and others, such partial 'schedules of reinforcement' were capable of producing such strong habits (for pulling levers or pecking discs, for example) that responding continued to the point of exhaustion. Whatever the nature of the reward from consumption of a potentially addictive substance or activity, it does not need to be experienced reliably every time. This is relevant to all forms of addiction but is most obvious for gambling or game playing, where winning is obviously not a reliable outcome. In fact, gambling winnings arrive according to what has been referred to as a random ratio (RR) schedule, which is particularly treacherous (Knapp 1997). Winning is highly unpredictable: all one knows is that the more one plays, the greater the chances of eventually having a win, but there is no way of knowing when, and nor do the chances of a win on the next play increase the greater the run of previous losses – despite the 'gambler's fallacy', which would have it otherwise. The second aspect of habit learning is its probabilistic nature. It is not the case that one type of action, such as taking crack cocaine at the weekend, totally replaces an alternative course of action straightaway but rather that it will gradually tend to do so as habit strengthens. This feature of habit development is probably of the utmost importance in understanding the power of dangerous consumption habits. The insidious nature of the growth of such habits makes it very difficult for everyone, the consumer him- or herself included, to recognise when the line has been crossed between a moderate and acceptable lifestyle habit and one that has become harmful, excessive and unacceptable. Indeed there *is* no single line but rather a whole succession of lines to be crossed, an enormous grey area where any statement about the excessiveness of consumption is disputable. That ability of addiction, as it develops, to blur the picture, hide its real intentions, mask its power and divide the opposition, is one of the most vicious bases of addiction's power.

The erosion of discrimination

Ordinary, restrained, unremarkable consumption behaviour which conforms to social norms is, above all, discriminatory. As restraint theory suggests, it is held in check by a host of rules and regulations, formal and informal, which dictate when, where, how and with whom these otherwise dangerous commodities should be consumed. The essence of moderation is discrimination. That's why I feel a tinge of guilt if I have my evening drink half-an-hour earlier than usual. It's why regular pub drinkers are alert for signs that they or fellow drinkers may have crossed the taken-for-granted boundaries of normal drinking; for example, by drinking alone, drinking early in the day, or becoming aggressive (Kerr et al. 2000). Much illicit drug use is controlled by time and place, confined to weekend evenings or nights out in the company of friends. Even those illicit drugs believed to be the most dangerous, including opiates, can be used in a controlled fashion for years provided restraints against uncontrolled consumption are carefully held in place. According to the classic US study of the 1970s which found evidence for that, key factors for maintaining control were keeping up regular ties with friends and colleagues, including non-drug users and other controlled users, with whom drug use 'rituals and social sanctions' were carefully adhered to (Zinberg et al. 1977).

One of the ways in which habits creep up on us is by a process of generalisation, the opposite of discrimination. The stronger the habit becomes the more pressure there is to break the rules, to shift the boundaries. Some tobacco users are occasional social smokers, but most developed a regular habit over a period of at most a few years in their teens during which time discrimination was dramatically eroded. Smoking only with friends, only when the opportunity arose, and often not inhaling, is transformed into daily smoking, at least every few hours, inhaling, performed with monotonous regularity irrespective of the presence of other people. Another way of thinking of this process is in terms of a gradual separation of the growing habit from the network of ordinary connections which mostly keeps such consumptions under control. As Alcoholics Anonymous lore has it, alcohol has for the 'alcoholic' become a 'cure-all'; any event, good or bad, is now a potential stimulus for drinking. The number of occasions and events which provide a cue for drinking has grown; in learning theory terms behaviour has become more widely 'cue-linked'. In power terms, this could be expressed by saying that the orderly management of appetitive behaviour is breaking down, the boundary wall between self-discipline and excess is being chipped away and the normal powers which restrain passions and maintain order are being challenged by the greater power of mood-modifying consumption.

One of the main ways in which habits can become more deeply rooted in people's daily lives, and one of the principal reasons why the power of habits should not be under-estimated, takes us back to Pavlov and his early experiments on dogs salivating merely to the sound of a bell that had previously been associated with the presentation of food. This cue conditioning, which confers secondary reinforcing properties or incentive value, as it is variously termed, on formerly neutral stimuli, is almost certainly a major factor in strengthening consumption habits. There is nothing intrinsically interesting about the sound of a can of beer being opened or the sights and sounds which accompany the pulling of a pint of best bitter, nor is there anything intrinsically attractive about an injecting syringe, nor the sight of white cocaine powder being lined up. With the development of drinking or drug-taking habits, however, these cues become invested with their own power to attract. Gambling offers some prime examples. In his autobiographical novel, *The Gambler*, Dostoevsky, who is often referred to as one of the most famous of all compulsive gamblers, has the hero, Aleksey Ivanovitch, say, 'Even while approaching the gambling hall, two rooms away, as soon as I begin to hear the clinking of money being poured out, I almost go into convulsions' (cited by Minihan 1967, p. 319). A young man addicted to gambling machines described much the same thing to his research interviewer:

> Although winning money was the first thing that attracted me to playing fruit machines, this was gradually converted to lights, sounds and excitement. I always received a great thrill from new machines with new ideas and new lights and sounds. (Griffiths 1993, p. 393)

Nor should consumption habits be thought of as simply discrete, isolated behavioural acts but rather as whole sequences and chains of actions which are involved in the preparation for or lead up to consumption or which are associated with the places where consumption occurs and the often complex nature of consumption itself, all accompanied by a host of cues, prompts and encouragements.

The role of cognition

Much of what has been said so far about learning and conditioning processes that underlie habit development is thought to apply to many animals, not just humans. But the human animal has such capacity to dwell mentally on his or her habitual attachments that modern addiction theory now puts equally as much emphasis upon how people think about the objects of their addictions, how they apportion attention to them and to the cues associated with them and how memories about them are stored. A much studied aspect of this has been the 'expectancies' that people hold about consumption objects, their consumption and their effects. Those with larger drinking habits have been found to have more positive expectations than other people that drinking would be associated with such things as social pleasure, sexual enhancement, aggression and power, social expressiveness, relaxation and tension reduction (Cooper et al. 1992). Those with stronger gambling habits have been found to have more positive expectations that gambling will make them feel excited, important, expert or 'in control'

(Walters and Contri 1998). For such expectancies to be powerful supporters of habit they need not be realistic, of course. In fact, commonly held beliefs are clearly unrealistic; the belief of some gamblers in the power of luck, or machine gamblers' belief that they have some control over whether a machine pays out, are largely fallacies. The latter belief, which has been referred to as the 'illusion of control' (Langer 1975), represents another of the many paradoxes that surround the power of dangerous consumption habits: the development of a habit which threatens to rob the player of the power to govern his or her own actions is supported by an illusion of precisely the opposite – that the player commands control of events that are in fact controlled by others.

Some of the mental ways in which we elaborate on consumption objects can be thought of as a kind of self-talk. It can take a number of different forms, including the following: 'Doing X is the only way I can feel . . .', 'All men like me do X', 'If he's going to be like that then I'm entitled to X', 'If I didn't do X, then I'd probably do Y', 'X is one of the best things in life'. Thoughts such as these may be openly publicly stated to other people, or they may be kept private, be semi-conscious or scarcely within consciousness at all. But expectancies, illusions and fallacies and self-statements are just part of what cognitive scientists now think of as neural networks or cognitive schemata which combine a great deal of interlinked information about a particular object of consumption (Munafò and Albery 2006). Such a cognitive schema controls attention, perception and memory to do with the object, biases the holder towards receiving information and stimuli pertinent to it, and represents the embodied consolidation of the habit. Much of this cognitive support for habit development most likely has its origins early in life, even before any actual consumption has taken place, not just through direct experience but by modelling behaviour on that of other people, particularly others who are in authority, who are looked up to or who are seen often. Expectations about the effects of alcohol, for example, are already acquired long before the teenage years (Jahoda and Crammond 1972). Adults with gambling problems often talk about how they were influenced by witnessing the gambling of parents and other family members. As one woman gambler said: 'I remember my Dad coming in on the odd time saying he'd won a £100 jackpot . . . I remember thinking ooh how great, I wish I could play those [fruit machines]' (Orford et al. 2003, p. 183).

In summary of this part of the argument, we can say that there exist a compelling set of processes – to which mood modification, cue conditioning, the erosion of discrimination, mental elaboration and social learning all contribute – which has the capacity to abrade with stealth the power to control one's own consumption behaviour, which most of us take for granted most of the time. This raises the question, central to this chapter, of whether, under the influence of these powerful forces, someone like David or Caroline or Amanda (Chapter 1) can be said to be exercising freedom of choice. Are they any longer acting rationally? Are they now behaving in a way which is contrary to their real interests? Are they, in Spinoza's seventeenth-century language, 'dupes', subordinate to the power of drink, drugs or gambling, no longer able 'to live as their nature and judgement dictate' (cited by Lukes 2005, p. 114)? It is implicit in the very word 'addiction', and perhaps even more so in the clinically favoured word 'dependence', that power over one's behaviour has been compromised. Yet, under the sway of a largely biomedical model of addiction, the implications of viewing it as a form of powerlessness have not been drawn out.

The creation of a conflict of interests and the amplification of powerlessness

These processes, responsible for a deepening dependence on alcohol, tobacco, other drugs, gambling or other objects of consumption, help explain how habits strengthen but they do not complete the addiction story. Addiction, in its fully developed state, has something more abnormal, or disease-like, about it. It is more than just an ordinary habit grown strong. The disempowerment is more profound. That is because unless new forms of restraint enter the picture or the person concerned for some reason develops a commitment to self-restraint, strong consumption habits of the kind we are dealing with here can set off vicious cycles capable of seriously undermining one's already diminished personal agency. This is the third key point of this chapter's argument. Although the time course of addiction varies greatly from person to person, it rarely comes into existence suddenly and fully formed; in fact it often takes years to develop. One consequence is that it cannot be fully explained in terms of the circumstances that pertained at the beginning of the process – when Amanda started to experiment with illicit drugs in her mid-teens for example – but needs to take into account the changing circumstances of her life, including the accumulating effects of her drug-taking and associated lifestyle, as her life progresses over the subsequent months and years. In my excessive appetites model of addictions, the key idea for understanding this is that of *a conflict of motives* (Orford 2001). The development of a strong habit brings costs which smaller habits do not. The costs may be largely financial, as in the case of gambling losses or the cost of maintaining a drug habit. Time may be the resource that becomes over-extended, as can be the case for those using internet functions excessively. The costs may be health-related, some of them being ones that are anticipated in the future: for example, worry about long-term serious effects of smoking, of psychotic symptoms from heavy consumption of cannabis or of serious infection from promiscuous sexual behaviour. David's work was adversely affected by his drinking and the threat of losing his driving licence was another potential cost. Amanda's studies were affected and finally abandoned and her whole lifestyle deteriorated. Caroline's mental health suffered as her gambling escalated and control of her life slipped away from her. Many of the costs are social, becoming apparent in the form of advice or criticism from family members, friends or others.

Whatever the nature of the costs, their existence changes things. No longer is the habit unremarkable, consonant with the rest of a person's life, requiring no special thought or executive decision. It is now the subject of a conflict of motives. An already strengthened appetite for the habitual activity is now pitted against equally strong motives of an opposite kind: to use money and time for more essential purposes, to be more careful about one's health or to behave acceptably in the eyes of family, friends and work colleagues. Much of the behaviour that we associate with addiction – much of David's, Amanda's and Caroline's behaviour, for example – is the consequence of that conflict of interests. Increasingly, the addicted person becomes more harassed and demoralised. In more and more trouble with other people, an increasingly addicted person is more likely to try to hide consumption behaviour from others, to use transparent justifications, to become defensive, inconsistent and unreliable in others' eyes, and to be suffering personally with mounting feelings of anxiety, guilt, desperation, depression and even suicidal ideas. It may become more congenial and practical, as Amanda did, to spend more time with other people who share the habit rather than with those who don't. All these changes have the capacity to intensify the addictive attachment. Whatever the original motivation – for example, to positively enhance mood or to gain social esteem – continued consumption now has new sources of motivation; for example, to relieve tension, provide distraction from guilt feelings or to fill in time left after losing a job or friendships. Research on the psychology of conflict has shown that recourse to alcohol or drugs is one of the ways in which people respond to intense conflict (Janis and Mann 1977). Hence, one method for dealing with the conflict produced by an increasing alcohol or drug habit is to drink more or consume more drugs! The vicious cycle could not be clearer. The trap is tightening. Power over consumption and over the lifestyle associated with it is increasingly forfeited to the power of the addictive activity.

Different forms of addiction suffer from their own brands of vicious cycle. Heavy regular use of a number of drugs of addiction, but not all, can produce a withdrawal syndrome – including the restlessness, 'cold turkey' skin, and stomach cramps associated with opiate withdrawal or the shaking and nausea associated with alcohol withdrawal. Since such symptoms tend to be relieved by further consumption of the same drug, the motivation to continue to consume is increased. In fact, for a long time it was that vicious cycle which was thought to be at the heart of addiction (Edwards and Gross 1976). Special to gambling – although with similar habit-deepening effects – is the phenomenon of 'chasing losses'. Some writers have put this at the centre of their understanding of the escalation of the gambling habit. According to one classic description of male gambling (women's gambling was less well known and little studied then) from the 1980s,

> . . . a new and catastrophic element now dominates his betting style. Before all this happened – before the losing streak began – he was gambling to win. Now he is gambling to recoup. He is doing what gamblers call 'chasing' – the frenetic pursuit of lost money. The pursuit is fired by many fuels. There is the loss of the money itself and what that money could have bought for him. There is the loss of what the money symbolizes – importance, prestige, acceptance, recognition, friendship, power . . . his addiction . . . has now been in force for a number of years, but the motivating force has changed. Before, it was propelled by the euphoria of winning and the devouring desire to perpetuate it. Now it is propelled by the depression and anguish of losing and the overwhelming need to quell those feelings. (Custer and Milt 1985, p. 106)

Others have emphasised how, with little to lose and much to win, for example, following heavy losses or the accumulation of debts, gambling becomes less careful, more desperate; as losses are chased, play becomes less sensible and inferior betting selections are made (Rosecrance 1988).

Addiction, once it is moderate to severe, obeys what has sometimes been referred to as *the law of proportionate effect* whereby the effect of any one growth-promoting influence is proportional to the already accumulated effect of all preceding influences (Aitchison and Brown 1966). There are many things in nature which follow this law: the amount of people's personal wealth, for example, the sizes of towns and cities, or the length of rivers. Once some wealth is accumulated, processes occur which make a further accumulation of wealth more rather than less likely. Once a river is large enough it has greater capacity to deepen its bed through erosion and is better placed to capture other smaller rivers. The vicious cycles associated with mounting addiction produce the same amplifying effect.

Cognitive scientists have emphasised the information-processing features of addiction, characterising the addicted person as an increasingly biased information processor. They are particularly interested in the way in which cues associated with the object of an addictive habit acquire an exaggerated capacity to grab the addicted person's attention – what they call 'attentional bias'. They have shown much ingenuity in devising experiments to demonstrate this. One of the simpler experiments has shown that dependent drinkers, to give one example, are better able than other people to memorise alcohol-related words, and are more likely to interpret ambiguous words, such as 'bar', 'pint', 'spirits', 'shot', in alcohol-related terms when required to incorporate each word into a sentence (Glautier and Spencer 1999). More complicated are experiments showing that heavy gamblers, for example, take longer to name the colour in which a word is printed when the content of the word is designed to distract them by relating in some way to gambling (McCusker and Gettings 1997). In other experiments, those with a drug addiction are better able to report a signal occurring in part of a visual field where a word or picture associated with their form of drug use has just been displayed (Munafò and Albery 2006). Cognitive scientists stress the way in which this growing information-processing bias is of an automatic nature, reflex-like, and not fully within conscious awareness. This just adds to the entrapment which is addiction. They point to the fact that actions that are automatic tend to speed up with practice and become more fixed and less variable, more readily triggered by a relevant cue and, therefore, more 'stimulus bound', tending to initiate a whole chain reaction or sequence of behaviour without time for thought and involving relatively little effort. One cognitive psychologist describes these processes as, 'autonomous and without intention, difficult to control, effortless and involving little conscious awareness' (McCusker 2006, p. 127). The human capacity for acquiring habits which are semi-automatic is of obvious evolutionary advantage. Storing complex sets of information in 'working memory' helps us get around a familiar world and efficiently do what we have to do every day. In these terms addiction might be thought of as a kind of 'infiltration' of working memory, a form of distortion of what is otherwise an adaptive and functional process. The same cognitive psychologist put it thus: 'The normal evolutionary advantages conferred by automaticity of appetitive responses, however, turns against the individual who crosses some threshold of appetitive behaviour rendering it an automatic addictive cycle of self-destructive proportions' (p. 138).

What appears to be being suggested here is that, as addiction develops, the capacity for rational judgement is being stifled. This comes close to one of the central themes about power discussed by social scientists and philosophers such as Spinoza, who thought that one manifestation of social power was the way in which its exercise blunted the capacity of the dominated 'to use reason correctly'. Steven Lukes, one of the most influential social science theorists of power in recent times, asks how we might objectively recognise failures of rationality. His answer is interesting: we might look for evidence, for example, of 'self-deception and wishful thinking, succumbing to cognitive biases, fallacies and illusions' (Lukes 2005, p. 116), all very much the kinds of things which cognitive scientists studying addiction refer to as biased information-processing. Although there would be fierce debate over the proposition that Amanda, Caroline and David have lost a significant measure of freedom to make calm, rational decisions about their consumption of certain drugs, gambling and drinking, respectively, inherent in the idea of addiction is the notion that rational judgement is at least to a degree impaired. This is captured by those behavioural economists, referred to earlier, who show that addiction is associated with an increased discounting of the value of delayed reward and the relative over-valuing of those received immediately. The person with an addictive habit therefore finds him- or herself in a situation where the harmful consequences (mostly delayed until 'tomorrow', 'Monday morning' or simply 'later') are now less powerful in counteracting the immediate pull of consumption – the latter now enhanced because the increased addictive attachment has resulted in an over-valuing of immediate consumptive activity relative to the delayed costs (Madden et al. 2007). Even those attempting to use more classic forms of economics – for example, when trying to estimate the benefits and costs to a nation of consumption products such as alcohol and gambling which product significant 'negative externalities' – have felt the need to factor in some element of loss of rationality on the part of those experiencing alcohol or gambling problems (Crane 2008). Most economists concede that not all consumption of such products follows the classic rational consumer model.

Addiction is full of paradoxes. One – perhaps the central one of all – emerges as addiction advances. As habit strength rises and behaviour becomes increasingly automatic, run off without thought, under the control of biased information processing, so does the cost or downside of behaviour force itself increasingly upon the addicted person's attention. Just when the processes described previously have conspired to make a consumption habit most difficult to break, the person at the centre of the matter may be most ready to break it. It is probably the accumulation of costs of various kinds associated with an increasingly strong consumption habit – the financial, social, physical and mental health costs associated with a very heavy drinking habit of the type which David had or a drug habit like Amanda's, for example – often combined with pressure from family or others such as health professionals and/or a triggering traumatic event of some kind, which is most likely to provoke a resolution to exert control. But for many addicted people this mix of self-generated and other-generated pressures to change comes too late. It is a case of 'When I could, I wouldn't; now I would, I couldn't'. The strength of the habit is simply too great to be mastered by resolve with or without help from others. What takes place for many, often for long periods of time, is a struggle to control an addictive habit. As a result of the conflict of motives involved, change is often contemplated but action not taken, or short-term change is success-fully made but followed by relapse. Hence, addictive behaviour can take on a new unstable, more compulsive character, characterised by fits and starts, resolutions made and broken, hopes raised and then dashed. This differs markedly from a low level, relatively unremarkable consumption habit which gives rise to little pressure for change. Some addicted people say that in the process the original enjoyment of the activity has been lost. It is now something which is the subject of attempts at control. Indeed, it now constitutes addiction in the full sense of the term: an attachment which is so strong that it cannot easily be broken despite the harms it is causing.

Testimonies, old and modern, to the disempowering effects of addiction

The recognition that some forms of consumption can be so overpowering that behaviour becomes out of the ordinary, disease-like in its ability to disable, involving a struggle for control, warranting the term *addiction*, goes back a long way. One historian has traced the conception of habitual drunkenness as an addiction as far back as the beginning of the seventeenth century. She quotes, for example, an English reverend writing in 1609:

> ... they who addict themselves to this vice, doe finde it so sweete and pleasing to the flesh, that they are loth to part with it, and by long cus-tome they turne delight into necessitie, and bring vpon themselues such

an vnsatiable thirst, that they will as willingly leaue to liue, as leaue their excessiue drinking; and howsoeuer the manifold mischiefes into which they plunge themselues, serue as so manie forcible arguments to disswade them from this vice, yet against all rules of reason, they hold fast their conclusion, that come what come may, they will not leaue their drunkenness. (cited by Warner 1994, p. 687)

That quotation seems to constitute an excellent, plain statement of what addiction is and one that has hardly been bettered since. It recognises how, by long use, the nature of consumption, originally pleasurable, has been transmuted into a necessity and that, despite the multiple harms it has brought, neither encouragement from others nor the exercise of reason has been sufficient to bring excessive consumption under control. Go back almost a century earlier and we find the following statement by Jerome Cardano in one of the earliest books on gambling, *Liber de Ludo Aleae* – A Book on the Games of Chance. Himself a physician amongst other things, he saw himself as a suitable case for medicine:

During many years I have played not on and off but, I am ashamed to say, every day. Thereby I have lost my self-esteem, my worldly goods and my time... Even if gambling is altogether evil, still, on account of the very many large numbers that play, it would seem to be a natural evil. For that reason, it ought to be discussed by medical doctors like one of those incurable diseases. (cited by Brenner and Brenner 1990, p. 139)

The end of the eighteenth and the beginning of the nineteenth centuries was a period when medications containing opium were legally available and widely used in the treatment of all manner of ailments (Berridge 1977). The romantic poets of that era have provided us with much material about addiction. The most frequently quoted of all is probably Thomas de Quincey's *The Confessions of an English Opium Eater*, published in the *London Magazine* in 1821. It contains one of the most detailed descriptions existing of the slow, insidious entrapment by a habit which started in a small, untroublesome way – initially used to relieve facial pain and then as a pleasurable accompaniment to trips to the opera and walks around London – into a habit of which he wrote:

... from this date the reader is to consider me as a regular and confirmed opium-eater, of whom to ask whether on any particular day he had or had not taken opium would be to ask whether his lungs had performed respiration, or the heart fulfilled its functions. (de Quincey 1897, p. 400)

Even Samuel Taylor Coleridge, who, unlike de Quincey, was very reticent about his opium habit – although his wife, Sara, and his close friends, such as William and Dorothy Wordsworth, were less so (see Chapter 3) – occasionally referred to it directly in letters to friends, as, 'a Slavery more dreadful than any man who has not felt its iron fetters eating into his very soul, can possibly imagine' and 'This free-agency-annihilating Poison' (cited by Lefebure 1977, pp. 51, 57). What all these early observers of their own or others' addiction have been impressed by is the surprising erosion of control or undermining of personal agency. To say that the power to make decisions about one's consumption has been completely annihilated is perhaps to exaggerate, although that may have been how it felt and how it continues to feel to those addicted in the present day. For example, Billy, a heroin user, told a researcher:

> At first, it was just great. Me and my mates . . . we didn't care about nothin', you know having a good time, having a toot and that. But then, it sort of turned round . . . you just have a smoke, smoke the gear, and that's it like. There's nothin' else to bother about. I stopped going to football . . . and I used to love football, you know, the match. I stopped going to concerts, going out like. That was it. (Pearson 1987, p. 28)

And a cocaine user:

> . . . in the first year, I only did it twice, then the year after, went mad for it: every night for three months. I spent about a grand (£1,000) a week, ludicrous when you think about it. Every night until about 6 in the morning. I even used to go out and score at 2 in the morning . . . and that would be the third time that night. That's the way cocaine gets you. That's why it's a complete waste of time. (Ditton and Hammersley 1996, p. 31)

And a woman in trouble with gambling:

> When you start spending every spare penny you've got, when you start deceiving, cheating and lying, that's when it becomes a problem . . . I had bank loans, credit cards debts . . . any credit I could get hold of and built up £1,000 in debt. They started chasing me and there was no way I could pay all the arrears as I was only on £60 a week . . . The downside of it is that I'm nearly 40 years old and I've got nothing . . . it's ruined relationships, because rather than go out with friends I go gambling. It's just ruined friendships . . . I started lying as to where I was going . . . purely so nobody would find out what I was doing. (Orford et al. 2003, p. 205)

What these various descriptions have in common is reference to the demanding nature of consumption which, once an effortless choice, has now become an imperative, expanding in importance to take on unwarranted significance in a person's life. Systematic study of the 'symptoms' of 'dependence' have repeatedly shown that it is the preoccupation with, or salience of, consumption which is central to addiction (Orford 2001). More and more time and attention is devoted to obtaining, consuming, and recovering from consuming a limited class of objects to which the person is addicted and correspondingly less and less time and attention is committed to otherwise important, alternative social, occupational or recreational activities. Life increasingly revolves around the addictive consumption. This heightened attachment is often likened to a love affair, so strong is its ability to control thoughts and determine activities, and so powerful the feelings of attraction to the object of the attachment and despair at the thought of giving it up. In short, a new source of power and influence has come into one's life.

It is surprising how the dominant models of addiction have bypassed this glaringly obvious aspect, the fact that it is disempowering. There may be a number of reasons for this myopia. Medical concepts of addiction, as well as the supposedly more sophisticated biopsychosocial models, have had scant place for power and disempowerment. In the spheres where those models hold sway there is little tradition of discussion in terms of power. In the social sciences, on the other hand, where power and disempowerment are common currency, there has tended to be resistance to the idea of addiction, or at least to the over-simple and now well-discredited idea that certain forms of consumption rapidly and inevitably destroy agency utterly. Between reductionist biomedical conceptualisations of addiction on the one hand and social science scepticism on the other, a central idea of power of choice undermined has been lost.

How can we understand addiction in power terms?

If we are to understand addiction in power terms, there exist a variety of concepts which may be of help. The simplest idea is that of an assault on a very basic human need to be self-directed, to be able to make one's own plans and pursue them, to shape one's life oneself rather than have it shaped by other people or external forces, to be able to aim for and hopefully produce outcomes that one desires. In psychological terms this could be called self-control, competence, or self-efficacy. This chapter has indeed been about personal power and its erosion; the focus has been upon individuals like Caroline, David and Amanda and the people whose testimonies were quoted earlier. But, as we shall see from the next chapter onwards, the power dynamics that surround addiction go well beyond those individuals who are at the sharp end of it. We shall need concepts which help understand how addiction involves distortions and redistributions of power in David's, Amanda's and Caroline's families, neighbourhoods and jurisdictions and in the global economies of which their communities and countries are part. The notion of loss of what Hobbs called 'agency' (Clegg 1989, p. 41) or what Sen (1985) and Nussbaum (2000) term 'capabilities' may serve us better. What I have tried to argue in this chapter is that those individuals who experience addiction at first hand can be understood to have lost a degree of sovereignty over their own actions, have had their personal agency restricted, and even, it could be said, forfeited, in the process, some degree of capability for leading a truly fulfilled human life in domains such as loving relationships and productive and meaningful work. Another way of thinking of what has happened is to see it as the development of an unequal power relationship with the object of addiction. As many addicted individuals will say, the drink, drugs or gambling is now in charge of the individual consumer rather than the other way around. It is as if Amanda were now dependent on a resource which only her drugs of choice can provide her. Her drugs have a hold on her because she sees no alternative source of that resource and from her dependent relationship with her drugs she sees no obvious exit.

Nor have philosophers who have considered addiction used the concept of power explicitly, although they have come close to it. Let us take two philosophical contributions to the debate, one by Wallace (1999) in the journal *Law and Philosophy*, the other by Levy (2006) in the *Canadian Journal of Philosophy*. Both repudiate what they see as the simplistic ideas of addiction as an irresistible compulsion or a force which completely undermines personal agency. Each, however, acknowledges the power of addiction without actually using that word. The first concludes that addiction does indeed constitute a volitional defect, a defect of the will. The second argues that addiction constitutes an impairment of basic autonomy, a compromising of self-government or self-rule. Each acknowledges the difficulty of the argument. If those who suffer addiction are not forced to seek out and consume the objects of their addiction in the way they do, and if the ability to deliberate and reason about action is not lost, then how can it be argued that will or autonomy is impaired? Isn't the simple answer to the questions 'Why does Amanda take drugs?' or 'Why does Caroline play fruit machines?' because they want to? Isn't the logical position that of the 'addiction sceptic', who believes that addiction is nothing more or less than a 'passion', a strong desire or preference, the idea of addiction as an entity with powers of its own little more than a 'myth', and the word 'addiction' simply an attribution which may serve well the interests of those who indulge in ways that convention disapproves of as well as the interests of their professional helpers? (Davies 1992).

How then do these two philosophers justify the positions they take? Wallace's argument rests on the distinction between the ability to deliberate and make a judgement about what one ought to do, which remains unimpaired, and the capacity to choose that course of action, which *is* impaired. Impulses associated with addiction, which Wallace calls 'A-impulses', have characteristics of persistence or resilience, intensity or urgency and close association with feelings of pleasure or pain. They present themselves as extremely pleasant, 'highly vivid candidates for action' (p. 643). Hence, although the ability to appreciate the moral, legal and material dangers involved remains intact, what is not is the capacity to weigh up the pros and cons of alternative courses of action and to choose judiciously. What is impaired, at least partially, is the capacity for practical rationality and reflective agency. It is the power of choice which is impaired:

> By making one vividly aware of alternatives for action that promise an immediate and visceral pleasure, A-impulses bring it about that compliance with one's settled better judgement would require effort, concentration, strength of will. In these ways, A-impulses represent potential impairments not only of our capacities for rational deliberation, but also of our volitional power to comply with the verdicts of such deliberation. (p. 649)

Although that formulation may not take us much further forward than Aristotle's concept of *akrasia* – the failure to comply with deliberated verdicts in the face of temptation (Wallace 1999) – it does illustrate how one modern philosopher has tried to grapple with the mystery of addiction. Although the distinction between unimpaired judgement and impaired ability to choose a course of action may be difficult to sustain in practice (for example, was David's judgement always unimpaired when his drinking was at its heaviest?) – Wallace understood the conflict which I believe lies at the heart of addiction and the way in which that conflict complicates and challenges the free operation of personal willpower.

Levy's more recent attempt to understand that conflict and its disempowering effects was able to draw upon developments in behavioural economics, although his argument is not dependent on them. The key idea was that an addict's preferences are inconsistent over time: the ability to make judgements about action is not impaired, but judgements shift from time to time. Sometimes, particularly in the face of cues which remind a person of, or which orient her towards the object of addiction, the judgement is that consumption is the preferred option. At other times the judgement is that consumption should be avoided. What characterises addiction, therefore, is an inability to consistently exert will across time. Agency is fragmented and the addicted person loses full capacity to effectively make plans, to put in place long-term projects, 'preventing her from extending her will across time' (Levy 2006, p. 440).

This raises an interesting philosophical question. If David sometimes chooses to drink but at other times decides he should not, which is the real David? Which aspects of his agency have the authority to speak for him as the agent? This is reminiscent of the question about 'interests' that has so exercised power theorists (Lukes 2005; Smail 2005). It could be said that addictive substances or activities manipulate people into believing that their interests lie in continued consumption. This is akin to what Lukes has called power's third dimension: the subtle exercise of domination in such a way that the powerless scarcely appreciate that their real interests have been subordinated. A criticism of this understanding of power lies in the difficulty of establishing what constitutes a person's 'real interests'. It is very common for addicted individuals to say, as Billy did about stopping going to his beloved football (see page 63), or as many others have said about addiction ruining family relationships and friendships, that addition has in effect blocked the pursuit of their 'real' interests. On the other hand, to suppose that they have not voluntarily chosen their consumption patterns and that their real interests are being subordinated to their addiction may be to run the risk of accusing them of 'false consciousness'.

Levy deals with this problem by drawing on the work of another philosopher, Michael Bratman (2000, cited by Levy 2006), who argues that true agency, or real interests, lie, as Locke might have had it, in 'the states and attitudes which have the role of constituting and supporting the connections and continuities which make up personal identity' (Levy 2006, p. 441). If addiction is a fragmenting, disunifying, experience, which distracts the affected person from pursuing a life course consistent with personal identity, then, Levy argues, there is a real sense in which it is true to say that consumption is contrary to a person's will, and self-government is impaired.

This chapter has tried to marshal the argument that addiction acts to undermine the personal power of those who are unlucky enough to experience it at first hand. There will be those who object to the way in which, in the process of making that case, I have endowed addiction, itself, with almost human powers. I have from time to time referred to the objects of addiction – drink, drugs and gambling – as dangerous. In places in this chapter I have referred to addiction as if it has the capacity to manipulate and lay traps for unwary victims. My defence of the use of such language is that it reflects the experience of those who have talked and written about their own addictions. Perhaps, in more measured language, it may be helpful, as Levy suggests, to think of the disempowering effects of strong habits of consuming or engaging with dangerous substances and activities in terms of the way in which such habits distract people from maintaining the pursuit of a satisfying life consistent with personal identity. As we shall see in the following chapter, those others who are most closely associated with addiction – family members and friends – also speak of it as having the capacity to distract from the pursuit of common interests, in the process spreading disempowerment still further.

CHAPTER THREE

Addiction subordinates the interests of family members and friends

Powerlessness, which is so central to the idea of addiction that I am propos-ing in this book, radiates outwards, impacting those who are most closely connected. In the case of David – one of the three hypothetical cases introduced in Chapter 1 – it is his wife, Marian, who bears the full brunt of this disempowerment at second-hand, along with their three children, parents, brothers and sisters and close family friends. In Amanda's case it is her parents who feel mostly keenly the erosion of control over their lives, as do Amanda's brother and sister and other family members and friends. With Caroline it is her daughter, Karen, and brother, John, who are most affected. Like the other more than 100 million people world-wide who are affected by the addiction problem of someone they live with or are very close to – the number is certainly colossal but only a very rough estimate is possible – they experience a range of uncomfortable feelings as they witness the hold over their relatives exerted by the addictive substance or activity and its power to undermine their own interests. In the course of research by the group that I am part of, in which approaching a thousand affected fam-ily members have been interviewed in a number of different socio-cultural groups in four different countries, family members have told us repeatedly how it has made them anxious, depressed and angry. They talk about being worried, preoccupied with thinking about the relative and the problem, feeling nervous and panicky, irritable and quick tempered, low and mis-erable, annoyed and resentful. They use expressions such as, 'wrung out', 'plays on your mind', 'nerves in pieces', 'on tenterhooks', 'dragged down', 'energy level and stamina low', 'cheated', 'let down', 'feelings of love and hate'. It is common for affected family members to feel a failure themselves or devalued. Some say they feel alone in facing the problem. Others feel frightened. It is not at all uncommon to hear thoughts of suicide expressed. It is hard to think of anything much more demoralising than witnessing at close hand a person you love, whose life is closely entwined with your own, and who you know is capable of many good things in his or her life, apparently being taken over by a seemingly senseless attachment to such a harmful form of consumption.

Those feelings are all indirect expressions of powerlessness. But very often, worried family members express their disempowerment directly. That is particularly the case when long periods have already been spent unsuccessfully trying to find ways to intervene. The wife of an excessive drinker, living in Mexico City, put it this way:

> I don't know how to deal with it. I ask myself if it's worth carrying on, but the truth is I have faith and hope. I always convince myself that he is going to give up his consumption. Now I view it with indifference, I just withdraw from wherever it is that he is. (Orford et al. 2005, p. 119)

A British Asian mother was so demoralised by her son's drug-taking and his stealing at home that she and the rest of the family now carefully locked all their doors, and she described herself as sitting in her 'dark, prison like house... upset, crying and depressed... [not wanting to] clean it or do anything' (Orford et al. 2010a, p. 173). The sister of a drinker in an Aboriginal Australian family expressed her feelings of impotence, as follows:

> I don't want him to die. I'd like to see him old and grey. I'd like to see that we'd spend another Christmas together. I just guess I want it all to go away, to share – you know, to have that sort of sharing in the family. I wish there was a way that I could help him ... but he's chosen not to have it. (Orford et al. 2005, p. 119)

Sara Coleridge and Caitlin Thomas: wives affected by their husbands' addiction

The people who volunteered to be interviewed in our research – the larger proportion women and many of them wives or partners of men with an addiction to drink or drugs – are a cross-section of ordinary people whose stories would otherwise be hidden from general view. Other affected family members are more famous and their accounts have had wider circulation. Two of them, from whom I have learnt a lot, were wives of great poets – Sara, the wife of Samuel Taylor Coleridge, and Caitlin, the wife of Dylan Thomas. Let us take Sara Coleridge first. We are very fortunate that a biography of Sara, *The Bondage of Love: A Life of Mrs Samuel Taylor Coleridge*, was published in 1986, written by Molly Lefebure, who herself had worked with young people with drug problems, had carried out research for work on the Lake poets and had previously written a biography of Samuel Taylor Coleridge (STC), subtitled *A Bondage of Opium* (Lefebure 1977). In that book she had made the case that STC was a classic case of opium addiction although his own reticence on the subject, lack of understanding about addiction at that time and a tendency to refer to an opium habit only obliquely – the euphemism 'indolence' was often used – meant that his addiction had been under-estimated. *Bondage of Love* is a goldmine of insights about the disempowering effects on a wife of a husband's addiction and about her struggles to maintain some control over her life and that of her family. The remarkable thing to me is how modern it all sounds.

It is not known for certain when STC began taking laudanum – perhaps at school, prescribed during a bout of rheumatic fever or perhaps while a student at Cambridge – but by the time he and Sara moved to the Lake District in 1800, their marriage by then five years old, Sara was coming to the realisation that something was wrong with her husband and that his taking of laudanum had something to do with it. Just like the often slow and insidious advance of the disempowering habit on the person addicted, this 'coming to realise' that there is a serious problem, and what its nature is, is also very often a long drawn-out process characterised by doubts and uncertainties. Also very typical of modern partners and other affected family members was how Sara reacted and the way her actions changed with the passage of time. She 'began to remonstrate with her husband, declaring that the opium, far from alleviating his sufferings, was clearly contributing to his languors and dejections' (Lefebure 1986, p. 135). She started to complain that he was failing to support her and their young children financially. STC met these criticisms by accusing Sara that she was giving him unhelpful 'blunt advice' and that all he got from her was 'dispathy and thwarting' – not exactly the words that would be used nowadays but nicely expressive, nevertheless, of the view that Sara lacked the sympathy that might be expected from a wife. Sara, however, persevered. As Molly Lefebure put it, 'Somebody had to tell him the truth!' (1986, p. 140). As STC's health deteriorated Sara found her assertive approach to be ineffective and she became more resigned, concluding that STC needed delicate handling, like a small child: 'Nothing but tranquillity keeps him tolerable, care and anxiety destroy him' (p. 155). Lefebure comments that, a few years later, Sara 'had long since learned the uselessness of reprimanding and upbraiding; or attempting, with coaxing or cajoling, to persuade him to cut down on his consumption of his drug' (p. 197).

Two further points come out which support what we have heard from our research participants. One is the sense of loyalty which family members often express towards the person whose behaviour they are concerned about – despite the destructive effects of that behaviour – and the attempts they make to hide the full extent of the problem from other people and to protect the relative from criticism. The following quote from *Bondage of Love* makes this point well:

> Sara knew that on many counts, she was pitied by her family and friends. This she spiritedly resented, she would not have anyone pitying her; above all she would not listen to a word against her husband. She, as his wife, maintained the right to speak to him bluntly in private (yet with discretion, now that she understood the effect that blunt speech had upon him) but to hear him harshly judged by others was a thing she would not tolerate. (p. 160)

The other point to emphasise here is about the assimilation of responsibility. Compounding the disempowerment felt by Sara, and countless other partners and other family members before and since, is a form of mental disempowerment so often experienced by the relatively powerless in the face of disempowering circumstances or powerful others. Once Sara realised how ill STC had become she started to regret her 'thwarting and dispathy' tendencies and even to beg her husband's forgiveness. Even their daughter commented years later that her mother had been too honest in speaking her mind and that she lacked the 'meekness and forbearance which softens everything' (p. 139). It is not uncommon in fact for wives and other affected family members to acquire an undeserved bad reputation amongst friends, neighbours and – sad to say, since they should know better – health and social service professionals, on account of their perfectly understandable reactions to their relatives' excessive consumption habits. In fact, much of Molly Lefebure's motivation for writing *Bondage of Love* was to try and restore Sara Coleridge's reputation, which had taken a battering over the years, largely due to the writings of STC himself and that of Dorothy Wordsworth, whose writings have become popular since and who thought she knew better how STC should be handled. Lefebure refers to Sara as 'amongst the most maligned of great men's wives' (p. 15).

Over 100 years after Sara Coleridge's experiences with her poet husband's opium addiction, Caitlin Thomas was having a not dissimilar experience living with Dylan's excessive alcohol consumption. Many of the two women's difficulties were the same and, in many respects, like that of other people who have lived with partners with addictions. As Caitlin put it in her book, *Double Drink Story: My Life with Dylan Thomas* – one of several autobiographical and biographical sources about Caitlin's life with Dylan, in this case published many years after Dylan's death:

> ... ours was a drink story ... just like millions of others ... the only signif-
> icant difference between our drink story and any of the other drink stories
> is that in the middle of it was a genius poet. Otherwise nobody would have
> taken a fragment of notice of it. (Thomas 1998, p. 169)

By all accounts Caitlin had much to put up with. Income was unreliable
and, 'Any money of his own went on drink' (Thomas and Tremlett 1986,
p. 56). Like most wives of men with drinking problems, her husband's
unreliability was a prominent complaint. As she wrote to her sister: '[he]
suddenly disappears, and I may not hear of him till perhaps several nights
later he strolls in a little battered and contrite but not one word of explanation' (Ferris 1995, p. 91). Later she recalled, 'He had completely let himself
go, physically' (Thomas and Tremlett 1986, p. 93). The question is often
raised why people put up with their relatives' addictions. That is often
asked of women who, if they are asked in the right way, will usually explain
the factors that constrain them from doing anything other than tolerating
it. As Caitlin explained in *Caitlin: Life with Dylan Thomas*, co-authored
with George Tremlett, and based on tape-recorded interviews carried out
with Caitlin:

> Because it was Dylan I was very tolerant. To me, he was so endearing, lovable
> and comforting that I could overlook this unreality ... I had an enormous
> amount of pride and self-will – inner resources, I called it. I was strong,
> and anyway, I had to put up with it; I had no choice. I had no skills; I had
> never been taught anything ... I don't know how I put up with it, but what
> alternative did I have? To go home to my mother's? I could have done, but
> I was still very attached to Dylan, and when the man you are living with
> is the father of your child it gives him a much greater hold over you ...
> There were times when I thought that if only I could manage to leave him,
> for a short while, he would soon see what life was like without me, and
> then perhaps he would come back chastened; but I didn't seem able to do
> that, somehow: I never had the money ... I was captured, and it seemed so
> unfair (pp. 56, 85, 106, 144, 153)

Like Sara Coleridge there are many signs that Caitlin Thomas had assimi-
lated a sense of personal responsibility. Like so many other family members
struggling to cope with an addiction problem, Caitlin was one of her own
severest critics. In place of Sara Coleridge's 'thwarting and dispathy', Caitlin
had 'carping and nagging'. In *Double Drink Story* she wrote, 'I carped at
Dylan like a fishwife, and if anything is guaranteed to kill love, carping will
do it' (Thomas 1998, p. 95). Her and Dylan's rows, sometimes amounting
to physical fights, became the talk of their friends and acquaintances. By
the time of Dylan's death, Caitlin was said to be at the end of her tether,

'permanently embittered', according to one woman friend (Ferris 1995, p. 114).

The disempowering effects of addiction, first on those who are themselves addicted to a dangerous form of consumption and thence on their closest family members, has, in my opinion, not been well understood. One of the effects has been the negative traits that have often been ascribed to family members and the negative reputations that they have consequently acquired. For me, therefore, one of the most notable features of the writings by and about Caitlin Thomas was the way in which one of her main biographers – Paul Ferris in *Caitlin: The Life of Caitlin Thomas* – used evidence of the tougher, retaliatory side of Caitlin's reactions to apportion blame to this 'hardened . . . harsher' side of Caitlin:

> . . . without the guarantee of her affection, he [Dylan] was in trouble . . . if her strength and security had been important to him throughout their life together, and there can be no doubt that it was, then the anger she displayed increasingly . . . can't have left him unmoved . . . her willingness to heap humiliation on him . . . This was the other element in his psychological downfall, which in turn made him reckless with his life, and would lead to his death. (Ferris 1995, pp. 116, 134–5)

Being blamed, directly or indirectly, for the addictive behaviours of their menfolk is a common experience for wives the world over.

The colonisation of family life and the subordination of family members' interests

We can see in these two famous, much written about, cases how the lives of women can be taken over by their husbands' addictions. This state of affairs is not normally seen in power terms by those who treat addiction or who carry out research. But it cries out for being theorised in such a way and there exists to hand a variety of ways of doing so. Social theorists talk of the domination of the powerless by the powerful and the way in which the interests of the powerless become subordinated to those of the powerful, the perspectives of the powerless becoming less visible and their voices less heard (Boehm and Flack 2010). Are those appropriate terms to use when thinking of Sara and Caitlin and the countless other wives, past and present, who live with partners with alcohol, drug or gambling addictions? Perhaps, but, if so, it calls immediately for an important note of clarification. If it is the case, as argued in the previous chapter, that the Davids of this world are themselves disempowered by their addictions, how can we explain their wives' disempowerment? By whom, or by what, are they disempowered?

The answer, I believe, lies in the notion of 'real interests' being subverted: the assumption that the effect of David's, Coleridge's and Dylan Thomas's addictions is to introduce into their lives a powerful new 'interest' which expands in importance and crowds out their real interests. As their dependence deepens, their new interest in the object of their addiction plays an increasingly commanding role, dominating both their own lives and those of the people they live with. At the same time, as mastery of their own behaviour is weakened, they may display the aggressiveness and other kinds of defensive behaviour which are characteristic of those whose power is threatened (Bugenthal 2010). The true source of their disempowerment and, consequently, that of their family members is the power of addiction to a dangerous product. But, to their partners, they appear to be exercising *greater* power of a dangerous, mystifying and unreasonable kind. This question of whether David and the poet-husbands Samuel Taylor Coleridge and Dylan Thomas were powerless in their pursuit of the substances of their addictions or, alternatively, whether they are to be seen as preoccupied with their own interests, more and more self-absorbed and tyrannical in their relations with their family members, is a moot point. Indeed, this question itself is one which wives and other affected family members ask themselves constantly: Why is he behaving so badly? Can he help it? What is responsible for the change which seems to have come over him? Whatever the solution to those conundrums, what is certain is that their wives' interests have become subordinated in the process. In deed, the idea of real interests subverted is much less problematic in the case of family members affected by addiction than is the case when we attempt to apply that idea to the addicted persons themselves. As we saw in the previous chapter, it is not at all clear where Caroline's, Amanda's or David's real interests lie: it may be best to think of them, now addicted, having divided or incompatible interests, which prevent them from wholeheartedly pursuing a coherent way of life. But for their concerned family members there is little doubt about it: their addictive patterns of consumption are in direct opposition to their family members' interests.

Social psychologists have studied the mental processes of the powerful and the powerless. Findings regarding the relatively powerless fit what we know about the experiences of affected family members rather well. The powerless have been shown to be constantly vigilant, needing to pay attention to what the powerful are doing, attending to their wishes, tending to converge in their attitudes and feelings towards those of the powerful, tending to display deference and politeness, and in the process inhibiting the expression of their own attitudes and qualifying any assertions that they make (Guinote 2010; Keltner et al. 2010).

Of particular relevance is *social dominance theory* (SDT), a broad ranging set of ideas which attempts to explain such issues as stereotyping, prejudice, discrimination and oppression of various kinds (Sidanius and Pratto 1999). The central idea of SDT is that all societies tend to be stratified in three ways: by age, with adults having social power over children and adolescents; by gender, with males having disproportionate power; and by some third source of stratification based on characteristics such as ethnicity, caste, social class or religion, which, unlike age and gender, varies from one society to another. These hierarchies are maintained by hierarchy-enhancing forces including beliefs and 'myths'. They include shared or societal beliefs such as racism, sexism, nationalism, but some of the hierarchy-enhancing myths are more subtle. They include, for example, beliefs that attribute responsibility for poverty or ill health to poor or unhealthy individuals themselves or to the communities in which they live; explaining the position of a minority in terms of the psychological characteristics of its members, such as bitterness, frustration, envy or resentment (psychologisation); or not accepting or minimising true facts or statements expressed by a minority who are then accused of being irrational or incoherent (denial). Those in subordinate positions, according to SDT, themselves participate in and contribute to their own continuing subordination; for example, by showing deference to those more dominant in the hierarchy, by being less clear and organised against the existing hierarchical arrangements than the powerful are in defence of them, and inadvertently expressing attitudes and engaging in actions which undermine their position. Others have described much the same psychological processes in a different context: that of the relationship between colonists and the colonised. They include Frantz Fanon, a psychiatrist connected with the liberation struggle in Algeria, and Steve Biko, the Black consciousness leader involved in resistance to South African apartheid (Hook 2004). Both described how the disempowering effects of colonisation, with dominating colonial ways of thinking and the marginalisation of the experience of the colonised, affected even the minds of the oppressed. The psychological consequences – described as the 'scars of bondage' or the 'mark of oppression' – had the effect of compounding the effects of colonialism and perpetuating those effects even long into the post-colonial era. When David's wife, Marian, asks herself whether she is to blame in some way for her husband's alcohol addiction, whether she has ignored his needs, failed as a wife, or when Caitlin Thomas berated herself for her nagging, were they displaying the mark of oppression, contributing to their own continued subordination and dependence? Have their family lives, in an important sense, been colonised by addiction?

An alternative way of trying to get to grips with the predicament faced by wives and other family members affected by their relatives' addiction is the capabilities approach developed by the economist Amartya Sen (1985; 1999) and the philosopher Martha Nussbaum (2000, 2011). In her book, *Women and Human Development: The Capabilities Approach*, Nussbaum (2000) explains that the approach is based on the idea of a set of universal values cast in the form of a common set of functions which each and every person should be capable of exercising to a certain threshold level. Basic is the idea that each individual should be respected in her or his own right and should not be so constrained by powerful other people or by circumstances in such a way that basic human capabilities are threatened. She lists ten central human functional capabilities. Looking through the list it is clear that living as a family member with addiction could undermine any or all of these capabilities. Some are instantly recognisable as highly relevant. The second, for example, is *Bodily Health*: being able to have good health, including reproductive health; to be adequately nourished; to have adequate shelter. The third is *Bodily Integrity*: including being able to be secure against assault. Number five is *Emotions*, including not having one's emotional development blighted by overwhelming fear and anxiety or by traumatic events of abuse or neglect. *Affiliation*, number seven, includes having the social bases for self-respect and non-humiliation; being able to be treated as a dignified being whose worth is equal to that of others. The ninth is *Play*: being able to laugh, to play, to enjoy recreational activities. The relevance of the capabilities approach for our present discussion is borne out by the fact that excessive drinking, and gambling in one case, figure in both of the human stories to which Nussbaum makes reference throughout her book. Both involve women in India. Of the first she writes, 'Vasanti's husband was a gambler and an alcoholic. He used the household money to get drunk . . . Eventually, as her husband became physically abusive, she could live with him no longer and returned to her own family' (p. 16). Of the other, 'Jayamma's husband usually used up all his income (not large in any case) on tobacco, drink, and meals out for himself, leaving it to Jayamma not only to do all the housework after her backbreaking day, but also to provide the core financial support for children and house' (p. 21).

Because of the universal existence, to one degree or another, of the gender-based hierarchical system, Nussbaum considered the capabilities approach to be particularly pertinent to the circumstances of women. And so have many writers on the subject of the impact of addiction on family members. For example, the struggle to understand what was going on in their marriages was the central theme of a book, *Women with Alcoholic Husbands*, based on in-depth interviews with over 50 women in the USA. One way of managing the confusing 'definitional ambivalence', as she called it, was what was termed 'personalizing':

> The generic questions involved in the ambivalence of definition and meaning with regard to self are, Am I an okay person? Wife? Mother? What's wrong with me? Why is he treating me like this? Why is my life like this? What can I do? What do I want? What have I become? And what is to become of me? . . . [for example] 'I took it very personally . . . that he didn't care enough about me; he would rather be out drinking than be home with me' . . . 'I really believed at that time the things that I was feeling, that I was mentally not all right'. (Asher 1992, pp. 10–11, 86, 107)

Commenting on the circumstances faced by wives in that situation, Ussher (1998, p. 153) viewed this as an aspect of disempowerment particular to women: 'the way in which women blame themselves for problems in relationships . . . [because of factors including] low self-esteem, depression, the impact of previous neglect or abuse, guilt, shame, fear of loss or separation, and the idealisation of both heterosexuality and of men'. Writers from John Stuart Mill, in *The Subjection of Women*, to modern writers such as Sen, Nussbaum and Bourdieu have written of the power of legitimate, traditional male authority to socialise women into a position of subordination, contributing to their own powerlessness by incorporating beliefs about their own more passive, feminine natures, 'yielding to the control of others' as Mill (1989 [1869], p. 174, cited by Lukes 2005, p. 138) put it, or, as Sen (1984, pp. 308–9, cited by Lukes 2005, p. 137) had it, displaying acceptance rather than discontent, 'conformist quiet' rather than 'hopeless rebellion'.

Parents and husbands: addiction's challenge to authority

Wives, especially in cultures or marriages where gender roles are traditional, can be thought of as doubly disempowered when their husbands have addictions. But what, then, are we to make of family members affected by addiction such as parents or husbands, in traditional relationships, who otherwise carry greater power or authority in relation to their addicted relatives? Do they, by virtue of their more powerful position in the family, escape the disempowerment otherwise associated with being an affected family member? Or do the two things – their normal position of authority and the disempowering stress of living with an addicted relative – cancel each other out? No doubt the answer for any one affected family member depends on many factors, but on the whole the evidence suggests that for many parents and for many male family members the experience of living with a relative's addiction is highly stressful and threatening to family resources and stability. Take, for example, the case of Amanda's parents, Mercy and Gilbert (see Chapter 1). Although having the authority of parents towards an adolescent child with a problem of drug addiction may protect parents against the worst of oppression which can be associated with being a wife of a husband with such a problem living in a traditional marriage and in circumstances of poverty, it is certainly not the case that parental authority shields them altogether from the debilitating effects of living with addiction. In fact, social psychologists have pointed to evidence that helps us understand how the authority associated with being a parent or a traditional husband is often quite fragile, sensitive to challenge by children and partners. Under those conditions the perception that rightful authority is being undermined is particularly stressful (as shown, for example, by chronically high cortisol levels) and sometimes leads to exaggerated efforts to reassert power, including aggressive actions (Rivers and Josephs 2010). Fathers are sometimes conscious of occupying a position in which assumed authority is challenged, as the following quotation from the father of a son with a drug problem illustrates:

> See, as a man, when it comes to the crunch in the house, the man makes the decisions most of the time . . . now we come to a situation where a little bit of grey comes in, because you cannot deal with the problem you have in your own house because the very person that is creating the problem isn't listening because of his drug problem . . . The difficult thing for the man, to me, is really the fact that he is not able to cope with the problem but will not admit it to himself or anybody else. (Dorn et al. 1987, pp. 10–11)

The disempowerment that parents experience in the face of a daughter's or son's drug use is similar in many ways to that experienced by wives in the face of excessive drinking. Common to both, for example, is the usually drawn out and disorienting process of coming round to a realisation of what is wrong. Partly because of the illicit nature of some forms of drug-taking and the highly negative connotations associated with use of certain dangerous drugs, and partly because of the inherent nature of parent-adolescent/young adult relationships, the process of realisation is often marked by one or more traumatic moments of 'finding out'. One British study based on interviews with parents, which resulted in a booklet for parents entitled *Coping with a Nightmare: Family Feelings About Long-Term Drug Use*, illustrated the strong emotions felt by parents when they first realised that a son or daughter had a drug problem. The feelings expressed included those of guilt, loss, sometimes betrayal, as well as worries about such things as stealing, unsafe sex, and the possibility that their children might overdose and die. One parent described feelings of 'Anger, angry that you can't do anything. My first response was anger that he was so weak to do it – horror, horror'; and another, 'A terrifying feeling of fear and a shot of desperate disappointment, you know, how can this happen – he was so lovely, my child, how can it have happened to my child?' (Dorn et al. 1987, p. 9).

One of the most detailed accounts of being a parent in that situation is the book *Pete Doherty: My Prodigal Son*, written by Jacqueline Doherty (2006), the mother of the popular musician Pete Doherty. In the first chapter the author describes the early signs of Pete's developing drug habit, signs which, with hindsight, she could see were clear warnings but which at the time were missed. The signs became clearer as time went on but, like most parents, she latched on to any sign that her worst fears were misplaced. For a while she hoped that his drug-taking was confined to cannabis; when it emerged that he was smoking heroin and crack cocaine she was, 'mortified. I wanted to hit him. I wanted to be sick; to be deaf; to be struck down; to hold him; to cry out to God' (p. 24). She then reassured herself that at least he was not injecting, another hope that was subsequently crushed: 'I simply don't have the words to articulate how learning that Peter was injecting heroin affected me; perhaps only another parent in the same circumstances could fully understand' (pp. 123–4).

This common experience of uncertainty about whether there is anything to worry about at all, how serious the problem is, and what part an addictive attachment plays is just one aspect of the disempowering uncertainty which family members experience. Another is the uncertainty of knowing where the using relative is, what he or she is up to, and what risks are being run and dangers faced. Jacqueline Doherty put that well:

> I'm always waiting, waiting, waiting. Even now. Never know what the next day will bring... You lie there, night after night, unable to sleep because you're thinking of your loved one, or waiting for the phone to ring, or worrying about them, or praying long into the night for them. (p. 220)

Parents of sons or daughters with large gambling habits describe much the same loss of control over their offspring and their own lives (Krishnan and Orford 2002). Once again, a regularly recurring theme is the slowly dawning realisation that something is seriously wrong and that a gambling habit is a big part of it. A mother says that for several years she and her husband put their son's difficult behaviour down to adolescent problems out of which he would surely grow. The possibility that gambling on 'fruit machines' was behind his unpleasant changes in behaviour and personality had been the last thing they had thought of. A father recounts how money kept on going missing at home; it was some time before he realised his son was taking it but even then for a long time had not traced it to his son having a gambling habit. Another couple could not understand where all their son's money was going, why he had lost his job or why he had unexplained absences at work and college. Like parents of those with alcohol or drug habits, feelings run high for these parents as well. A mother admits, with shame, to feelings of hatred and anger, and another to feelings of desperation and frustration. A father says, 'It ruins your life', and describes feeling so strongly that he had wanted to throw things. They each feel guilty at times thinking that they have failed as parents. Their own health and relationships have suffered. It is common for these parents to feel that they cannot safely go away on holiday for fear that possessions might be taken and sold while they are away. Mothers have been tearful and depressed and fathers frightened by their own irritability and loss of temper. Sleeping is often disturbed and social life restricted.

Regarding men who are partners of women with alcohol, drug or gambling problems, can the metaphor of disempowerment be extended to cover their case? The conclusion that my colleagues and I have come to, as have several other research groups, is that they have very similar experiences to those of women who are partners of men with such problems (Estes and Baker 1982; Orford et al. 2005; Philpott and Christie 2008). Just as wives do, they describe their feelings of frustration, bitterness, anger, being wound up and at the end of their tether, preoccupied with the problem, feeling hopeless, exhausted, depressed, concerned about the deterioration in their relationship and family functioning and particularly worried about possible effects on their children. They, too, describe the difficulty of getting help or support from others and the way other people can be critical of their ways of coping. They also experience some relief when they find out who they can talk to. As one husband said, 'You don't feel you're on your own so much. It doesn't feel so much of an uphill struggle. There are other people in a similar and worse situation than myself' (Orford et al. 2005, p. 148).

Coping dilemmas: the struggle to stand up to addiction

One of the greatest sources of uncertainty is simply the feeling that something should and could be done but not knowing what that something is. Just as the development of an addictive habit disables the addicted person's ability to choose, so does the experience of being closely connected to someone who is developing such a habit undermine the control which the connected person normally expects to be able to exercise over her or his life. Almost every family member who is desperate with worry about a loved one with an addiction problem has entertained the thought that there must be some way of retaking control. Surely if one was more determined, forceful, single-minded, the person who is of concern could be rescued, he could be forced to come with you to a place of safety, submit to order and discipline or at least enter rehabilitation. When parents and other family members do try to engage in efforts to stand up to the problem in some way, they are faced with very difficult decisions – 'coping dilemmas' I call them (Orford 2012) – about exactly what to do. Because the addictive habit is so demanding, most attempts fail most of the time, leaving parents and others feeling further impotent and frustrated, agonising about whether they have done the right or wrong thing, perhaps even exacerbating the problem in the process, and, sadly, often inviting disagreement and criticism from the addicted relative, other family members, friends, neighbours and advisors. One form which this uncertainty about coping takes for parents – although partners and others also experience something very similar – is the struggle to reconcile the need to impose some order on family life, with, at the same time, the wish to maintain a positive, caring relationship with the addicted relative. That dilemma, of course, is endemic to parenting generally, perhaps to all close relationships, but when the disempowering effect of addiction is added, the dilemma is greatly heightened. For example, parents of adolescents receiving treatment for drug misuse have to weigh up their wish to enforce rules for appropriate behaviour in and out of the home against their fear that they might provoke their offspring to leave home, thus exposing them to greater dangers. Parents have told me and my colleagues of the compromises they reach when faced with such dilemmas, and how uncomfortable they are about doing that, often feeling manipulated or blackmailed in the process. It is difficult for a mother to see her son or daughter without sound footwear or warm outdoor clothing for the winter, or without the fare to travel to a job interview or a doctor's appointment, without offering some help, even though she is sure that an excessive habit is the cause and even if she suspects that any help offered may be subverted into funds to support the habit. Being 'tough' under those circumstances is not easy. Staying strong in the face of a relative's addiction is very likely to provoke charges of what Coleridge referred to as 'thwarting' or what Caitlin Thomas's biographer called 'hard' and 'harsh'.

A good example is to be found in a newish biography about Charles Baudelaire, the nineteenth century French writer. A new biography was necessary according to its author, Frank Hilton (2004), because, although most who had written about Baudelaire knew that he used laudanum, and many described him as an addict, none of his previous biographers had grasped the importance of his addiction. The relevance here is Baudelaire's relationship with his mother, which constitutes a major theme of Hilton's biography, *Baudelaire in Chains*. It seems that Baudelaire was even less forthcoming about his addiction than Coleridge had been and Hilton thinks it likely that his mother never knew about his drug habit, although Baudelaire wrote much about drug-taking in the third person, famously in *Les Paradis Artificiels*. In so many respects, however, it is clear that Baudelaire's mother experienced much of the impotence that is common to mothers and other family members who are only too well aware of their relatives' drug habits. For all of Baudelaire's short adult life they maintained a relationship, much of it by correspondence, a great deal of which seems to have revolved around Baudelaire's requests for money and his mother's resolve to resist – resolutions that were often broken in the face of Baudelaire's persistence. Eventually, though, she adopted a tough stance, one which most of Baudelaire's biographers have been critical of, viewing her as hard-hearted, as, not surprisingly, did Baudelaire himself. Specially draconian was thought to be the strategy she finally decided upon in order to control her son's finances. At the time he left the parental home at the age of 21 Baudelaire had come into a considerable inheritance, most of which he had squandered within just a few months, and his need of money remained one of the main issues between them from then on. With the help of Baudelaire's half-brother and the family solicitor, a *conseil judiciaire* was imposed on Baudelaire, a legally binding arrangement whereby financial decisions would be made by Baudelaire's mother and the solicitor, and income from his remaining capital given to him in monthly amounts for the rest of his life. This enraged Baudelaire as his mother knew it would, but it was the result of years of frustration. The case of Baudelaire's mother illustrates rather nicely the point that, although the manner and degree of an affected family member's disempowerment is highly variable, very few family members escape addiction's disempowering effect.

Baudelaire's mother, living apart from him, well supported emotionally and financially by her husband (Baudelaire's step-father, who advocated taking a strong line with his step-son), and perhaps unaware that drug dependence was a major part of the problem, nevertheless experienced some of the same struggle and sense of impotence experienced by other family members who are much more closely affected by their relatives' addiction.

Baudelaire's mother has been criticised for the tough line she eventually took with her son. If, on the other hand, parents or other family members affected by a relative's addiction do not take a tough line, they equally expose themselves to criticism – including self-criticism, in fact, most particularly self-criticism – on the grounds that they are 'colluding', 'co-dependent', or 'enabling'. In fact Hilton, in his biography of Baudelaire, falls into the familiar trap of assuming that all partners, parents and other close family members of relatives with addiction problems fall into one of two camps, the 'doves' or 'enablers' and the 'hawks, the un-enablers' (Hilton 2004, p. 107). In fact, family members struggle with a set of circumstances to which there is no obvious, societally approved, 'right' way of responding, usually finding their own way which seems right for them in their particular circumstances, a position they reach only after much struggle and soul-searching.

The counter-positioning of the tough and tender roles which occupies the minds of affected family members, was made very public in the course of a BBC television programme some years ago on the subject of the Tough Love approach to the question of how parents should respond to their children's drug misuse (Orford 2012, pp. 15–20). A number of parents in the studio had in various ways adopted a tough stance, one father in particular having reported his son, who had developed a serious drinking habit, to the police for stealing from the family firm. As a result, he had served six months in prison. The following is part of the exchange that took place between the programme presenter and the father:

> *Presenter.* But the idea, it's repugnant to many people I think instinctively, the idea of parents informing on their own children. It's the sort of thing we'd associate with a totalitarian regime perhaps, with George Orwell's *1984*. It just doesn't seem right for a parent to do that, to many people.
>
> *Father.* Why not? At what stage do you draw the line? . . . When you've tried all the nice things . . . I thought there was no alternative. We'd tried all the nice things . . . We tried to be nice with [our son]. We talked together. And [he] would always say, 'Yes, what I did was wrong. I accept that. I won't do it again. I'm sorry'. Sorry was the famous word. We had sorry for ten years.

Despite full discussion, involving a Tough Love expert from the USA and one of his staunchest critics, as well as a number of parents who had adopted different approaches, and their offspring, the question of which was the better approach remained unresolved, as it was bound to be. Could caring parents do what that father had done and were there great risks in that approach, including his son acquiring a criminal record? Or is it the case that a more caring approach runs the greater risk of slipping into accepting what should not be accepted, putting up with it, not examining it objectively or resolving to stand up to it if that is what is needed? Might the tougher approach in the end be the more caring one? Differences of opinion about the best way of coping was also a theme in Jacqueline Doherty's (2006) book. She contrasted her own desperate attempts to stay in touch with her son – often involving exhausting and mostly frustrating attempts to 'chase' him, tracking down his whereabouts, having a brief meeting if possible and doing whatever a mother could – with his father's refusal to allow his son home and his policy of distancing himself physically and emotionally. Not surprisingly their different approaches put a great deal of strain on the parents' marriage.

Amongst the many coping dilemmas faced by parents of sons or daughters with gambling problems, those revolving around money are prominent (Krishnan and Orford 2002). Most talk about watching money very carefully. Some have simply stopped giving their offspring money but others are not so firm. Those who have been advised by Gamblers Anonymous, or who have attended GamAnon – for family members or friends of compulsive gamblers – know that the recommendation is not to give gamblers money under any circumstances. But these parents worry that their offspring will suffer as a result, perhaps even starve, or that they will start stealing and getting into trouble. Some have, therefore, lent their gambling children money although they believed there was little chance of being repaid. Some have covered their children's debts or rent, sometimes to the tune of several thousand pounds. Some have successfully taken over their children's finances, only handing out money for what are thought to be reasonable expenses. A research paper entitled, *Ripples in a pond: the disclosure to, and management of, problem internet gambling within the family*, provides several examples of parents and other family members taking actions to attempt to reassert control. The following quotation is from a son in his thirties describing the way his father assumed financial control of his affairs:

[W]hen I went home [to his parents' home following a gambling related suicide attempt], within five days all my debts were consolidated into one

payment to my Dad per month, no interest. It's just a massive weight off
and all my cards were cut up, all my accounts were closed. (Valentine and
Hughes 2010, p. 284)

If the addiction experienced by one person – a David, an Amanda or a
Caroline, for example – can be thought of as the source of a contagion-
like spread of disempowerment which most affects those in the immediate
vicinity, how far does the contagion spread? Certainly David's and his wife's
relations, for example, their sisters and brothers and their families, felt some
of the same sense of impotence in the face of David's alcohol addiction as his
wife, Marian, did. But they were not living under the same roof with David
and perhaps the ripples progressively decline in force as the distance from
the source of disempowerment increases; 'distance' being meant here in a
general sense, to include, but not be limited to, the geographical distance
separating the parties. But we should be careful not to underestimate the
capacity of addiction to engender widespread concern amongst circles of
kin and non-kin associates. Recall, in Chapter 1, the important roles played
by Amanda's sister and by Caroline's brother. In studies of adult family
members affected by addiction, wives and mothers have been the largest
groups, with fathers, adult children and husbands also well represented. But
a wide array of others have also appeared, including sisters and brothers,
aunts and uncles, grandparents, cousins, in-laws and others. Children and
adolescents, living with a parent with an addiction problem, have been the
subject of a great deal of separate study (Kroll and Taylor 2002; Velleman
and Templeton 2007). Sisters are a group who not uncommonly take
responsibility for trying to re-establish order and control, as this sister did:

> She said she'd had some debts; she was sorry she'd gone on the gambling
> again. She needed so much to bail herself out . . . would I be willing to do
> it? . . . So I spoke to my mother, I spoke to my husband and we all came
> to the conclusion that she needed a loan. I'd get her the loan but it had to
> be, you know, there had to be certain regulations or conditions to getting
> the loan. And I made her wait for about a week before I told her. And then
> another condition was she had to tell her husband because her husband had
> no idea what she'd been doing . . . I took a loan out from my bank and made
> sure it was a secured loan for £5000. (Valentine and Hughes 2010, p. 280)

Beyond kinship: impotence in the face of addiction

The disempowering waves created by addiction can be felt still further
afield beyond the ties of kinship. In a large multi-centre trial of treatment
for alcohol addiction (the UK Alcohol Treatment Trial (UKATT) Research

Team 2005), one of the treatments being compared (Social Behaviour and Network Therapy, SBNT) was based on the principle that recovery from such an addiction benefits from the addicted or 'focal' person being able to draw on the support of a small network of concerned others who may be asked to attend treatment sessions to discuss the support they can provide. We had expected that *some* of these 'network members', who were identified as potential supporters by the focal person and who were sufficiently concerned to subsequently come forward to help, would be other than close kin. What was surprising was that nearly half of all the network members who took part were friends, bound to the addicted person by ties other than kinship.

The experiences of concerned friends have not been studied in any detail, but again we can have recourse to published biography to provide some insight. Once more, Samuel Taylor Coleridge and his friends have given us one of the best examples. Molly Lefebure's biography of Sara Coleridge, although it deals with Sara as the main protagonist, has much to say about the Coleridges' network of friends, several of them famous names. Probably the most famous are fellow poet William Wordsworth and his sister, Dorothy. The two families' lives were entwined over many years and they were neighbours in the Lake District. Addiction has the effect of driving wedges between people and the triangular relationship among Coleridge, his wife Sara, and the Wordsworths is a perfect example. William and Dorothy thought Sara unsuitable for Coleridge and accepted the idea that it was she who was partly responsible for his addiction. They thought they could do better in looking after Coleridge and, indeed, they took him in under their roof for substantial stretches of time lasting for a total period of a year or more. It has to be said that many people criticise the close 'carers' – if that is the right word – of people with addiction problems, and think they know better how to handle them, but very few have the courage the Wordsworths had to put their ideas to the test. According to Lefebure, they soon discovered, however, that they lacked the power to turn things around in the way they had hoped. At the end of the experiment it seems that Dorothy, who had been particularly strong in her criticism of Sara, was completely disillusioned. She wrote to a friend,

> We have no hope of him . . . His whole time and thoughts . . . are employed in deceiving himself, and seeking to deceive others . . . This Habit pervades all his words and actions, and you feel perpetual new hollowness, and emptiness . . . It has been misery, God knows, to me to see the truths which I now see. (Lefebure 1986, p. 196)

The Coleridge story also offers a good example of how different friends can adopt very different positions. Robert Southey, fellow poet and youthful radical thinker of Coleridge's, and subsequently brother-in-law through marrying Sara's sister, was one whose attitude to Coleridge's addiction appears to have moved from that of concerned support to one of tolerant resignation, later hardening into something more like angry indignation. This differed substantially from the attitude of another longstanding friend from Somerset days, Thomas Poole, who seemed to have consistently adopted the position that Coleridge was a highly strung genius who should be encouraged and protected from upset. Indeed, Coleridge had what we might now call an extensive network of supporters. There were others who offered him accommodation or tried to raise money for his treatment. Although those are perhaps unusually generous offers of support, it is not uncommon to find that people who are disempowered by their own addictions are surrounded by well-wishers who recognise the absurdly disempowering effects of their friends' addictions, who feel that something should be and can be done and who are prepared to offer what help they are able to.

One of the best accounts that I know of, written by a concerned friend, relates to another of the poets whose life has been much written about and who has already been referred to – Dylan Thomas. In this case, the friend, unlike the Wordsworths, had at no time lived under the same roof with Dylan, making him in some ways more typical of the generality of concerned friends. He and Dylan were related, however, via their work as poets. The friend I am referring to is John Brinnin, who arranged and managed all Dylan's tours to the USA and got to know him extremely well in the three or four years between their first meeting and Dylan's death during his final tour. The book which Brinnin later wrote, *Dylan Thomas in America*, makes it clear that he admired Dylan greatly and was proud to be responsible for bringing him to the USA. It is equally clear that the experience was immensely frustrating for him on account of Dylan's drinking and unpredictability. He found himself having to sort out numerous problems, including dealing with hosts at the speaking venues angered by Dylan's behaviour. He describes at one point his state of indecision about how to respond to Dylan's drunkenness at a party, a state which many close family members would well recognise:

> Should I somehow force him to leave? By what right could I force him to do anything? I did not know it then, but I was in the dead centre of a dilemma that was to recur a hundred times. It had become impossible for me to carry on conversation with anyone. To turn my eyes from Dylan was but to

encounter faces the spectacle of him made sad and uncomfortable, eyes that implored me to do something. Goaded by them and by my new ill-fitting sense of responsibility I still could do nothing but loathe my indecision and wish that I were miles away. (Brinnin 1957, pp. 18–19)

Brinnin even found himself having to help Dylan out with financial expenses, despite knowing that Dylan was earning two or three times as much as Brinnin was himself. Like close family members, he began to wonder what his role had become; was he now simply Dylan's nursemaid, lowly assistant, or just bar companion? He asked himself whether he was wrong to put up with what was going on: 'it . . . appalled and saddened me . . . I had become ill-tempered, insomnious for the first time in my life, neglectful of my friends . . . and unable to concentrate upon my work' (pp. 57–8). As an alternative to putting up with a relative's or friend's addiction, one of the ways that people inevitably think of responding is by withdrawing from the situation, putting greater 'distance' between oneself and the disempowering source of the problem. Those who already live at some 'distance' from the addiction – more distant relatives, for example – usually find it easier to keep their distance or increase it. In the first example in Chapter 1, several of David's and his wife's friends did just that, as did Amanda's brother in the second example. For the closest family members, withdrawing is more problematic and may require more dramatic action: partners contemplate separation, for example, and parents think of telling their young adult children to leave home. Finding himself almost in the role of 'wife' to Dylan Thomas when he was on tour, Brinnin also dwelt on the possibility of telling Dylan that he had had enough. But like so many wives, his attitude towards Dylan was full of ambivalence and there were many reasons for continuing the relationship and reasons against terminating it.

Also very telling is what Brinnin said about his relationship with Dylan's wife, Caitlin. They both had very close relationships with Dylan and both wrote books about it. They had many of the same experiences. Although they might have shared much, their relationship was a difficult one, partly because of Caitlin's dislike of Dylan's US tours and, hence, her suspicion of Brinnin and also because Brinnin was party to knowing about several romantic attachments which Dylan formed in the USA and which were kept secret from his wife.

A last twist to this tale which intrigues me is that John Brinnin has come in for some of the same criticism which Caitlin Thomas, Sara Coleridge and other close family members have been subject to. In 1997 there appeared a book, *The Death of Dylan Thomas*, written by James Nashold, a doctor who thoroughly investigated the circumstances of Dylan Thomas's death, and George Tremlett, the same author who helped Caitlin Thomas write the most interesting of her autobiographies (Nashold and Tremlett 1997). Not only did they conclude that Brinnin had exaggerated Dylan's heavy drinking, but, in much the same way as Dylan's biographer, Paul Ferris, appeared to be blaming Caitlin for contributing to Dylan's decline, they accused Brinnin of failing to look after him properly during his last, fatal visit to the USA and for failing to get him appropriate treatment (they argued that a good doctor would have detected his diabetes, which they believed was the major underlying cause of his ill health).

John Brinnin and Dylan Thomas were not only friends but also colleagues engaged in a work-related task, albeit a less than mundane one. Those who are affected by a colleague's addiction often have a special perspective on its undermining effects. Their concerns may partly be for the health and well-being of their addicted colleagues, but in addition they are likely to be worried about the health of the joint project on which they are engaged. With other colleagues they are members of a team and the addiction of any one member threatens team performance. The threat is not unlike the threat to family and home; addiction constitutes a danger to any group in which the addicted person plays any kind of significant role. In work settings which are at all hierarchical – which means nearly all of them – addiction is most threatening when it is a senior person, or one who otherwise plays a key role, who is the focal, addicted person. There have been some highly publicised examples in the worlds of English football and British politics. In the most famous of all football cases, George Best, star player and leading goal scorer of one of the top-flight teams, became a liability and eventually lost his place in the team. He was already a legend then, and his legend lives on in his native Northern Ireland and in the rest of the UK, but there are many other sports people who have had similar problems.

The politician I have in mind, Charles Kennedy, was leader of one of Britain's political parties, the Liberal Democrat party, from 1999 to 2006. He eventually resigned because of the effect drinking was having on his ability to lead the party. The difficulty of standing up to addiction is well illustrated by a biography of Kennedy written, shortly after his resignation, by a journalist who had followed events closely (Hurst 2006). Throughout the period of his leadership there had been a series of complaints about his drinking – uncharacteristically poor performances, smelling of drink or evident drunkenness – and rumours that he had a drinking problem. A small group of his immediate staff and advisers knew of the problem and for some years managed to protect him from unwanted attention from the media and other members of the parliamentary party. But doing so was a strain. Several of the inner circle considered resigning unless Kennedy did something about his drinking. One small but telling indication of their concern was the fact that wine was banned from the office. A key person – the only person, apart from his wife, whom Kennedy thanked by name in his resignation speech – had this to say:

> It was often very tense in our office. Charles and I have known each other for twenty years, it was like brother and sister. I did tell him he had to sort things out or I would not stay, not because I had lost confidence or wanted to leave. I wanted him to sort himself out and was determined to make him. I did it to scare him into sorting himself out. The reality was I would never, ever have walked out on him. He was always saying to me: 'You promise you won't leave?' I would never have left him and he knows it. (Hurst 2006, p. 183)

He did seek treatment and, strongly advocated by his immediate group, he was on the point of making a public statement about it over two years before he was finally forced to do so. Hurst's opinion is that, had he taken that opportunity to make a public confession and clear the air then, the confusing and damaging events which threatened to split the Liberal Democrat party following the 2005 general election might have been avoided. The year 2005 was a bad one with things finally coming to a head in November. Kennedy had given a series of poor performances – most notably when launching the party's election campaign and when giving his leadership speech at the party conference – and questions about his drinking had become more public, to which he had responded with outright denials. There was now a larger group, consisting of the Liberal Democrat shadow cabinet, who were well aware of the seriousness of his drinking and its effect on his performance and that of the party as a whole. Even then, however, concerted action to stand up to his addiction was problematic. This was partly due to a conflict of interests for most senior members of the party, a number of whom would aspire to leading the party should Kennedy resign. Nor was there agreement about what should be done. A letter, addressed to Kennedy, asking him to 'consider his position', was drafted but never delivered. Some were of the opinion that individuals should make their views known to the chief whip, whilst others thought the proper course of action was for individuals to speak to him personally. His drinking and his future as leader were by then the subjects of numerous conversations. Several senior colleagues did speak to him personally, telling him that his position was unsustainable and citing his drinking. The crisis in the party was prolonged by the fact that the majority of Liberal Democrat MPs, outside of the shadow cabinet, had not known what was going on, and most had not known about the seriousness of their leader's drinking; when the crisis became evident, they supported Kennedy's continued leadership. The final days of his time as leader, further prolonged because of the Christmas break, were tortuous and uncomfortable for all. He tried to cling on by announcing a leadership election in which he would stand against other candidates – thought to be an empty gesture since the strongest other candidates would not wish to stand against him. The meeting at which he made that announcement was followed by threats of resignation from several senior colleagues and he was put in the position of having to resign two days later.

What is important for present purposes about the addictions of such prominent team players is the way in which addiction undermines their ability to play their roles and the quandary of impotence and indecision into which that throws their fellows. For one thing, addiction at work may remain hidden or partially concealed for a long time, as it can in the family context. A number of colleagues may have some degree of knowledge or concern about a person's addictive behaviour, perhaps over a period of many months or years. But – and this is what seems to have happened in the Kennedy case – if those who have partial knowledge do not share this with others or fail to agree with others about what should be done, then the organisation's coping strategy is very likely to be one of inaction. Concern is likely to rise as team performance declines and future threat – of slipping down the league or losing popularity with the voters – grows. The spotlight increasingly falls on the team manager or chairperson of the party who may be blamed for failing to act earlier or for acting too precipitously.

The constraints on rebelling against the illegitimacy of addiction

This chapter has advanced the argument that family members, friends and colleagues affected by addiction – a group, of colossal size globally, of people who have seen addiction at close quarters – are appropriately thought of as people whose power to control their own lives has been undermined, at second hand if you will, by the alien, external power which has entrapped their addicted relatives and associates. If that is a reasonable formulation, what further is there to be learnt from the great body of social theory and social science research about how people react in circumstances of disempowerment?

One of the questions which has preoccupied theorists of that subject is the question of how obvious inequalities in power are perpetuated despite the fact that the powerful are not constantly having to maintain their privileged positions by the use of force or other coercive tactics. Attention then turns to the powerless. Are they in some way consenting to these unequal relationships? Why are they are accepting things as they are, tolerating a position of subordination, putting up with such indignity? (Lukes 2005; Spears et al. 2010). This immediately suggests relevance to our interest in addiction and the family. As noted earlier, professionals have often asked – rather insensitively we can now see – why family members (it was usually women they were talking about) put up with their relatives' behaviour which seemed to the professionals to be entirely unacceptable. Knowing now much more about the actual experience of living with addiction and the strength of the emotional and material constraints that family members are often under, we can understand why affected family members often describe ways of reacting in the face of a relative's addiction which have been variously described as 'tolerant-accepting', 'inactive resignation' or 'resigning and maintaining façade' (Orford et al. 2005). Can this at all be equated with the apathy, acceptance and resignation in the face of powerlessness, even in democratic countries, which political theorists in the USA wrote about? (Dahl, 1961). Is it similar to the passivity, conformity and fatalism and lack of critical consciousness of their unacceptably deprived circumstances, which Latin American activist-theorists such as Martín-Baró (1994) and Freire (1972) wrote about? Is the question the same one that Gramsci (1971 [1926–37], cited by Lukes 2005) grappled with in his *Prison Notebooks*: how can consent to capitalist exploitation be explained? Does the explanation lie in the focus that subjugated people, with very limited resources, need to maintain on simply surviving, keeping safe, protecting children, preserving what little income one has? Or is it that the relatively disempowered usually know 'which side their bread is buttered': things may not be perfect but there are material and other benefits from coexisting with, and constantly renegotiating in small ways, an unequal relationship? Or is acceptance of disempowerment more deep-seated as many – from Gramsci with his influential concept of 'ideological hegemony' to modern social theorist Lukes (2005) with his 'third face of power' – have concluded? The powerless have so internalised predominating values, definitions and beliefs, so the argument goes, that they have accepted that things are the way they are for good reasons and that there is no feasible alternative. Hence, challenges to the status quo and rebellion are stifled.

Once allowance is made for the very different terms used in political and social theory, on the one hand, and family psychological and social science, on the other hand, there is much in what we know of the experience of family members and others affected by addiction which fits that way of thinking. There is a view, predominant especially in western thinking, that health problems, of which addiction is one, are individual matters, the responsibility of individual consumers. Addiction therefore represents a failure to 'drink sensibly', 'gamble responsibly' or not to 'misuse' or 'abuse' drugs. As will be argued in later chapters, this represents a gross distortion of the true state of affairs, masking as it does the power of those who benefit from the supply of dangerous products. Affected family members have internalised this hegemonic ideology and, as good wives, good parents or other good family members, much of the time they take upon themselves a large measure of responsibility for what has gone wrong. This is compounded by a whole complex of dominant beliefs about, for example, the rights of people (mostly men) to drink heavily and the appropriateness of family members (mostly women) to put up with it. Is it helpful, therefore, to think of family members affected by addiction – and, to a lesser degree, friends and associates – as a subordinated class, a subjected group of people whose consciousness about what their real interests are and how they are being subordinated under existing conditions needs awakening? If it is, then it is certainly a class currently without a collective voice, consisting most of the time of isolated individuals scarcely aware of the enormous number of other people who share their predicament – an 'atomised' class if ever there was one.

There are a number of theories in social psychology which are relevant here. Social dominance theory (SDT), with its useful ideas including that of hierarchy-enhancing myths, has already been mentioned. A variety of other theories give an important place to the concept of *legitimacy*. One view is that 'legitimate power' is one amongst a number of forms of power (force, coercion, reward, expertise, charisma, persuasion and manipulation are others): certain roles in society are invested with power legitimately, by general consent, not because it allows some people to wield power over others malevolently but because it allows some people to play more of a leadership, decision-making, role in the group's interests ('power for' rather than 'power over') (Wrong 1979). Others have given legitimacy an even greater role, arguing that differences in power are largely benign and are necessary for societies to function at all. One social psychological theory which has stood the test of time is social identity theory (SIT). SIT puts emphasis on identifying with a group, or groups, of people with common interests. One reading of the theory is, therefore, that a group will challenge other groups which threaten its own status position but only if power differences are perceived as illegitimate. Identity is, therefore, seen as the key factor helping to maintain consent with power inequality or, alternatively, promoting dissatisfaction with the status quo (Spears et al. 2010). Unfortunately, the relevance of this otherwise influential theory is seriously limited by the fact that family members affected by addiction are mostly isolated and have no collective sense of identity (although some counter examples are offered in Chapter 7). Other theories, such as resource dependence theory, see power differentials as being based on the greater dependence for important resources of one party on another: A has more power than B if B is more dependent on resources which A controls than vice versa (Pfeffer and Salancik 1978, cited by Overbeck 2010). But, again, this theory may be of limited relevance for our present discussion because, in the case of addiction, the source of a family member's disempowerment is obscure and confusing: the disempowerment may be keenly felt, but where power lies is less clear.

More relevant is system justification theory (SJT). According to SJT, there exists a quite basic psychological motivation to legitimise and defend the norms, rules or policies of the social systems which form the status quo within which people live. The idea is that it is uncomfortable, indeed threatening, to keep on thinking that the world is unfair and that existing social structures are illegitimate, undesirable, random or haphazard. A series of studies has shown that people in low power positions often justify the system which puts them in that position – for example, they subscribe to the view that high-power people are virtuous and deserving and/or that low-power people are less virtuous or less deserving – particularly if they believe that the system of which they are all part is under external threat or if they believe that the system in which they play a relatively lowly part is inevitable or unchangeable (Kay et al. 2010). This last factor – the perceived unchangeableness of the system – may be particularly relevant for addiction and the family since affected family members are very susceptible to the idea that their relatives' addictions are unchangeable and that they, as family members, have little or no control over their relatives' behaviour.

In his book, *Power: A Radical View*, Lukes (2005), following Tilly (1991), lists the following five answers to the question 'Why are subordinates compliant rather than continuously rebellious?'

1. The premise is incorrect: subordinates are actually rebelling continuously, but in covert ways.

2. Subordinates actually get something in return for their subordination, something that is sufficient to make them acquiesce most of the time, including valued ends such as esteem or identity.
3. As a result of mystification, repression, or the sheer unavailability of alternative ideological frames, subordinates remain unaware of their true interests.
4. Force and inertia hold subordinates in place.
5. Resistance and rebellion are costly; most subordinates lack the necessary means.

Only the third of those answers corresponds to an internalisation of disempowerment or, as one social theorist has called it, the 'thick' form of false consciousness (Scott 1990, cited by Lukes 2005). The other four acknowledge in different ways that false consciousness is really quite 'thin'; the powerless are more often dependent, coerced, realistic or actually quietly rebellious. Many social scientists have questioned the thesis that the powerless are passive, accepting the legitimacy of the status quo, inclined to justify the system in which they are relatively powerless, or that they are victims of false consciousness. They point to the many ways in which the powerless rebel in ways which disguise their resistance, constantly devising strategies to minimise or reduce their powerlessness, expressing their dissatisfaction and resentment in ways that will not lead to direct confrontation, including using humour and sarcasm and, wherever possible, expressing their true feelings to others of their class or group. Family members and others affected by addiction find many ways of coping which do not involve simply putting up with it, despite their opportunities for escaping the problem altogether being constrained. These ways of standing up to addiction include at least the following: finding helpful ways to talk to the addicted relative about the problem; deciding upon a strategy for resisting requests for money; setting rules or limits about substance use in the home; finding ways to reconcile firmness with kindness; adopting ways of protecting children and other family members; protecting oneself from harm; and looking for opportunities to support the relative in his or her efforts to control consumption of drink, drugs or gambling.

It is undeniable, however, that force and coercion are not uncommonly used to prevent affected family members from using methods of resistance such as confiding in others, seeking help for oneself, or separating. It is also incontrovertibly true that many lack the ability or resources to escape or to rebel openly. That is, of course, true for most children but is also the case for millions of wives and other family members affected by addiction. They may then undergo a process of preference adaptation, settling for a position which is manifestly unjust but which appears to be unchangeable. This is the process that Sen has written so vehemently about. As he has put it:

> [The] underdog learns to bear the burden so well that he or she overlooks the burden itself. Discontent is replaced by acceptance, hopeless rebellion by conformist quiet, and . . . suffering and anger by cheerful endurance. (Sen 1984, pp. 308–9, cited by Lukes 2005, p. 137)

The process is much aided by philosophies, including religious ones, which cast loyalty, meekness, patience, self-sacrifice and humility as virtues.

In this chapter I have tried to expand the idea that addiction is disempowering by applying that perspective to include wives, parents, husbands and other family members and friends and colleagues affected by someone else's addiction. I conclude that this enormous group of 'affected others' can be thought of as a subordinated class whose interests are compromised by the power of addiction. They are confused – as are all of us who contemplate addiction – about the source of their disempowerment. The immediate source appears to be the unacceptable behaviour of the addicted relative, who may be acting in an increasingly tyrannical and domineering fashion. But the addicted relative's apparent power is an illusion. It is not his or her real interests that rule but rather the demands of a new, conflicting interest, artificially created by attachment to an addictive substance or activity. Both those addicted – the Davids, Amandas and Carolines, the Coleridges, Thomases and Kennedys – and their families, friends and colleagues, are disempowered in the process, one because their true life interests have been compromised by a demanding new master, the other because their relatives' now divided interests have consequences for them which undermine their capability for effective management of their lives and that of their families and teams. In the following chapters the power perspective is expanded further, beyond the family and friendship and work groups, to include the wider context in which addictive objects are made available.

CHAPTER FOUR

Inequality in the power to resist addiction

The argument of Chapters 2 and 3 was that addiction is best thought of as an external source of power which undermines the capacity of the consumer for autonomous action (Chapter 2) and which, from thence, erodes the control which other members of the family, as well as close friends and colleagues, have over their lives (Chapter 3). But that says nothing about already existing power differences: it implies that addiction strikes randomly irrespective of people's power to resist. In this chapter it will argued that, far from showing such a disinterest in the structure of power, addiction flourishes where power to resist is already weakened. The argument will draw on a wide range of research evidence, derived from different traditions, some of it epidemiological and statistical in kind and in other instances of a qualitative and ethnographic sort. It engages us in examining the influence of power differentials by social class, gender, ethnicity and sexual orientation. It requires us to focus on individuals, their households and the neighbourhoods and areas in which they live. It forces us to consider the weight of the political and economic history and current context in which addiction can thrive. It raises the question of the extent to which free will and the exercise of autonomy are possible in resisting addiction in the face of structural forces of which those who suffer from addiction may be scarcely aware.

Socioeconomic status and the power to resist harm

Let us begin with some evidence of the relationship between socioeconomic status (SES) and alcohol problems. A good demonstration of the relationship is contained in the results of a Swedish study which examined records of hospitalisations and mortality related to drinking using survey data from the early 1970s to the mid 1980s (Romelsjö and Lundberg 1996). By the end of that period manual workers were showing standardised alcohol-related hospitalisation and mortality rates several times those of medium or high-level non-manual employees. What was particularly interesting was that, in the earlier part of that period, these social gradients, although less extreme than later, were nevertheless quite marked despite the fact that the gradient for average volume of alcohol *consumption* was in the reverse direction – those of *higher* SES being on average the greater consumers. This latter trend diminished over time in Sweden: in fact later, by the early 1990s, it was manual workers who were also the heavier consumers. This finding of a strong, negative SES gradient in alcohol-related mortality, despite fluctuating and often inconsistent relationships between SES and indices of consumption, is something that has been found in many countries. For example, in Finland (much of the best research of this kind has been done in the Nordic countries) a three- to four-fold difference in alcohol-related mortality has been found between the lowest and highest SES groups amongst men, and a two- to three-fold difference for women, despite lack of systematic differences between SES groups in levels of reported alcohol consumption (Mäkelä 1999). In Britain, the relationship between social class and alcohol-related mortality became clearer from the 1980s onwards. In one study which examined records of deaths from 1988 to 1994, a clear social class gradient was found for men, particularly for men under 40 years of age: young men in unskilled manual occupations were found to be 10–20 times more likely than those in the professional group to have been recorded as dying from alcohol-related causes. The results were in the same direction for younger women, although less clear cut, and for women over 40 the trend was in the reverse direction (Harrison and Gardiner 1999). People who are unemployed may be at special risk: the Swedish study found rates of alcohol-related hospitalisations and mortality amongst the unemployed to be 5–10 times normal.

Socioeconomic status bears on gambling problems also as illustrated by the results of British Gambling Prevalence Surveys conducted in 1999/2000, 2006/07 and 2009/10 (Sproston et al. 2000; Wardle et al. 2007, 2011). Average estimates of the amounts spent on gambling are generally positively related to SES but the estimated prevalence of gambling problems trends in the reverse direction, with highest rates of prevalence to be found amongst those in semi-routine or routine occupations. Those who are unemployed have a particularly high rate of problem gambling – more than three times the rate amongst those in paid employment according to the last of those surveys.

Drug problems too have often been shown to be related to SES. For example, one large US survey of adults with a 10-year follow-up showed the onset of drug dependence during that interval of time to be very strongly related to years of education: a massive odds ratio of 15 for those with fewer than 12 years of education compared to those with more than 15 years of education (Swendsen et al. 2009). A large French study of 17-year-olds showed that it was not experimenting with drugs – tobacco and cannabis in that study – which those of higher social status avoided but rather the *regular* use of such substances (Legleye et al. 2011). The results for cannabis were particularly clear in that respect: compared to teenagers from managerial/professional families, those in all other groups were actually significantly *less* likely to have experimented, but amongst those who had experimented, the transition to daily use was significantly *more* probable, particularly so amongst those from families where adults were unemployed or occupationally inactive.

Such studies of the SES–addiction link, of which the foregoing is just a tiny selection, are themselves just a small part of what is now a huge litera-ture on the relationship between SES and physical and mental ill health of many kinds in people of varying age groups in many different countries. In Britain, where this type of work has been particularly strong, it started with the publication of the *Black Report* published in 1982, followed by *The Health Divide* in 1988 and subsequent studies, especially the Whitehall studies of London civil servants (Townsend et al. 1992; Whitehead 1988; Davey Smith et al. 1990). But there are many debates about the idea of SES, not least how to measure it. Most popular have been measures based on a person's occupation, such as job grade in the Whitehall studies or, more generally, a scale such as the Registrar General's classification of occupa-tions in the UK, now superseded by the National Statistics Socioeconomic Classification of occupations. Other measures are based on an individual's income or years of education or qualifications. One source of controversy has been the question whether a more appropriate index of social posi-tion is one based upon the household, such as the occupational position of the person in the household whose occupation is of highest standing, or household income, accumulated family wealth, housing tenure, area of residence, or some index of standard of living (based on a single item such as access to use of a car, or fuel poverty, or a combined index such as one based on possession of a number of household durables and amenities). The Finnish study cited earlier (Mäkelä 1999) was unusual for including a number of separate SES indicators – education, occupational status, hous-ing tenure, personal income and household income – finding mortality from both acute and chronic alcohol-related problems to be independently associated with each of the SES indicators.

More important for present purposes is how those associations are to be explained and how those explanations fit with theories about social class and its influence and what role power occupies. The author of the Finnish report considered a number of possibilities. One was the idea that heavy drinking might be the cause and lower social position the effect – sometimes called the 'social drift' hypothesis. But that kind of explanation has mostly been rejected in the body of work on health inequalities generally and in the case of the Finnish alcohol results it seemed unlikely to provide much of an explanation since all the social indicators showed an association with mortality, including education, which is perhaps least likely to be an effect rather than a cause of social standing. Even in the case of relationships between addiction and unemployment, which certainly can be caused by excessive drinking, drug use or gambling, there is overwhelming evidence that unemployment leads to mental health difficulties such as anxiety and depression (Fryer 1990) which are likely to increase the risk of addiction.

More favoured than a social drift explanation was one based upon a form of drinking more prevalent in lower SES groups, namely drinking large quantities on a single occasion to the point of intoxication. That might go some way toward explaining the recurring finding that the frequency and overall volume of drinking have not consistently been found to be higher in lower SES groups whereas alcohol-related illness and mortality have been. As we shall see later, a similar type of theory, based on an understanding that some modes of consumption may be more harmful than others, has been advanced to explain the different impact of drug-taking in different social groups.

But, sticking to the example of alcohol, social class and health for the moment, what is the nature of the link between drinking and intoxication and social class? Is it something to do with class 'culture', a matter of values, beliefs, norms, customs and lifestyles, more prevalent in one part of the social class hierarchy than another, passed on within peer groups who share the same social and geographical spaces, even passed on from one generation to the next? Or, to pursue a line of thinking which brings power more into focus, has it more to do with there being more life stresses the lower one's position in the social hierarchy, more frequent reminders of one's lower status, or fewer alternative affordable opportunities for 'having fun'?

Or are power and control at the very heart of the matter? Two of the theories put forward to explain the general relationship between occupational status and health are relevant here. The first, the job demand-control (JDC) theory, gives a central place to job control – the degree of a worker's autonomy in making decisions on the job, the variety of skills that are used and the discretion that can be employed in their use (Karasek 1979). In the second Whitehall study, for example, job control and civil service grade were highly correlated: those in lower grades were very likely to report low job control (78% of men, 76% of women) and those in the highest grades were least likely to do so (9% of men, 10% of women) (Marmot et al. 1997). The second theory – effort-reward imbalance (ERI) – goes further, linking characteristics of a job itself with macro-economic labour market conditions, including factors such as salaries, career opportunities and job security (Niedhammer et al. 2004). It therefore addresses questions of fairness and distributive justice as well as issues of power and division of labour in the workplace. Power is least, according to this type of explanation, in jobs of lower status, particularly so amongst those who are employed by others, without any budgetary control, who not only lack authority over other workers but have little autonomy in their own work. Power is yet lower under labour market conditions which result in 'job insecurity, forced occupational mobility, short-term contracts and increased wage competition' (Siegrist et al. 2004, p. 1485). The rise of neoliberalism and economic globalisation, many argue, has exacerbated class differences, increased income inequality, and at the same time undermined public sector institutions which act to reduce inequalities or buffer their effects on health and welfare (Coburn 2004).

Closely related to work on social class and health, including that which relates specifically to addiction, is the comparatively recent idea that inequality is in itself bad for public health. This idea, particularly associated with the writings of Wilkinson, notably in his 1996 book *Unhealthy Societies*, goes beyond the finding that health is negatively related to SES within the population of a country or area. The new finding is that the health of the country or area taken as a whole is worse, the greater is the extent of inequality there. This is, therefore, not just about the existence of a social class health gradient but rather about the steepness of that gradient. Although neither their evidence nor their interpretation has gone unchallenged (Judge et al. 1998), Wilkinson and colleagues have now produced a lot of evidence suggesting that signs of poor public health and well-being – including infant mortality, childhood pregnancies, obesity, mental illness, imprisonment, homicide, to name only some – are higher in those amongst the richer countries of the world and amongst those states in the USA, which, compared to other countries or states, have the higher levels of income inequality. Much of this evidence is collected in the more recent book, *The Spirit Level: Why Equality is Better for Everyone*, by Wilkinson and Pickett (2009). Included is a graph, constructed from information contained in a UN World Drug Report for 2007, showing a significant relationship between an index of a country's rate of drug use – the index combines data on use of opiates, cocaine, cannabis, ecstasy and amphetamines – and the extent of income inequality in different countries – the ratio of the income received by the top 20 per cent of the population to that received by the bottom 20 per cent. The graph shows that the use of illegal drugs is more common in the less egalitarian countries such as the USA, UK and Australia and least common in the most income equal countries such as Japan and the Scandinavian countries (Portugal is an exception as one of the most unequal rich countries where use of illegal drugs is fairly average according to the UN report). Wilkinson and Pickett also report a tendency for illicit drug misuse and deaths from drug overdoses to be more prevalent in the states of the USA which are more unequal in income distribution.

Risky drug injecting environments

Because of the overriding public health concern about HIV and other forms of infection such as hepatitis C, there has been a surge of research into the factors which make drug injecting particularly risky for such infections. What these studies repeatedly show is that risk is associated with the methods and circumstances of drug-taking and that the riskier styles and environments are associated with those groups of people most lacking in the power to defend themselves against risk. One such study was carried out amongst injecting drug users in Marseilles, France, in the late 1990s, a few years after the city had embraced the harm minimisation aim of reducing risky injection practices (Lovell 2002). The latter included injecting with syringes and needles used by someone else, passing on a syringe or needle which had already been used for injecting, and sharing rinsing water, cotton or other material used in the preparation and injecting of the drug. The study was notable for its use of the concept of 'acquired cultural and economic capital', defined as the formal knowledge, qualifications, competencies, job status, assets, and other forms of wealth accumulated by an individual over his or her life course. The exact measure of acquired capital was based on highest employment level, educational level, monthly income, and absence of a prison record. This was one of two factors associated with avoiding risky injecting practices, the other being 'social stability', a variable made up of stable housing and 'social capital'; that is, having at least one person in his or her social network who was formally employed (or retired) and who was not a drug user. The power of the social network was further demonstrated in that study using a sociometric method which required each of the approximately 100 injecting drug users recruited for the study to nominate others in their social networks. Those who were involved in a large network of other injectors were significantly more likely to be engaging in risky injecting practices.

A review of network factors associated with sharing drug injecting equipment showed there to be several, including factors to do with the structure of the social network (such as how near to the centre of a relatively dense network of injecting drug users a person is), the composition of the network (for example, the presence of drug-using family members or others whom a person has known for a long time), as well as the extent to which sharing is the norm in the group and the degree of a person's drug addiction. Amongst other factors related to sharing was lower income, thought to be a factor because those with fewer resources to acquire drugs or purchase clean injecting equipment (if no free syringe exchange programme is available) are more dependent on others. As the review suggested, 'The power imbalance inherent in drug-sharing relationships governs the process of preparing, dividing and consuming drugs, which ultimately influences an individual's exposure to used injecting equipment' (De et al. 2007, p. 1734).

Qualitative data from the French study threw interesting light on how social disadvantage might make risky practices more probable. For example, amongst the most disadvantaged were some who appeared to lack the resources to procure drugs regularly for themselves. They received 'tastes' of heroin or cocaine in return for services or for some of their own prescription medication. Tastes might consist of a small amount of drug left over in someone else's syringe. Disadvantaged drug users might pick up used syringes or pick up or ask for other injectors' used cottons in order to extract drug residue for injection (Lovell 2002).

Studies from a number of countries have now helped to improve our understanding of drug use 'risk environments' and their association with a lack of material and other resources (Rhodes et al. 2005). The illegality of drug dealing and the stigmatised nature of the taking of some forms of drug, such as heroin, cocaine and crack, serve to augment those associations greatly. Studies from countries which include India and Vietnam as well as the USA have shown how the desire to avoid the gaze of non-users and the need to avoid police surveillance are among the factors which encourage the taking of drugs in semi-public settings where risks are greater. 'Shooting galleries' have been shown to be especially risky, particularly where injecting equipment is rented or stored for re-use or where injecting is administered by a 'hit doctor' who may be drawing the solution from a common pot. Injecting in abandoned buildings or other outdoor settings is associated with risk. Homelessness or imprisonment increase risk still further. Drug injecting in prison has been linked to HIV outbreaks in a number of Eastern European countries and in Thailand. Police activity, just part of the 'war on drugs', frequently increases risk, for example, by making people fearful of using public health syringe exchange programmes – as was found to be the case in the French study cited earlier – or by confiscating a user's personal injecting equipment or moving users on from comparatively safe areas to others where the risks are greater.

The often powerless position of women with problems of drug addiction

A number of studies of drug addiction from the 1980s onwards have noted the position of women illicit drug users, like Amanda (Chapter 1), as a particularly powerless one, more likely than male heroin users to have partners who also used, and more likely to have been influenced by their partners who may have introduced them to a new drug or made drugs more available or acceptable. One study focused on women heroin users in three cities: London, Amsterdam and Sydney. The report of that research noted that women's initiation into drug use had often been by men:

> The most frequently occurring type of induction was the he-gives-and-she-uses pattern. 'He' is usually a powerful figure, often a pimp or a dealer (economically powerful), or he is the object of her love (emotionally powerful), or he provides protection (powerful support). (Sargent 1992, p. 90)

One woman is quoted as saying, 'I used to think it so romantic that he would fix me. I used to feel so close to him that I would trust him to stick this needle in my arm, and when we first used it felt so great together' (p. 92). Others have noted that it is difficult in these circumstances for women to negotiate the circumstances of shared injection, leaving themselves open to pressure to engage in risky practices (Bryant et al. 2010).

A later study of heroin and speed injectors in the Haight Ashbury district in San Francisco documented the way in which a young woman's initial excitement at being involved on the edge of the drug scene could quickly develop into a life in which intimidation and violence were the norm (Bourgois et al. 2004). Having a sexual partner who was also an injection partner was associated with infection risk; the ethnographic part of the study showed why. Male partners usually exerted control over obtaining, preparing and injecting drugs, even when they were economically dependent on their women partners' income, including income from sex work. As one woman said, 'For three years, I didn't even watch my boyfriend prepare the drugs. He would just present me with a loaded syringe and fix [inject] me every time. It's the same with everyone out here. The guys like it this way. They like the feeling of having all that control over somebody' (p. 259), and as one man admitted, 'The guys like it when the girls can't fix [inject] themselves. It's power; the guys have power over the girls' (p. 255).

The diminished power of indigenous and minority groups to defend against addiction

The association between risky substance use – especially drinking – and a relatively powerless social position is at its most starkly obvious among indigenous peoples such as Australian Aboriginal and Torres Strait Islanders and Native USAmericans, who have been subject to invasion and subsequent oppression. Just one striking finding from a survey of teenage indigenous USAmericans across five sites was that the great majority of students – seven of every eight – reported that either a parent or another adult who was important to them had had problems with alcohol or drugs, either in the past or currently (O'Neill and Mitchell 1996). In Australia, although some improvements have taken place, the state of health of indigenous people has been a cause of great concern. Life expectancy is much lower than for other Australians and alcohol is thought to play a major role. For example, of all deaths of indigenous people living in town camps in Alice Springs, as much as 46 per cent were thought to be attributable to alcohol at least in part (Saggers and Gray 1998). The effect of drinking on violence – including alcohol-related domestic violence towards Australian Aboriginal women – has been a particular worry. But it is the total impact on family life and whole communities that indigenous people have increasingly been speaking out about. The brother of one of the all-too-many Aboriginal men who died in police custody – a national scandal – spoke at the Central Australian Aboriginal Congress: 'Couldn't sleep last night after listening yesterday. Thinking about how grog is killing people, family problems, culture dying, lost respect . . . Grog is tearing Aboriginal people apart' (Langton 1992, p. 3). The following was said during a research interview by a father, recruited to the study because of his concern about the excessive drinking of his son:

It [grog] is killing our life, our culture, our Aboriginal people. And people are getting carried away by drinking at what you might call the white man's drinking waterhole. It has taken away our life, the lives of my country-men . . . taken away the life for Aboriginal people. And now it's the crying time, people crying for their land, but that grog, people have to watch or control their lives, because if we want to live for another hundred years or more, us Aboriginal people, maintain our language . . . white men came into Australia, took away our rights, but the main one is the grog, took away our lives, for Aboriginal people. That's the main one, that big waterhole where we're getting drunk and into trouble. (Orford et al. 2005, p. 180)

Many reasons have been offered up in explanation of the harmful nature of indigenous Australian drinking but few deny that it cannot be understood without considering the sociohistorical context which has led to the present disadvantaged position of Aboriginal people:

> In every available measure of social and economic disadvantage, Aborigi-
> nal and Torres Strait Islander people record worse outcomes, face greater
> problems and enjoy fewer opportunities than the rest of the Australian
> population. The poverty and relative powerlessness of Australia's indige-
> nous people is reflected in inferior education, employment, income and
> housing. (Roberts 1998, p. 266)

Surveys of indigenous communities in Alaska and other parts of the USA have reported a high prevalence of excessive drinking, attributing this to social and historical factors such as being blocked for obtaining leadership positions in US society; response to the deterioration of a society under conquest; learning drinking behaviour from whites; and using intoxication to achieve Aboriginal goals (Segal 1998; Frank 2000). One piece of research, which involved two reservations in the upper midwest USA, used the concepts of 'historical trauma' and 'historical grief', drawing an analogy with the Jewish holocaust of the Second World War (Whitbeck et al. 2004). The focus was on regular reminders of the losses that their people had experienced and the feelings of distress caused by those reminders. 'Loss of our language', 'losing our culture' and 'loss of respect by our children for traditional ways' were amongst the losses that were most frequently on people's minds, but 'loss of our land' and 'loss of trust in whites for broken treaties' were not far behind. The single loss of which people were most frequently reminded was 'losses from the effects of alcoholism on our people'.

Indigenous groups may also be especially vulnerable to the risks posed by modern forms of gambling. There is evidence that Maori people spend more per head on gambling than New Zealanders of European heritage even though Maori median incomes are roughly half that of non-Maori people (Dyall and Hand 2003). It is probably no accident that casino development in the USA and Canada has particularly flourished in Native USAmerican and Canadian First Nations territories (Eadington 2003).

Russia offers a dramatic example of a country where excessive drinking has been affected by social change. The fluctuations that have occurred in alcohol consumption and health in that country since the mid 1980s have been described as unprecedented in peace time (Leon et al. 2009). Life expectancy rose sharply with the Gorbachev anti-alcohol campaign in the mid 1980s, falling dramatically in the years immediately after the collapse of the Soviet Union, recovering briefly in the mid 1990s, declining again due to the economic crisis in the late 1990s, and fluctuating again since then. At a low point, in 1994, life expectancy had dropped to 57 years for males and 70 for females. The huge difference in life expectancy for the two sexes is widely attributed to the much greater drinking of Russian men than women. Indeed, a conservative estimate attributes 30–40 per cent of deaths among working age Russian men to alcohol consumption. Vodka and other strong spirits are the most popular beverage type and a common pattern of male drinking that involves remaining intoxicated for two or more days at a time – a rather more extreme pattern of drinking than the one we have come to know as 'binge drinking' in the UK and elsewhere – is known in Russian as *zapoi*. Consuming alcohol in forms not intended for consumption (non-beverage alcohol) is also reported to have become more common. In one survey conducted in a single medium-sized industrial town on the western side of the Ural mountains, 11 per cent of men between the ages of 25 and 54 were reported to have gone on *zapoi* at least once in the last year, seven per cent to have consumed non-beverage alcohol, and 13 per cent to have had frequent hangovers (Tomkins et al. 2007). But, unusually dramatic though the Russian case may be, it provides yet another example of how the dangerousness of addictive forms of consumption tends to bear more heavily on those who are more socially disadvantaged. Each of those three indicators of excessive drinking was related to less education, to unemployment and to poorer amenities (possessing neither a car nor central heating). The association with education was particularly strong: after adjusting for the other social factors the odds of those in the lowest educational group experiencing *zapoi*, consumption of non-beverage alcohol and frequent hangovers, respectively, were 5.2, 7.7 and 3.7 compared to those in the highest education group.

There are, of course, many examples of groups around the world who are in a minority and disadvantaged position and vulnerable to further disempowerment through excessive engagement in dangerous forms of consumption. Immigrant groups under high stress through a combination of the experiences they have undergone before and during immigration, and the struggle to adapt to a new country, are often found to be vulnerable. Cambodian women now living in the USA is just one such group. Often finding themselves culturally isolated in their new country and having endured the traumas of the Cambodian holocaust, grieving for family members or worrying about those left behind, this group of women were found to be at high risk of misusing prescription drugs such as sleeping pills or drinking excessively (D'Avanzo et al. 1994). Immigrant groups in European countries – Sweden is one example – have been found to have higher-than-average rates of problem gambling (Rönnberg et al. 1999). In Britain, black and minority ethnic groups have a higher rate of problem gambling than the white majority despite also having higher proportions who do not gamble at all (Wardle et al. 2011).

Lesbian, gay and bisexual people (LGBs) are a minority group which has often been oppressed and victimised. There is ample evidence of the continued existence of homophobic or heterosexist attitudes, worse in some countries where the law supports discrimination and LGBs are subject to being terrorised, but continuing in some form and degree almost everywhere. It is not surprising to find, therefore, that there is now a considerable body of evidence showing that LGB people are at greater risk of taking up alcohol and drug use more quickly than other adolescents (Marshal et al. 2009) and meeting criteria for substance dependence as adults. For example, in one large national US survey the odds of meeting the criteria for alcohol dependence were three to four times as high for LGB adults as they were for heterosexuals (McCabe et al. 2009). A similar association between sexual orientation and alcohol use (and tobacco) was found in a large national survey of young adults in Mexico (Ortiz-Hernández et al. 2009). That study was of further interest because it tested the hypothesis that the relationship was at least in part due to the exposure of LGBs to homophobia. It was found that LGBs were more likely than others to report having had prejudicial, discriminatory and violent experiences – having been a victim of crime in the previous 12 months, answering affirmatively to a question about violence in the family and feeling that 'your rights have not been respected because of your sexual orientation'. Several of the associations between sexual orientation and alcohol and tobacco use could be explained by the mediating link with homophobia exposure. Another US national study similarly found that the substantially higher rate of last-year substance disorders amongst LGB people could, to a large extent, be accounted for statistically by their significantly greater lifetime exposure to victimisation experiences (Hughes et al. 2010).

Social status confers advantage in resisting and quitting addiction: the case of smoking

Because the supply of tobacco cigarettes has mostly been legal and because the prevalence of smoking has been so high, a relatively great deal of relevant information on smoking has been available of a kind that can be analysed by epidemiologists. The trends over the later part of the twentieth century were intriguing and may tell us a lot about how dangerous consumptions bear most heavily upon those who are already relatively powerless. For example, a whole special issue of the journal *Drug and Alcohol Dependence* focused on smoking among women and the emergence of a clear social class gradient towards the end of the century (Chilcoat 2009; Graham 2009). In accordance with the idea of stages in the rise and fall of the engagement of populations in dangerous forms of consumption like smoking, there was a period, roughly from the mid 1950s to the mid 1960s in the USA, when men's smoking prevalence was starting to decline but women's was still on the increase. The suggestion is that the negative social class gradients became clear only once a stage was reached when the popularity of the habit was in decline. The US data show that, from the 1970s onwards smoking was decreasing for both sexes and differences between those in different social positions were opening up for both. When social position was indexed by years of education, the difference was appearing for men because those with the most years of education were now taking up smoking much less often than others, whereas among women the difference was attributable to the group with the least education continuing to take up smoking at a high rate, indeed at a rate that continued to increase at least until the 1980s. Not only that, but also, amongst smokers, a social gradient in terms of heavy smoking – at least 25 cigarettes a day – started to appear in the mid 1980s and became stronger over the next decade. The less education women had had the more likely they were to take up smoking and if they did so the heavier their smoking was likely to be. Similar trends were detected in Europe with the familiar negative social class gradient emerging first for men and later for women, the whole process being relatively delayed in some southern European countries where smoking by women remained relatively taboo for longer. Herein lies another of addiction's power paradoxes: the increased social and economic power of women has led to them following men's bad example and adopting a habit which in the case of tobacco not only deprives most consumers of the ability to fully control their consumption but which for many will also turn out to seriously damage their health.

Tobacco is, of course, particularly deadly. Changes in the smoking habits of different social classes were reflected in changes in social gradients for lung cancer mortality. Up until the 1960s for men in the USA and up to the 1980s for women, the relationship between SES and mortality from lung cancer was positive, reversing only thereafter, and reversing more slowly for older people (Chilcoat 2009). There is evidence also that social disparities in smoking have increased in Russia since the early 1990s and that much the same may have taken place for smoking in China. For example, figures for women smoking show increased prevalence in the decade between the early 1990s and the early 2000s in all educational groups in both countries, but steepest increases in those with least education – less than secondary education in Russia and less than five years education in China (Graham 2009).

One theory, which may help explain these changes, talks of social conditions emerging as a fundamental determinant of disease and forms of behaviour which are risky for health, once knowledge about the risks becomes widely known and when methods to treat the disease or to help people change risky behaviour become available. When those things happen, those 'who command more resources of knowledge, money, power, and prestige, and beneficial social connections are able to gain a health advantage to a greater extent than those who lack these resources' (Chilcoat 2009, p. S22). As one prominent UK epidemiologist has put it, 'The decline of cigarette use in countries like the USA is leaving behind a population of smokers which is increasingly female and poor' (Graham 2009, p. S15).

Differences in prevalence rates between population sub-groups may be due in part to different rates of taking up consumption in the first place and partly to differences in rates of giving up consumption or consuming in a less risky way. Data from a study carried out in the USA, Canada, the UK and Australia threw some light on the relationship between social conditions and quitting smoking (Siahpush et al. 2009). At one wave of this longitudinal study participants were asked whether they were planning to stop smoking or not: two-thirds to three-quarters in each of the countries expressed such an interest in quitting. When next interviewed two years later around half of that proportion (between 32 and 41 per cent of all those interviewed) reported having made any attempt to stop smoking since the previous interview, and a slightly smaller proportion (between 27 and 40 per cent of all those interviewed) reported having been successful in stopping. The particular interest here lies in the relationship between the process of quitting smoking and an index of social position. The index used in that study was financial stress: ' because of a shortage of money, were you unable to pay any important bills on time, such as electricity, telephone or rent bills?' Those answering positively to that question (between 6 and 16 per cent of all participants) were significantly more likely to express an interest in quitting but significantly *less* likely to subsequently report having made an attempt to stop and also significantly less likely to have stopped successfully between one wave and the next. Those under financial stress were more likely to be in the lowest of three income groups and were more likely to say that they had spent money on cigarettes that they knew would be better spent on household essentials like food – a rather staggering 18 to 20 per cent answered affirmatively to that question.

In France, between 2000 and 2007, five national telephone surveys about smoking were carried out (Peretti-Watel et al. 2009). In those seven years smoking prevalence decreased most amongst executive managers and professionals: a decrease of 22 per cent, mostly occurring between 2000 and 2003. The decrease was less marked among manual workers: an 11 per cent decrease, mostly occurring between 2003 and 2005. There was no decrease amongst unemployed participants. These data also provide a clear indication of how costly a cigarette habit is for those on lower incomes. Between 2000 and 2005 the proportion of household income (the measure used was equivalised household income, which corrects for the number of people in the household) spent on smoking by professionals and executives who smoked rose from three to five per cent. For manual workers the equivalent figures were 9 and 13 per cent. For those unemployed, the figures were 13 and 21 per cent. Taking all smokers together, the proportion devoting at least 20 per cent of household income to the purchase of cigarettes had gone up from five to 15 per cent.

The UK Millennium Cohort Study includes children born in the first two years of the new millennium. What their mothers did about smoking during and after pregnancy provides further evidence of the influence of social disadvantage (Graham et al. 2010). Whether or not mothers smoked before pregnancy was strongly negatively related, as we would expect it to have been by then, with social indicators such as the mother's occupational status and household income: those in the lowest of three occupational categories were 2.5 times more likely to be smokers than those in the highest category, and those in the lowest income category were four times more likely to be smokers than those in the highest. But smoking prior to pregnancy was also significantly related to childhood circumstances as indexed by their fathers' occupations when they were young teenagers and by a life course variable thought to be crucial in the link between childhood and adulthood disadvantage, namely age of leaving education. Those who left education before the age of 17 were more than four times as likely to be smokers as those who remained in education beyond the age of 21. Being a relatively young mother was also strongly related to smoking: those under 20 at the time of first giving birth were nearly four times as likely to be smokers as those who first gave birth at age 30 or above. These social disparities in smoking were enhanced during pregnancy since, among the smokers, quitting was significantly more likely amongst those of higher occupational status, greater household income, higher childhood SES and more years in education. Furthermore, among those who gave up smoking during pregnancy, greater household income and more education were significant predictors of remaining as non-smokers at nine months post-partum.

There is also recent evidence for an area effect on drug use cessation. A 10–20 year prospective study of injecting drug users in Baltimore, USA, showed that those who achieved long-term injection cessation, defined as three consecutive years without drug use, were significantly more likely to live in less deprived neighbourhoods. Relocating from a highly deprived to a less deprived neighbourhood was also associated with cessation (Genberg et al. 2011). The places where people live and consume dangerous products may be important.

Place matters: some neighbourhoods are riskier for addiction than others

So far in this chapter powerlessness and disadvantage have been treated either as individual-level properties, indicated by variables such as a person's occupational status, education, financial resources, sex, ethnicity or sexual orientation, or as a macro-level property of a whole nation or ethnic group. But powerlessness, as it relates to the risks associated with dangerously addictive forms of consumption, may also be a matter of the particular areas or neighbourhoods in which people live. It has long been known that mental ill health, suicide attempts and most forms of crime show a strong tendency to be concentrated in poorer areas (Orford 2008a) and there has been a growing interest amongst epidemiologists in exploring the relationship between place and all manner of health and social indicators (Macintyre et al. 2002). That research has had to contend with the criticism that what may appear to be place effects are really just due to the 'selection' into poorer areas of vulnerable or already ill individuals and families, combined with selective migration out of such areas by those who are less vulnerable. This has led to the use of complex multi-level statistical techniques to try to detect place effects independently of individual-level variables. But that can become an unhelpful exercise since it may reasonably be argued that factors such as individuals' levels of education, occupations or income are themselves partly determined by where people live: controlling them out statistically may, therefore, remove part of the area effect that is being looked for (Oakes 2004). It may be artificial to contrast place explanations with those based on individual-level factors. In practice, it becomes impossible to separate the influence of neighbourhoods and knowledge about the people who reside in those neighbourhoods: it may be better to think of area effects as emergent properties of the social interactions of the people who live there.

Addiction research on area effects is comparatively limited but what exists is interesting and varied – some epidemiological, some qualitative, some ethnographic – and it provides support for this chapter's thesis. In the early 1960s Chein and his co-investigators wrote one of the first detailed accounts of what was then a small and localised narcotics problem in New York. The book was generally known by its sub-title, *The Road to H*, and it became a classic text. Their work showed convincingly for the first time that drug problems were concentrated in certain areas, notably Harlem in Manhattan and the south-central area of the Bronx. These 'epidemic areas', as they called them, were

> ... on the average, areas of relatively concentrated settlement of under-privileged minority groups, of poverty and low economic status, of low educational attainment, of disrupted family life, of disproportionately large numbers of adult females as compared to males, and of highly crowded housing; they are densely populated and teeming with teen-agers. (Chein et al. 1964, pp. 55–6)

Within the epidemic areas and those immediately adjacent to them, they found highly significant correlations across census tracts in each of the three boroughs of Manhattan, the Bronx and Brooklyn between rates of drug problems and the percentage of the local population that was black as well as the percentage of households on low incomes and of men employed in lower SES occupations, dwelling units without television and dwelling units that were highly crowded. In another chapter of their book they reported the finding that young teenage boys in areas of the city with relatively high rates of drug problems were more likely to express attitudes implying futility, rejection of middle class values and orientation towards delinquency. They were more likely to endorse statements such as, 'There is not much chance that people will really do anything to make this a better world to live in' and 'Most policemen can be paid off'.

A good example from Europe is a study which estimated the prevalence of opiate addiction in the 30 or so areas within the city of Barcelona. Areas with the highest rates were mostly those near the centre of the city where rates were up to 10 or more times those in low rate areas. A very high correlation was found between addiction prevalence and the unemployment rate in the area (Brugal et al. 1999).

One national US study from the early 1990s found evidence supporting the hypothesis that ethnicity and poverty interact when it comes to alcohol-related problems. Census data were used to assess the proportion of households in the area – these were small areas corresponding to residential blocks of about 400 households – which were below the poverty line. Black men living in more impoverished neighbourhoods reported more alcohol-related problems than white men but there were no differences between black and white men living in the more affluent areas (Jones-Webb et al. 1997). One explanation examined by the authors was simply that there were more social problems in predominantly black inner city neighbourhoods: black men living in poorer areas and who reported alcohol-related problems were more likely than white men to live in blocks with low family incomes, fewer people in the labour force, higher population densities, and greater numbers of establishments serving alcohol. Other evidence from the USA suggests that black men report higher rates of drinking problems than white men at the same level of consumption and are put at relatively greater risk by lower SES, lower incomes and unemployment (Herd 1994). As discussed earlier, this might be due to styles of drinking which are riskier, and/or to local norms which encourage riskier forms of consumption, or to a host of factors associated with social marginalisation which decrease resilience in the face of risks to health. Interaction effects are not uncommon in the literature on place and health (Orford 2008a): it is often found to be the case that relatively disempowered groups such as black or minority ethnic groups, in the UK, for example, are comparatively less healthy in poorer areas, but sometimes it is found to be the case that minority groups are less healthy in better off areas where they are in a smaller minority and perhaps living in an area where inequality is greater.

What evidence there is suggests that the drinking or drug-taking of adolescents is also affected by the areas in which they live. One study followed up African USAmerican school students in their mid teens in Baltimore, Maryland. A measure of neighbourhood disorganisation, which included questions about the frequency of violent crime, feelings of unsafety and the visibility of drug use, was predictive of a combined measure of the frequency of a student's tobacco, alcohol and marijuana use two years later. Part of the effect for the boys, and all of the effect for the girls, was mediated by the students' beliefs about drugs: those in the less disorganised neighbourhoods were more likely to perceive substance use as harmful and were more likely to disapprove of it, beliefs which protected them against higher levels of personal substance use (Lambert et al. 2004).

Area deprivation has also been shown to be associated with problem gambling. The analysis of data from a national survey in the USA divided respondents' areas of residence into ten groups according to level of deprivation, finding problem gambling to be 12 times as prevalent amongst those living in the most extremely deprived areas compared to those living in the very least deprived (Welte et al. 2004). Analysis of data from the 2006/07 and 2009/10 British Gambling Prevalence Surveys divided respondents into five roughly equal sized groups depending upon the deprivation index assigned to the areas of England in which they lived. Area deprivation was found to be related both to the respondents' own problem gambling and to the frequency with which they reported having a close relative with a gambling problem. The second of those relationships was particularly strong: those in the most deprived areas being two to three times as likely to report a close relative with a problem compared to those in the least deprived areas (Orford et al. 2010b).

Two studies carried out in the early 1990s provide additional snapshots of how risk might vary with neighbourhood. One was carried out with residents of four different areas in Glasgow, Scotland (Sooman and Macintyre 1995). They varied from an area containing some of the most desirable addresses in the city, consisting of nineteenth-century villas and tenements built for the Victorian middle classes, to the poorest of the four areas and the one most remote from the city centre, one of the city's post-war peripheral public housing estates, built to a low standard in an era of acute housing shortage and for many years lacking quite basic amenities. The first area was, unsurprisingly, viewed most positively by residents. It was the most likely to have easy access to resources such as a bank within walking distance. The latter area had the highest score on a scale of 'incivilities', which included problems of rubbish and litter, vandalism and disturbances by youths. The problem of discarded drug injecting needles was reported by four to five times as many residents in the latter area than in the former. Although most residents in all areas had easy access to a pub, that was nearly universally the case only in the latter, poorer area. At about the same time, a large sample of sixth and seventh grade pupils (young teenagers) in Baltimore, USA, were being asked about the neighbourhoods in which they lived and specifically whether they had ever been offered alcohol, tobacco, inhalants, marijuana, and crack or cocaine (Crum et al. 1996). They also answered 18 questions which made up a scale of neighbourhood disadvantage – not unlike the scale of incivilities used in the Scottish study – and the sample was divided into three roughly equal-sized groups on the basis of their answers. Offers of each of the types of substance were reported most frequently in the highest of the three neighbourhood disadvantage groups and least frequently in the lowest. For example, nearly twice as many young people had been offered alcohol in the most compared to the least disadvantaged of the three neighbourhood groups, and in the case of crack/cocaine the odds were five to six times greater.

Outlets for the sale of legal addictive substances and activities tend to be concentrated in areas where resistance is weaker

One line of research on place that has become popular because of its special relevance to addiction concerns the geographical spread of sales or supply outlets. This has produced an accumulation of evidence that outlets for dangerous but legally available forms of consumption, such as alcohol and gambling – the objects of David's and Caroline's addictions – are concentrated more heavily in poorer areas and, furthermore, that a greater density of outlets in an area is related to indices of heavier consumption or of harm related to consumption. Sometimes this research has involved adults, from younger to older, and sometimes it has been confined to young people (sometimes teenagers only and sometimes 'youth' which can include those in their early twenties). Typical of the research on smoking was a study of adults living in 82 neighbourhoods in four northern Californian cities which had been part of a well-known heart disease prevention programme (Chuang et al. 2005). Neighbourhoods with a relatively high density of convenience stores (which, according to the authors, were the types of retail outlets accounting for the largest volume of tobacco sales), where participants in the research were more likely to live within a short distance of such a store, were much more likely to be lower SES areas (more people with less than high school education, blue collar workers, unemployed, lower annual income, and lower housing values). Average number of cigarettes smoked a day was correlated with both lower neighbourhood SES and higher neighbourhood convenience store density, independently of individual variables such as a person's educational level, ethnicity, age and sex.

A study of 12–17 year olds living in Auckland, New Zealand, is one of those that have focused on alcohol consumption (Huckle et al. 2008). Areas for the purpose of this study were defined in terms of ten-minutes travelling time by car, and outlets included all on and off-licences where alcohol could be readily purchased: bottle stores, grocery stores, supermarkets, hotels and taverns, night clubs and some sports clubs, such as pool halls available to the public. Outlet density was highly correlated with score on a measure of the material and social deprivation of the area which included income, employment, communication, transport, support, qualifications, living space, and owning a home. In fact, outlet density and area deprivation were so highly correlated that it was meaningless to try to estimate which was the more important influence on young people's drinking. Both were correlated with the amounts young people said they drank on typical occasions. In another study of adolescents, this time carried out in California, alcohol outlet density – calculated as the count of active off-premise outlets per roadway mile within each zip code (postcode) area in the state – was, independently of area median household income and a number of relevant individual variables, correlated with both the frequency of drinking and the frequency of getting drunk at the first wave of this longitudinal study when the adolescents were aged 14–16 (Chen et al. 2010). Although there was a significant tendency for those in areas with lower outlet density to catch up in terms of their drinking in the following two years, the earlier start for those adolescents in the areas with more alcohol outlets is important because there is overwhelming evidence that the earlier the take-up of a potentially addictive form of consumption in adolescence the greater the risks for later problems. Another study, carried out in the city of Baltimore, found the concentration of off-premise establishments – typically selling alcohol chilled, in larger quantities than in taverns or restaurants, and ready for immediate consumption on the street, in a park or in a motor vehicle – was higher in those residential census tracts with a higher percentage of African USAmerican residents, and also in those census tract areas where median incomes were lower. Ethnic composition and median income were correlated but independently related to alcohol outlet density. There was an interaction effect such that outlet density was highest in those areas with the higher proportion of black residents *and* lower incomes (LaVeist and Wallace 2000).

Australia has been the setting for some of the best research suggesting the importance of the concentration of facilities for gambling. Most of the research there has been about the Australian type of electronic gambling machines or 'pokies'. Provision has varied greatly from one state or territory to another and, not surprisingly, the number of machines per head of population was found to be strongly related to per capita expenditure on machine playing across the eight states and territories (Marshall 2005). Later research in New South Wales showed that the concentration of machines in different towns and suburban areas was correlated with the proportion of residents who reported in surveys that they had recently played gambling machines and also with median expenditure on machine playing and the average number of sessions of machine playing in a period of a year. As has been found in the tobacco and alcohol studies, it was areas with less advantaged resident populations which tended to be those with the higher density of gambling machines (Marshall 2005). More recent research has shown, for the first time in Britain, that gambling machines are more heavily concentrated in poorer areas (Wardle 2011).

Closeness of access to gambling facilities and the prevalence of gambling problems have been found to be correlated in national surveys in the USA (La Plante and Shaffer 2007). For example, one found that having a casino within 50 miles of home was associated with nearly double the prevalence of gambling problems, and another found that having a casino within ten miles was one of several factors associated with problem gambling. In Canada also it has been shown that there is a significant association between rates of problem gambling in the different provinces of the country and the provision per head of the population of each of several different categories of gambling such as casinos, gambling machines and horse race venues (Williams et al. 2007). There is also now a body of research attesting to the relationship between density of alcohol outlets and the incidence of problems which are either alcohol-related by definition, such as drunken driving, or which are known to be at least partly alcohol-related, such as violent crime, motor accidents, pedestrian collision injuries, child abuse and neglect, domestic violence and sexually transmitted disease (Gorman et al. 2001).

Of course, it will be argued by some that it is oversimple to think of outlet density as a major cause of excessive forms of consumption and the incidence of consumption-related harms. Since outlet densities are so often associated with area deprivation or disorder, it may be that providers are simply responding to the wishes of those who live in those areas. They would like us to see alcohol outlets, for example, as, 'the connecting point... between individuals' proclivities to use alcohol and commercial and social markets for alcohol in community settings' (Gruenewald 2007, p. 873). The same might be said in the case of tobacco or gambling or, indeed, for illegal markets in prescribed drugs. The power of the providers is the main topic of Chapter 5.

Becoming involved in an illicit drug use scene: free choice, choice constrained, or coercion?

A number of studies report the results of carrying out detailed, in-depth interviews with users of illicit drugs in an effort to understand the processes involved in taking up the use of 'hard' drugs, becoming involved in an area drug 'scene', or undertaking the transition to drug injecting. Amanda, from Chapter 1, or someone just like her, would have been a very suitable participant in such research. Two such studies have been carried out in Canadian cities. One involved interviews with young people, aged between 14 and 16, all recent users of illicit drugs other than or in addition to marijuana and all by then fairly well entrenched into the downtown Vancouver drug scene. The process of becoming so involved is broken down into two parts: 'Coming down here' and entering the local scene and transitioning from being a 'Weekend warrior' who frequented the scene but was not resident in it to becoming fully engaged in it. The report discusses the interplay of choice in becoming involved – pulling factors – and factors which appear to have pushed people towards involvement. Some described living in the area from an early age, having parents who were addicted to drugs and/or alcohol; they emphasised the inevitability of their involvement and absence of choice. Others described escaping from involvement with law enforcement in other Canadian cities or escaping abusive or unhappy circumstances at home or in care. It was common for interviewees to describe the attraction of the famous Vancouver scene with its reputation for excitement, fun, being 'a wild place'. Several described an immediate sense of belonging when they arrived and many were able to obtain temporary accommodation quickly. Reflecting on the balance of pulling and pushing factors, the authors say:

> In sum, stories about 'coming down here' speak both to the ways in which young people exercised agency in *choosing* to becoming involved in the local drug scene (and in shaping the nature of that involvement), and to the ways in which their choices were powerfully constrained at the time of their entry into this drug-using milieu. (Fast et al. 2009, p. 1207)

Participants reflected on how quickly they became integrated into the social networks and practices of the local scene. A number recalled being quickly approached and introduced to places and people that connected them with drugs and with opportunities to generate income, mainly through illegal activity – some busking or recycling but mostly drug dealing, sex work, theft, and exchange of stolen goods. There was often reflection on their naivety upon first arriving and recall of a sense of intimidation felt when interacting with older or more experienced youth. These were described as critical moments. For example, 'that's when I got hooked on crystal meth'; 'By the end of the week I was selling anywhere from an eight ball of coke to a quarter pound of coke a day' (p. 1208). The ubiquity of drug use was consistently referred to as an important factor in redefining previously held 'risk boundaries'. As time went on, young people had found themselves increasingly established within the local scene, experiencing homelessness and difficulty obtaining stable accommodation, destabilisation of social networks due to arrests and periods of incarceration, loss of opportunities for legitimate employment, increasing reliance on illegal methods of income generation and accelerating addiction. The authors were struck by 'how quickly young people move from being willing players in the context of the local drug scene to circumstances where autonomy is severely limited – a theme that emerged (albeit in different forms) in each participant's story' (p. 1208). Hence:

> ... many young people find themselves suddenly and unexpectedly entrenched within a drug scene of which they want no part ... they emphasized that, although street life does offer opportunities for excitement and income generation, these benefits are greatly outweighed by the accelerating negative consequences of 'life on the streets', including exposure to violence and blood-borne infections such as HIV and hepatitis C, and immense emotional suffering. (p. 1209)

Nevertheless, as others have found, participants in this study rejected social determinants as explanations for their involvement in the drug scene, emphasised the possibility of exiting or avoiding some of its most destructive aspects and claimed that they maintained a high degree of autonomy.

From the other side of Canada comes a study based on interviews with injecting drug users recruited from a variety of sources, including syringe exchange programmes and by outreach methods. The interviewees were, on average, in their mid thirties but the average age of first injecting had been 17. They spoke about the factors they believed had contributed to their illicit drug-taking in the first place, a mix of unstable and sometimes abusive early family lives, an 'escape' from poverty and poor neighbourhoods and the attraction of what seemed like an exciting lifestyle – 'bad guys driving like Porsches and wearing Versace suits and freebasing cocaine' (Khobzi et al. 2009, p. 555), as one participant put it. Much of the report of this study is then about the process of initiation into injecting drugs. It is stated that in every case this transition was, 'accomplished out of a relationship with their social group' (p. 550). In a small number of cases the person had been introduced to injecting by a family member at a very early age, but mostly a combination of the 'harsh street culture' and the 'drug-filled environment' in which many of the participants had lived meant a natural progression leading almost inevitably to injecting being accepted and fears and inhibitions about injecting overcome. Although some learnt to inject on their own, most learnt directly from others and typically it was another injecting member of the social group who injected a novice (the often relatively powerless position of women in these circumstances was discussed earlier in this chapter). As the following two quotations from participants illustrate, there was sometimes an element of coercion involved but more usually interviewees described the desire to belong to a social group, looking up to older and 'cooler' members, or viewing injecting as part of the formation or strengthening of a bond with the group or an individual person within it.

> I was hanging out with an older crowd and I thought they were just the ultimate cool. I said, 'oh, I'd like to try that sometime' . . . [they] sat on my knees, grabbed my arm and said 'now is the time'. I didn't protest much cause it was something I really wanted to do myself. (p. 551)

> I was with a girl one day and I wanted to be accepted by everybody – it was an older crowd, 25, 30 years old . . . one day it was just me and her alone and she asked me if I wanted to try it and I jumped at the chance. She hit me up. (p. 550)

An interesting British study involved interviews with heroin users from five different user networks, recruited through treatment contacts, each now in his or her late thirties or forties (Best et al. 2007). They spoke about the different social networks in which they had used heroin and helped recruit five further interviewees for the study, each a member of one of the five networks. Heroin use had spread rapidly within these local social networks, based on siblings and friends who lived on the same housing estate. A recurring theme was the naivety of the participants, looking back, about the nature of the drug and its potential to create dependence. Almost all had used heroin for the first time in the presence of at least one other person, and several felt 'tricked' into using heroin, for example, being told that it was something other than heroin or by the use of a pseudonym for heroin with which the person was unfamiliar at the time. Another theme in these interviews was the effect of heroin use on the rupture of previous social networks and the gravitation to exclusively heroin-using groups.

Addiction as a reflection of social and economic structures of power

Just over 30 years after Chein et al.'s (1964) study of drugs in different New York neighbourhoods, by which time the city's drugs scene had expanded and undergone a number of changes, the anthropologist Bourgois (2003a [1996]) wrote another classic, *In Search of Respect: Selling Crack in El Barrio*. The research methods he employed differed substantially. Provoking the concern of his friends, he lived for a number of years in the late 1980s in a predominantly Puerto Rican part of east Harlem which had a history of being a heroin and cocaine epidemic area and which by then was becoming notorious for crack cocaine dealing. During his participant-observation ethnographic study he spent a great deal of time in and around one of the several local crack houses, getting to know well a number of those involved in dealing drugs there, recording interviews with them and family, friends and neighbours, managing in the process to overcome suspicions that he was an undercover policeman and avoiding the police, who suspected him of being a drug dealer himself. The result is one of the most detailed accounts available of a local, inner-city drug dealing environment. Bourgois is one who has made a strong case that drug-taking is not itself a problem but is, rather, an epiphenomenon, reflective of deeper problems of social structure. He describes in detail the emigration of Puerto Ricans, forced by loss of traditional livelihoods, their settlement in some of the poorest parts of New York historically settled by black USAmericans and Italians and other immigrants, the erosion of traditional working class employment, the difficulty of adjusting to working in service industries located in the richer parts of the city, and the prejudice experienced there, and the decline in rights to and the value of social security benefits. It is against that background, he argues, that drug dealing could be seen as part of the huge, unregulated and untaxed underground economy, which allowed poor New Yorkers to get by. Cocaine and crack dealing he describes as 'the fastest growing – if not the only – equal opportunity employers of men in Harlem' (p. 3). At the same time as providing financial opportunity, drug dealing could offer a certain respect amongst peers, part of the

inner-city 'street culture of resistance'. At the same time, Bourgois fully documents the downsides to drug dealing and drug addiction: the violence,
erosion of capacity to find legitimate employment, the domestic abuse and
neglect of children. He nicely expresses a power paradox when he writes:

> Illegal enterprise, however, embroils most of its participants in lifestyles of
> violence, substance abuse, and internalized rage. Contradictorily, therefore,
> the street culture of resistance is predicated on the destruction of its par-
> ticipants and the community harboring them. In other words, although
> street culture emerges out of a personal search for dignity and a rejection of
> racism and subjugation, it ultimately becomes an active agent in personal
> degradation and community ruin. (p. 9)

> Self-destructive addiction is merely the medium for desperate people to
> internalize their frustration, resistance, and powerlessness. (p. 319)

The environment described by Bourgois is one mainly dominated by men.
He is far from alone in seeing such a drug culture as providing young men
with a way of maintaining masculine dignity, albeit ultimately a disastrous
way for many. A similar conclusion was reached in the study, referred to
already in Chapter 2, of gang members in slum areas in the city of Makassar,
Indonesia:

> Maybe because it's really hard for many *lorong* [slum area] boys like us to
> demonstrate good achievement. You know, many of us are unemployed
> or just do low jobs, go to bad schools and then drop-out. What can we
> say? . . . We're just very keen to prove ourselves as *rewa* [braveness or tough-
> ness as vital indications of manhood] boys through heavy drinking, fearless
> in fighting and doing any other stupid things. Those are the only things
> that can make us popular. (Nasir and Rosenthal 2009, p. 240)

> Because *putaw* [heroin] is the hardest drug. It is the top drug among others.
> You need certain guts and a really good hand to inject it. You need to ensure
> that you're man enough to handle it . . . You play with your blood and it's
> quite dangerous. That's why I said injecting *putaw* is more *rewa*. (p. 241)

Drug economies do vary from place to place and have changed markedly
from time to time. The crack smoking epidemic which Bourgois witnessed
in east Harlem had partly replaced cocaine injecting and was itself partly
displaced in the 1990s by the greater availability of relatively cheap heroin.
In some parts of North America, such as the downtown eastside area of Vancouver, crack cocaine appeared not to have replaced cocaine injecting to the
same extent (Bourgois 2003b). But the concentration of problems related
to the use of illicit drugs in areas of disadvantage – often, but not always,
areas where a high proportion of residents are black or of minority ethnic

or immigrant groups – is a regular and continuing feature. Another anthropologist, Singer (2001), echoes Bourgois' thesis when describing the high prevalence of drug addiction in Hartford, Connecticut, which she describes as a now 'impoverished and economically marginalized urban center near to the east coast epicentre of the US drug injection and HIV epidemics' (p. 202). A once wealthy industrial city, Hartford was now one of the poorest medium-sized cities in the USA, with poverty concentrated amongst the black and Latin populations. The number of accessible, entry-level jobs for those without skills suitable for white-collar insurance or banking occupations had declined, producing high rates of unemployment and poverty. It was these large-scale forces, including gender inequality, racism and poverty, which in her view created the conditions that promote and sustain drug dependence. At the root of it was the restructuring of the global economy, which had caused the collapse of traditional pathways to dignified employment for inner-city populations, contributing to growing inequality. This state of affairs she refers to as 'structural violence' and drug addiction as an example of an 'oppression illness' which spreads along 'vectors of disadvantage', disproportionately striking those already burdened by unemployment, neighbourhood decay, inadequate housing and homelessness, racial discrimination and street violence. Under these circumstances, problems such as drug dependence rarely occur alone as a single epidemic, but rather as part of the broader 'syndemic', an interrelated set of diseases and noxious social conditions. Alexander (2008), a psychologist, has developed a not dissimilar general view of addiction as caused by the 'social dislocation' which has been a consequence of the hegemony of free market thinking and policies.

On the other side of the Atlantic, studies of heroin users in the late 1980s and early 1990s had pointed to the importance of the growing availability of the drug and the concentration of drug problems in more deprived areas, for example, in the Wirral area of Merseyside (Parker et al. 1988). That period and the remainder of the 1990s had seen the availability of class A drugs such as heroin, cocaine and crack spread from the bigger cities of the UK to smaller centres of population. Amongst the latter was 'East Kelby' in northeast England, which was the subject of one study which involved interviews with young people between the ages of 15–25, other interviews with drug workers and probation officers and a year's participant observation in the area. Like Hartford in the USA, this had been a thriving centre of heavy industry, but large-scale re-structuring and redundancies had led to a high level of chronic unemployment and poverty. Until the mid 1990s the town had not been thought to have a major heroin problem, but from then on the increased trading of cheap heroin and a relative drought of cannabis thought by some to be attributable to successful police targeting of local cannabis dealers, plus the arrival of crack cocaine, was described as having had a major impact. Amongst the young people interviewed were a number who had used heroin, combined with cocaine and/or crack cocaine, usually daily over months or years, plus others (the largest number) who reported recreational drug use. The latter often expressed the view that it was now a normal part of growing up to try at least some drugs and abnormal not to do so. That study concluded by suggesting that, in the context of young people growing up in that town at that time, heroin had appeal, 'as a poverty drug: a form of self-medication for the socially excluded' (MacDonald and Marsh 2002, p. 36). Another leading British drugs researcher states:

> Where drugs such as heroin and crack-cocaine are concerned, the most serious concentrations of human difficulty are invariably found huddled together with unemployment, poverty, housing decay and other social disadvantages. (Seddon 2006, p. 680)

Although the picture of drug problems in the UK has been less dominated by black and minority ethnic groups than has been the case in the USA, there have been a number of reports of increased drug misuse amongst young British Asian men. One study, which involved interviews with a number of British South Asian men, some convicted of drug offences, concluded that the majority of dealers, 'had experienced [occupational] instability, low wages and unrewarding or menial occupations. Most had found occupational opportunities in the informal economy and engaged in semi-legitimate income raising activity' (Ruggiero and Khan 2006, p. 476).

In 1997 the British journalist Nick Davies wrote a book which achieved considerable notoriety at the time. It was entitled *Dark Heart: The Shocking Truth about Hidden Britain*, in which he exposed the unacceptable conditions to be found in some of Britain's poorest urban areas. In one part of the book he focused on the damaging effects of a crack cocaine epidemic in one community in London:

> In a community where people worked and had a purpose to their life, it would never have spread so fast, but in this black ghetto, where the unity was still so frail, it was perfect. It was not so much that it filled their brains with pleasure for a minute or two – though that was important – but the really big point about crack cocaine was that it became the most saleable commodity in the neighbourhood. An entire economy grew up around it, of

suppliers and street dealers and consumers, all of it linked to the supply and sale of other drugs, all of it linked to the sale of prostitutes. This economy was a source of income on a scale that income support and dead-end jobs on factory floors could never match. (Davies, 1997, p. 218)

Communities disempowered by drug addiction

The subject of the previous chapter was the way in which the erosion of control over one's life, experienced by someone who has become addicted, spreads to those around them. In the same way, that feeling of losing control can extend to a whole neighbourhood, such as the one where Bourgois was carrying out his ethnographic research in the 1980s. He wrote that

> . . . hardworking, drug-free Harlemites have been pushed onto the defensive. Most of them live in fear, or even in contempt, of their neighborhood. Worried mothers and fathers maintain their children locked inside their apartments in determined attempts to keep street culture out. They hope someday to be able to move out of the neighborhood. (Bourgois 2003a, p. 10)

Elsewhere he writes of a 'culture of terror' which works to silence the peaceful majority of the neighbourhood population. He describes teachers at a local middle school covering classroom windows with black paper so that children should not see drug injecting taking place. He describes walking down his block crunching under his feet plastic crack vials and the occasional hypodermic needle and, as a father, realising that he either had to keep his child locked inside their cramped apartment and adopt a hostile attitude towards what was going on in the street or he would have to accept that his child would witness drugs and violence daily. Others have included the signs of drug and alcohol use on the streets as just one of the indications of neighbourhood disorder which provide the 'visible signs and cues that social control is absent' and which 'takes its toll in feelings of depression and anxiety' (Ross et al. 2000, p. 594).

Addiction and the agency versus structure, free will versus determinism, debate

In this chapter I have attempted to make the point, with a number of illustrations, about the way in which the risk of addiction is unequally distributed amongst the different groups which make up a society. The exact way in which the prevalence of addiction varies by social position depends on many factors, including the nature of the particular addictive commodity and the era under investigation. But nearly always the direction of the findings is one way: it is those who experience poverty and relative deprivation, who are economically and socially marginalised or 'socially excluded' – to use a modern and much debated and often criticised term – who are at highest risk from the harms associated with addiction. They are suffering, as writers such as Singer (2008) and Bourgois (2003a) see it, from the injuries that the existing economic and social order inflicts on people. With others who have carried out detailed ethnographic or interview studies with drug users (Fitzgerald 2009), they have been sharply critical of the prevailing, officially sanctioned, view that drug misuse should simply be seen in terms of the lifestyle choices of individuals who are failing to make rational or responsible decisions about their use of substances.

But does this mean that those who experience addiction are often, because of their social position, merely passive victims, 'dupes' of political-economic structural forces? Few would put it quite as starkly as that but there are different takes on that question within the field of social science drug research. Bourgois (2003a,b) and his colleagues (Bourgois et al. 2004) take a strong social structural position, appearing to see drug users and local dealers as helping, through their activities, to reinforce the social oppression that they are subject to or, worse, responding to their social circumstances in psychologically harmful ways, including fatalism and self-deprecation. Others have criticised Bourgois' account for making it appear that drug use is somehow 'produced' by the social environment rather than being part of it. Such critics are more inclined to stress the rationality or survival value or identity-promoting functions of active engagement in the irregular economy. Far from being totally powerless in the face of structural oppression, people are often displaying, it is argued, a considerable degree of personal agency and are often showing evidence of considerable economic and social competence. It is noticeable, however, that studies which support that line of argument have tended to be studies of drug users who are also local drug dealers and it might be more difficult to sustain that argument when thinking of someone like Amanda, whose role in her local drug economy was solely that of customer. As we shall see in the next chapter, enormous power inequalities typify drug markets.

As an aside here, it is interesting to note that even Bourgois (2003a) in the course of his study found it difficult from time to time to avoid slipping into individual blame mode, particularly when his feelings of friendship towards his participants and his appreciation of the social structural determinants of their lives were challenged by revelations of gross gender prejudice and sexual misconduct or when directly witnessing the neglect of children. He knew his research participants well enough to be able, on those occasions, to vent his indignation and to exhort individuals to behave better.

This discussion draws us in to the debate about structure and agency which is longstanding and unresolved in the social sciences generally and which has been discussed more recently within a part of the discipline of psychology – community psychology – with which I am familiar. In the latter field, a strong structuralist position has been taken by Smail, a British former psychotherapist turned community psychologist. His view is that the personal autonomy that we like to credit ourselves with is largely an illusion, shaped as our lives are by powers historical and contemporary. Some of these powers are comparatively 'proximal' and within our understanding, much as the activities of the New York police and the difficulties of entering the downtown job market were known to Bourgois' east Harlem drug users. Most, however, are, in Smail's terms, 'distal', too far over the 'power horizon' to be appreciated, much as the participants in Bourgois' research seemed oblivious to, or unimpressed by, explanations in terms of the history of the immigration of poor people, including Puerto Ricans, to some of the most deprived areas of New York. According to Smail, what the powerless need, therefore, is not psychotherapy to develop insight, but rather 'outsight' – raised awareness of how their interests have been 'hooked' by powerful influences and how the powerful have exploited their 'situation as isolated individuals locked within proximal worlds' (Smail 2005, p. 54).

In the wider field of the social sciences, two names – Giddens and Bourdieu – are associated with serious theoretical attempts to reconcile structure and agency. Giddens (1991) rejected the idea of social structure as something separable from individual actions. It was not a case of social structures bearing down upon individuals in a deterministic fashion but rather a case of the activities of individuals constantly reproducing, and in the process changing, social structures. That 'structuration theory' has been criticised on a number of grounds for example, for paying too little attention to cultural influences, for being more relevant to those living in a new era of 'high modernity' in richer countries and for leaning too far in the direction of free will associated with the actions of individual 'selves' (Best 2003).

Bourdieu was also critical of a forced choice between structural determinism and individual free will although his theorising has greater room for cultural influence: he is well known for the use of terms such as 'cultural capital' and 'social capital'. He wrote of 'symbolic domination' – whether ethnic, gendered, cultural, or other – which exerts a form of power on individuals, shaping what he termed their *habitus*. The latter term, the meaning of which is not altogether easy to grasp, refers not only to people's common sense, taken-for-granted, view of the world and ways of thinking and feeling but also the very way in which people use their bodies to stand, to walk and to express themselves. Bourdieu (2001, p. 39, cited by Lukes 2005, p. 141) wrote of the way in which structures of dominance and subordination were 'durably and deeply embedded in the body in the form of dispositions'. The dispositions that make up habitus are, according to this theory, 'spontaneously attuned' to the social order, perceived as natural and self-evident. This influence of the dominant social order is not necessarily intended and the process is largely outside of individuals' consciousness.

The Davids, Amandas, and Carolines (see Chapter 1) of this world are perhaps relatively untouched by these theoretical attempts to reconcile structure and agency, leaning mostly, I suspect, towards a view that privileges an explanation of their behaviour in which their own responsibility for their own actions plays a large part.

Whether in the form of differences in the social standing of individuals or households, the relative wealth or deprivation of neighbourhoods, which constitute risk factors for addiction, or in the form of the experiences of those who become engaged as consumers in illicit drug scenes – just some of the topics touched on in this chapter – power is never far away. In the next chapter the focus is widened to consider how power relations are manifest in the nexus of connections which surround the supply, legal or illegal, of substances and activities with addiction potential.

CHAPTER FIVE

Power and powerlessness in the addiction supply industries

Beyond the immediate awareness of most people who suffer from addiction, there exists a vast network of people and organisations through whom the commodities to which people are addicted are supplied. David, Amanda, and Caroline, whom we met in Chapter 1, have only a very hazy understanding of the routes and means whereby the objects of their addictions are made available to them. Nor do their family members and friends, increasingly aware of how addiction undermines autonomy, know very much at all about how the substances or activities to which their relatives are addicted are produced, transported and marketed. Indeed, a telling aspect of their relatives' powerlessness, and the powerlessness they as family members and friends experience at second-hand, is that the supply chain remains mostly beyond their horizon. David and his wife know little about the international drinks trade beyond their local pub. Amanda's parents, sister and friends are largely in the dark about the markets for illicit drugs, and even Amanda knows nothing beyond her immediate local suppliers. Likewise, Caroline, her daughter, her brother and her friends are largely ignorant of national policy debates about the regulation of gambling and certainly they know little about the gambling industry and how it operates. Caroline's brother has found out something about these things but he has had to work hard to uncover the information. The focus of the concern of these people, disempowered to one degree or another by alcohol, drugs or gambling, is much more local. If they hold anybody responsible for what has happened, it is likely to be themselves. Most people in their circumstances are far too taken up with their own affairs, which in the context of addiction are often confusing and disorganising, and are too inclined to apportion blame to themselves or to their relatives or family members or immediate circumstances to have the resources or motivation to investigate how the supply side works.

This chapter is about the supply side. Within the vast networks involved in supplying alcoholic beverages, illicit drugs and the means to gamble are to be found some very powerful people and organisations, and some who are getting very rich on the proceeds of activities and substances to which other people become addicted. There are many more people, however, who are not particularly wealthy or powerful, and some, particularly in the case of the trade in illicit drugs, who are themselves poor and exploited. David's and Caroline's suppliers – of alcohol and gambling respectively – will be considered first and Amanda's – of illicit drugs – later in the chapter. The fact that the former trades are legal while the latter is not makes a difference, although it can be argued that the two kinds of trade are, on closer inspection, much more similar to one another than might be supposed (Singer 2008).

The power of the legal addiction-creating industries

The alcohol industry is all-powerful, as demonstrated by its enormous size and increasingly world-wide reach, which give it the capacity to devote huge resources to promoting its policy interests. In recent years the industry has become increasingly dominated by a relatively few mega-corporations. In 2005 the 26 largest alcoholic beverage companies had a total net revenue of US$155 billion and a total operating profit of US$26 billion. Although much of alcohol beverage production is still local and outside the scope of the big brands – that is particularly the case in the Indian sub-continent and Africa and to a lesser extent in Latin America and Eastern Europe – national markets for alcohol are now generally led by an industry that has become more international and more concentrated. In 2006 the ten largest beer companies accounted for two-thirds of global beer production by volume and the ten largest spirits marketers held over half of the global market share. Concentration has been on the increase in the last 20–30 years, particularly in beer marketing and particularly in some parts of the world, such as Latin America, where one or other of the two largest world beer marketers controls over 90 per cent of the domestic market for brewed beverages in at least seven Central and South American countries (Jernigan 2009).

The power wielded by big alcohol and big gambling businesses has become well recognised by those who are critical of globalisation such as Merrill Singer. She defines globalisation as:

> . . . transnational, capitalist economic processes, including resource extraction and trade, which override local decision making, traditional ways of life, and indigenous cultural histories and promote uniformity, impose externally

devised social changes, and elevate the market and the needs of transnational corporations as the socially legitimized determinant of social values and ways of life. (2008, p. 10)

For the alcohol industry there are many advantages of globalisation, including standardisation, diffusion of technological advances and product developments and economies of scale in production, marketing, and distribution. The advantages include close links with the agriculture, trucking and packaging industries and coordination with local companies – although in practice control tends to remains in the hands of the global corporations:

> ... globalization can lead to an increase in international trade, but this trade rarely benefits developing nations. Global trade figures suggest that the overwhelming majority of global trade in alcoholic beverages occurs among the developed countries themselves, with very few middle- or low-income countries (e.g. Chile, Mexico) breaking into the ranks of the leading exporters. (Jernigan 2009, p. 9)

The leading alcohol marketing companies nearly all have their main headquarters in richer countries (Jernigan 2009).

The case of gambling differs somewhat because of its quite recent and virtually world-wide liberalisation in the last decades of the twentieth century, a move which has undoubtedly been driven by the same processes of free market globalisation as have fuelled the commercialisation of alcoholic drinks production. The growth of gambling in a few years, and the current size of the market, are staggering (Orford 2011). Net expenditure on gambling in Australia, for example, was AU$11 billion at the turn of the millennium and in the USA the figure was US$60 billion, a six-fold increase since 1980. In Britain, by 2008, gross gambling industry revenues totalled over £10 billion. Around £3 billion of that came from betting and gambling machines in betting shops, a sector of the British gambling industry which is dominated by a small number of enormous companies.

The resources that large corporations can devote to marketing are huge and the nature of marketing is becoming broader. In the USA the Federal Trade Commission has recognised no less than 22 different marketing methods, including advertising on television and radio, in magazines and newspapers, transit, outdoor and direct mail advertising, promoting products via company-sponsored or other internet sites, point-of-sale advertising and promotions, sponsorship of sporting events, sports teams or individual athletes and product placements (Jernigan 2009). The biggest US beer marketer reported on its website product placements in more than

20 popular films, and other companies are doing the same thing. Advertising in traditional media may have fallen but that reflects not a decrease in advertising budgets but a diversification into new media, including placing commercials on sites such as YouTube. In the case of gambling, it has been noted how sites with special appeal for teenagers are being used to promote betting, either directly or more subtly by, for example, encouraging betting for the artificial 'money' used in multi-player games (Downs 2008).

There are now a number of studies which seem to show that exposure of young people to alcohol advertising, whether on television or more generally, speeds up the initiation of drinking in the early teenage years and increases the prevalence of heavy drinking later on. Studies in the USA have estimated that a 28 per cent drop in exposure of youth to alcohol advertising would lead to a real decrease in binge drinking of somewhere between 8 and 33 per cent (Saffer and Dave 2006, cited by Babor et al. 2010), and, according to the estimate reached in another study, a complete advertising ban would reduce alcohol-related years of life lost by 16 per cent (Hollingworth et al. 2006, cited by Babor et al. 2010).

One of the features of any successful industry is its ability to develop and innovate. Industries whose products are potentially addictive are no exception. In the face of declining demand for tobacco cigarettes, the promotion of smokeless tobacco, increasingly popular in the USA and in Sweden, provides one example (McNeill and Sweanor 2009). Developments in the gambling industry are particularly impressive. Britain, already by the 1980s a country with a broad array of gambling on offer in the form of casinos, betting, bingo, and gambling machines, has seen the development since then of new types and ways of gambling, including spread betting, betting exchanges and internet gambling sites (Orford 2011). Gambling machines have become much more sophisticated and almost certainly more dangerous. Not only has a completely new type of machine come on the scene – the 'fixed-odds betting machines' which allow casino-type games to be played on machines in high-street betting shops – but the more traditional slot or fruit machines have become more intricate, allowing players many more options in the course of play, designed to encourage the illusion that the outcome can be controlled (Parke and Griffiths 2007). There is bound to be more to come. The Australian gambling machine industry is particularly vigorous. The Australasian Gaming Machine Manufacturers Association (AGMMA) has lobbied hard, declaring that it should not be prevented from taking advantage of current and future technological advances in designing and supplying gambling machines for the international market. In 2007, when giving evidence to the New South Wales and Australian governments, it stated that it was expecting its members to release new products on the international market. They would include new generation gaming machine terminals and gaming platforms, client-server gaming systems, gaming venue management systems and new-generation games (AGMMA 2007).

Massive resources are put behind particular innovations, especially those that promise to capture new markets. An infamous innovation of recent times has been flavoured alcoholic drinks – 'alcopops', which turned out to be particularly popular amongst teenage girls. In the USA, several hundred million dollars were spent on television advertising of such drinks in the early 2000s and drinks companies were criticised for using marketing tactics that employed stars popular with young people and promotional materials accessible to all ages on social media sites (Babor et al. 2010; Singer 2008). In 2008 an Australian report suggested that Independent Distillers, a leading producer of alcopops, had developed new sweet-tasting beverages using alcohol derived from lower-taxed beer in a bid to appeal to younger drinkers whilst at the same time finding a way around the new Australian tax on pre-mixed drinks (News and Notes 2008; Singer 2008). Although they deny it, big businesses, even when their products are potentially addictive, are bound to see the next generation of young people as an important market to aim for. Indeed, many would charge the alcohol industry with deliberately targeting legally underage drinkers with their promotion of flavoured and pre-mixed drinks. The industry has been equally accused of deliberately targeting poor and ethnic minority groups through their marketing of a cheap wine or 'malt liquor' which was a prominent feature of drinking in east Harlem when Bourgois was there doing his research in the 1980s (see Chapter 4) (Singer 2008).

Two scientists from the Department of Community Medicine and Health Care at the University of Connecticut, Jahiel and Babor (2007), have suggested that, rather than viewing addiction problems in personal terms, as has mostly been the case in the past, we might see them as constituting an example of 'industrial epidemics'. Unlike natural epidemics, industrial epidemics are associated with the commercialisation of a dangerous product such as tobacco, alcohol, gambling, illicit drugs, unhealthy food, cars or guns. Hence the epidemic is driven, 'at least in part by corporations and their allies who promote a product that is also a disease agent' (p. 1335). In classic public health terms this shifts the focus from the 'agent' (alcohol in this case) or the 'host' (i.e. the addicted or problem drinker) to the 'disease vector', which is responsible for the exposure of potential hosts to the risks posed by the agent. In this case, the disease vector is the alcohol, or gambling, industry and its associates. In the case of industrial epidemics there is a built-in conflict of interests between the industry, motivated by the need for profit, and public health, motivated to reduce the risk of harm to health. The analogy can be taken further by referring to 'targeted epidemics', in which corporations single out particular groups for increased product consumption, and 'transnational epidemics', where the targets are foreign countries that offer new or as-yet unsaturated markets or which are subject to less stringent controls.

The powerful use of lobbying, free trade and corporate social responsibility

Corporations are wealthy enough to buy favours with legislators. According to Singer (2008, p. 105), the alcohol industry contributed over $37 million to campaigns for offices in the US Senate and House of Representatives between 1999 and 2004, the major objective being the prevention of tax increases on alcohol sales and restrictions on advertising. The alcohol industry is powerful enough to be a major influence on government policy. A letter from Brazilian scientists which appeared in the academic journal *Addiction* expressed their concern about such influence in their country. A few years earlier, the authors claimed, the biggest beer company in Brazil – AmBev, which after a merger with Inter-Brew became the second biggest in the world – approached key figures in the scientific and professional alcohol fields in Brazil, one of whom subsequently started an AmBev-funded website, the purpose of which was 'to generate a source of information on health and alcohol'. The government department responsible for alcohol policy also engaged a consultant to that website to manage its own website and information policy and, at the same time, published a booklet for distribution to schools to educate young people about alcohol and its 'responsible' use. The authors of the letter pointed to the lack of evidence to support such 'educational' initiatives and to what they saw as an over-emphasis in these materials on the positive aspects of alcohol. A further worrying development was the sacking by her university of the then-President of the Brazilian Association for the Study of Alcohol and Other Drugs (ABEAD), which had begun to challenge the government about its alcohol policy and the influence on it of the alcohol industry. As part of its campaign ABEAD had adopted a policy of refusing to work with the alcohol industry or to accept funding from it. The authors acknowledge that such a position may be controversial around the world but that 'here in Brazil it is essential to set clear boundaries between public health interests and those of such a powerful and wealthy industry, which operates here with a free rein' (Laranjeira et al. 2007, p. 1502).

Much of the alcohol industry's weight is exerted through trade associations and what one reviewer has called 'social aspects/public relations organisations' (SAPROs). The latter, of which more than 20 had been identified at the time the review was being written in 2007, are national or international groups funded by the drinks industry 'to manage issues that may be detrimental to its interests, particularly in areas that overlap with public health' (Babor 2009, p. 35). The International Center for Alcohol Policies, supported by an international consortium of alcohol producers, is one example, and the Portman Group, established by the UK's major alcohol producers in 1989, is another.

The British government's industry-friendly alcohol policy under the New Labour administrations of the last few years of the twentieth century and the first few of the twenty-first have been severely criticised by expert academic commentators (as has European Commission alcohol policy, on similar grounds). One described the 2004 Alcohol Harm Reduction Strategy for England as a recipe for ineffectiveness (Room 2004). Combined with the derestricting 2003 Licensing Act which permitted up to 24 hour-a-day alcohol sales, it had had the effect of 'disabling the public interest'. Another concluded that the government's approach, 'rather than reducing alcohol-related harm, has not only failed to stem the increasing trends that it inherited but has positively encouraged major increases in harm' (Anderson 2007, p. 1515). It had done that by adopting a policy which frames alcohol-related problems in individual terms, ignoring the evidence that the increased affordability of alcoholic beverages – such as occurred in Britain between the early 1990s and the early 2000s – is associated with increased alcohol consumption, an earlier age of starting to drink amongst young people, heavier per-occasion drinking, more deaths from liver cirrhosis and more car accidents and evidence that the amount of exposure to alcohol advertising is associated with increased drinking and harmful drinking amongst young people (the government introduced stricter rules about the content of alcohol adverts but did nothing about the volume of advertising). Meanwhile, the Government Alcohol Strategy focused on the least industry-challenging subjects, such as alcohol-related offending, and actions to raise public awareness through the DrinkAware Trust, the latter funded almost entirely by the alcohol industry. This same expert commentator pointed out how British Labour Party thinking has changed over the years on this question of the relationship between government and industry when it comes to a potentially dangerous form of consumption product such as alcoholic beverages. He quoted from a Labour Party policy statement of 1923:

> It must be recognised, even by those holding diverse views as to the plan or method of temperance reform, that the enormous vested interest in the manufacture and sale of alcoholic beverages constitutes, in itself, a serious obstacle to every kind of reform. It can be forcibly argued that no effective temperance reform is possible so long as so great an interest as the liquor interest is in private hands. If therefore we do nothing on this point, we must look forward to a long period during which the efforts of private persons who desire any kind of temperance reform will be opposed by the money and organisation of one of the most formidable vested interests in the country. In fact, the political power of the 'trade' is now a standing menace to promoters of reform of any kind in Parliament or at Parliamentary elections. (cited by Anderson 2007, pp. 1515–16)

Even in the late 1970s, towards the end of the Labour administration of that period, a policy review was recommending that alcohol taxes should at least be kept level with changes in the retail price index and that alcohol licensing should not be relaxed any further – a report that was, in fact, never published in the UK and was only available in a Swedish publication (Room 2004). By 2003 the new Licensing Act was being prefaced by the statement that licensing should not interfere with the free operation of the market and that new outlets should not be constrained by any considerations of 'need' other than perceived commercial demand. In 2004 the new Government Alcohol Strategy was premised on the belief that, 'a more effective strategy would be to provide the (alcohol) industry with further opportunities to work in partnership with the government to reduce alcohol-related harm' (Anderson 2007, p. 1516). The commentator's first recommendation, on the contrary, was that clear water should be created between government and the alcohol industry when making alcohol policy. Public health policies should be formulated without any commercial interference. This is hardly a radical suggestion. Even the *Economist* argued in 2005 that businesses should get on with business and governments should govern, including setting goals for regulators, dealing with externalities, mediating among different interests, attending to the demands of social justice and providing public goods: 'the goals of business and the goals of government are different – or should be, and thus partnership between the two should always arouse intense suspicion' (cited by Anderson 2007, p. 1516).

The power of free trade agreements

It has been suggested that World Trade Organisation (WTO) law regarding trade and health represents a potential threat to the ability of countries to maintain measures designed to protect citizens against the harmful effects of a potentially addictive form of consumption. WTO agreements, such as the General Agreement on Tariffs and Trade (GATT) and the General Agreement on Trades in Services (GATS) state that nothing in them should be taken to mean that measures to protect health should be prevented, but they also state that any such measures should not represent a 'disguised restriction on trade' and that measures taken should be 'the least trade-restrictive... reasonably available in the circumstances to meet the objective of protecting health' (Baumberg and Anderson 2008, p. 1953). It has been pointed out that in practice the WTO is most accommodating of country policies that are unequivocally and solely motivated by health considerations. But in the case of the dangerously addictive forms of consumption which we are concerned with here, policies are usually complex balances and compromises with multiple aims, including both protection against health harm and trade protection. Policies including protection of alcohol monopolies, banning imports, or banning new products are unlikely to pass the WTO 'necessity test'. WTO is a powerful force behind liberalisation, therefore, and 'the degree of protectionism will decline as liberalization proceeds, which will raise alcohol consumption. It is in this sense... that it can be argued that the goals of trade liberalization are inherently in conflict with public health' (Baumberg and Anderson 2008, p. 1957).

From an officer of the Long Range Health Care Trends at the American Medical Association has come a review of the implications of the alcohol industry and trade agreements for public health. The review marshals the argument that the alcohol industry, particularly associations of distilled spirits producers, such as the European Spirits Organization (CEPS) and the Distilled Spirits Council of the United States (DISCUS) and the World Spirits Alliance, which comprises national associations from Australia, Canada, the Caribbean, Europe, Japan, Mexico, New Zealand, South Africa and the USA, use their power, together with the influence of the EU and the USA, to bring pressure on economically less powerful countries who may wish to improve their circumstances by gaining membership of WTO. CEPS is quoted as saying, 'WTO accession negotiations provide a "one off" opportunity for our industry to secure the spirit industry tariff and non-tariff objectives in countries wishing to join the organization'

(Zeigler 2009, p. 14). CEPS has been a strong supporter of the WTO since its formation in 1995, which is hardly surprising since membership of WTO obliges member countries to move in the direction of policies which are in the interests of the alcohol industry; for example, reducing government restrictions, privatising ownership and production of goods and services and reducing public funding generally. The article gives a number of examples. For example, Algeria lifted a ban on alcohol imports to help its negotiations on WTO membership, and Vietnam's submission was questioned by the US on the grounds that its tax policies favoured domestic spirits. Canada lowered minimum prices and allowed access for cheaper US beer in Ontario's monopoly beer retail system. WTO rules were used by the US, Canada and the EU to eliminate Japan's higher tax on imported spirits. A WTO panel ruled that Chile's tax system favoured a form of domestic liquor. Besides the power to have import tariffs removed, international trade agreements require a move towards eliminating 'technical barriers to trade' (TBT), many of which cover health, safety, environmental and consumer regulations. There is also a requirement that countries must treat equally the products and their suppliers from all other WTO countries, even if that runs counter to the wish, on public health grounds, to limit citizens' exposure to a new product which might be dangerous (such as beverages of higher alcohol content or flavoured alcoholic drinks). Similarly, there is a prohibition on placing limitations on the number of suppliers, thereby making it more difficult to reduce harm by regulating supply, for example, by limiting the number or concentration of retail outlets.

The threat to the ability of governments to maintain or introduce policies for the benefit of the public's health is even greater, suggests the same article, from trade agreements which are bilateral or regional rather than global. Such agreements, led largely by the US and the EU, expanded six-fold in the two decades up to 2005, and their rules often offer even greater flexibility to pursue 'trade-expanding policies not addressed well in global trading rules' (Zeigler 2009, p. 20). The North American Free Trade Agreement (NAFTA), for one, defines investor rights and property rights in such a way that public regulation – such as regulation of alcohol sales – is seen as the 'taking' of private property tantamount to expropriation. For example, NAFTA was used by tobacco companies to successfully challenge Canadian regulations that would have required plain cigarette packing with health warnings, on the grounds of expropriation of intellectual property worth hundreds of millions of dollars.

The influence of transnational drinks corporations is described in the same article as 'pervasive but largely behind-the-scenes' (p. 22). Trade agreements were said to be primarily negotiated in secret by government, often under intense industry lobbying or in close consultation with corporate interests. For example, the distilled spirits groups were represented as non-governmental organisations (NGOs) at several WTO ministerial conferences. Advisory committees on Consumer Goods, Distribution Services and Intellectual Property in the USA had until very recently six alcohol industry representatives and no public health voice at all. Commitments that countries are making in WTO negotiations are not always publicly disclosed. Trade lawyers move in and out of government service, working on the texts and laws which they often use later in the service of corporate clients. The article concludes that:

> Free trade policies, the basis of our global economy, have objectives that are fundamentally incompatible with alcohol control measures . . . Civil society should expect coherence between trade and public policies and demand health assessments of trade. (p. 22)

A good example of rapid derestriction associated with joining a free trade area – the EU in this case – and the effects that can have on alcohol consumption, is described in a journal article about the changes that occurred in Finland between the late 1960s and the early 2000s (Mäkelä and Österberg 2009). Until 1969, as in other Nordic countries, physical availability of alcoholic beverages was strictly controlled and the alcohol trade was controlled by a comprehensive state monopoly. From 1969 medium-strength beer could be sold in groceries and cafes and the legal age limit for alcohol purchases was reduced. Since then alcohol availability had increased further with a rise in numbers of liquor stores and licensed restaurants, controls of on- and off-premise sales of alcoholic beverages had decreased and opening hours had been extended. In 1995 Finland joined the EU and the state monopoly was dissolved, remaining only for the off-premise retailing of stronger beverages. The most dramatic change occurred in 2004, when Finland's southern neighbour, Estonia, joined the EU. The 5,000,000 Finns were making approximately 2,500,000 trips to Estonia every year: compared to prices in Finland, prices of cheap brands of vodka, beer and wine in Estonia were, respectively, one fifth, one third and two-thirds as great. In line with EU rules, quotas on tax-free imports by travellers arriving in Finland from other EU countries, including Estonia, were abolished. At the same time, the Finnish government cut taxes on alcoholic drinks by an average of one third in the hope of curbing the expected growth of travellers' alcohol imports and to maintain alcohol industry jobs and tax revenues at home. A time series analysis showed that alcohol consumption increased in Finland by ten per cent that year, clearly more than in previous years. A number of forms of alcohol-related harm also increased: alcohol-induced liver disease deaths increasing by nearly 50 per cent in the following three years, for example. As the evidence presented in Chapter 4 would lead us to expect, some sections of the Finnish population were less well able to resist the effects than others. Moderate to heavy alcohol consumption increased most in that sub-group of the population with the lowest level of education, and increases in alcohol-related deaths were most marked for those in long-term unemployment and for pensioners, somewhat less for other unemployed people and those living alone, with negligible increases for those in employment.

The influence of the industry in lobbying for fewer regulatory restrictions and for more liberal laws affecting their trade is, in a way, even clearer in the case of the gambling industry. Whereas attitudes towards drinking alcoholic beverages are generally positive in western countries, and there is always considerable public resistance to restrictions, in the case of gambling there is rarely much support for its expansion and little resistance to restriction. Gambling laws have progressively been liberalised in the UK, the USA and many other countries despite lack of public demand (Goodman 1995; Orford 2011). The liberalising 2005 Gambling Act in Britain was largely the result of gambling industry lobbying, the government's susceptibility to free trade arguments and the prospect of government income from taxation. The push for dismantling controls on gambling around Europe has mainly come, not surprisingly, from spokespeople from the gambling industry. A chapter in a book on European and national perspectives on gambling regulation written by the founder of a leading German law firm specialising in gambling law, whose clients include many private gambling operators licensed in the UK, Austria, Malta, and Gibraltar, provides an example (Arendts 2007). He bemoaned the continued existence of state gambling monopolies which still exist in a number of European countries. He viewed these as impediments to the creation of a fully free market in gambling products within the EU and accused some Member States of using their laws to bar foreign private gambling operators from advertising in their countries. Two of the big British betting companies had been forced to close down their German language internet sites, for example. Private companies were appealing to the European Court of Justice and submitting complaints to the European Commission. A number of Europe-wide gambling industry associations had sprung up, including the European Betting Association and the Remote Gambling Association.

One of the most controversial gambling policy issues in Britain is the continued legality of enabling children and young people of any age to access gambling machines, of the lowest stake and prize kind, to be found in 'amusement arcades' in seaside towns and elsewhere. Despite widespread unease about this anomaly, the gambling industry, particularly in the form of the British Amusement Catering Trades Association, has successfully argued that such low-stake/low-prize machines are trivial, not to be regarded as gambling at all, an essential feature of British family leisure, the removal of which would seriously damage local leisure economies (Gambling Review Body 2001). In Australia, where what are widely referred to as 'poker machines' or 'the pokies' – fast, high-maximum-stake-prize machines – are widespread in pubs and clubs (although, as we saw in the last chapter, more heavily concentrated in poorer areas), AGMMA has lobbied strongly against such suggestions as capping the overall number of gambling machines in an area, restrictions on multi-terminal gaming machines, restrictions on the numbers of machines allowed in clubs and hotels and limitations on stake and prize sizes (AGMMA 2007).

The paradox of CSR

Many of the largest providers of potentially addictive products now argue that they are responsible providers and have corporate social responsibility (CSR) policies to prove it. Much of CSR in the case of potentially dangerous forms of consumption consists of minimising the harm – often referred to as harm reduction or harm minimisation (HM). The term has found favour in the field of drug misuse where it embraces such programmes as those that provide clean and sterile syringes and needles so that those addicted to a drug such as heroin are less likely to contract and spread blood-borne diseases such as hepatitis C and HIV. Alcohol HM includes such things as the serving of beer in plastic rather than glass containers so that alcohol-related fights are less likely to result in serious injury, or the encouragement of drinking groups to nominate a non-drinking member who will be responsible for driving home. In the case of gambling, it includes measures to control crime associated with gambling, providing counselling for the few people who win National Lottery jackpots or those aimed at helping families of addicted gamblers. But the concept of HM has been hotly debated (Cantinotti and Ladouceur 2008; Weatherburn 2009). There are those who would define it tightly to include only those measures which attempt to minimise the harm associated with consumption but which do not aim to reduce the *volume* of consumption per se. Others would use the term to embrace a much broader range of measures, all aimed at reducing harm, many of which would, if successful, be expected also to lead to a reduction in overall consumption volume. Some would be supply reduction measures, aiming to control or limit the supply of the product in some way; others would work through demand reduction, acting on consumers so as to limit their demand. These are far more than academic or semantic considerations. HM programmes, in the narrower meaning of the term, are addressed to the harm – the 'negative externalities' to use the economists' term – associated with the dangerous activity but do not challenge the extent of the activity itself. HM in the broader sense does represent such a challenge and this is what alcohol and gambling promoters with CSR policies which embrace HM, and governments which are in favour of supporting their commercial activities, have not faced up to. Big business and governments often want to have their cake and to eat it. It is often an explicit part of policy to reduce harm using a range of measures. Whether in the process total population consumption may have to be reduced, along with the profits from consumption and government revenues, governments have not thought through and usually avoid being explicit about. Needless to say, it is not part of the industry's CSR policies that their growth should be curtailed.

Is there not, therefore, an inherent paradox in an industry, and its government supporters, espousing HM measures which, if successful, might limit expansion, whilst at the same time, as with any industry providing a commodity, aiming to innovate and expand? In fact, there are many who believe that the very notion of CSR contains an inherent contradiction. In the past its critics have included mainstream economic papers and magazines such as the *Financial Times* and the *Economist*. They often quote free-market guru Milton Friedman, who is reputed to have said such things as, 'Few trends could so thoroughly undermine the very foundations of our free society as the acceptance by corporate officials of a social responsibility other than to make as much money for their stockholders as possible' (cited by Caulkin 2003). There has been scepticism about the CSR policies of alcohol and gambling companies, as there has of tobacco firms. Critics see how CSR is to the advantage of corporations wishing to portray themselves as socially responsible, holding policies in line with those of government, and being seen to 'build partnerships' with non-government and government agencies involved in health, education and the environment (Barraclough and Morrow 2008). An important effect is that of impression management: an aim is to appear well able to engage in self-regulation, forestalling calls for tighter external regulation. Critics point to the lengths that such companies will go to in order to resist any HM measures which would threaten overall consumption, such as advertising restrictions, significant price increases, restrictions on easy access sales such as drinking happy hours, limiting the maximum stake or the speed of operation of gambling machines or banning the sale of small packs of cigarettes. It appears to many that the preference of the industry and its supporters is for those measures, such as educational ones, which are least threatening to supply or demand and which often have the least evidence in support of their HM potential (de Bruijn 2008; Babor et al. 2010).

At best, according to the most sceptical of critics, CSR is little more than a cover-up exercise. It may be much worse than that, some would argue. If companies are successful in building a comfortable working relationship with other bodies and institutions, particularly with the only ones in a position to stand up to the power of large corporations, including determining the very language with which the issues are discussed publicly, then an important aspect of democratic society itself may be in danger. As Naomi Klein (cited by Barraclough and Morrow 2008, p. 1793) says in her book *No Logo*, 'looking to corporations to draft our collective labour and human rights codes [means] we have already lost the most basic principle of citizenship: that people should govern themselves'. As one set of critics put it,

> Voluntary regulation by the industry is often faulty, and industrial support of public health approaches may give companies a positive image that they can then exploit to build political support... [whilst using their]... considerable financial resources that allow them to conduct their own investigations, retain major law firms, set up public-relations organizations and threaten to file lawsuits against their critics. (Jahiel and Babor 2007, pp. 1337–8)

The power to co-opt: seven ways to co-opt scientists

One of the effects of power being wielded by large companies trying to expand markets for potentially dangerous products is the way in which a wide variety of individuals, organisations and institutions are co-opted in support of industry expansionist interests. The dangers of having independence compromised are all too obvious in the case of governments subject to trade agreements and dependence on tax revenues. But the dangers do not stop with governments and their employees and consultant advisors. Attention has recently turned to focus on the potential pitfalls for the academic research community. The dangers were nicely summarised in an article in the academic journal *Addiction* which described seven ways in which alcohol science is in danger of being co-opted by the alcohol industry (Babor 2009). Some represent more transparent ways in which the industry uses its influence. The most obvious is research conducted directly by industry scientists or by research organisations contracted to industry. Also clearly serving the interests of the industry, although providing scope for less than perfect transparency, is research conducted by trade organisations and SAPROs. Such research is more likely to masquerade as serious science although methodology tends to be poor and there is clearly a bias towards enforcing positions favourable to industry. More serious is the fact that industry sponsorship may not be acknowledged when findings are published or that apparently independent scientists who endorse the findings may not declare that they have received support from the industry themselves.

More insidious – because the co-option of researchers and academics is less obvious although conflicts of interest are undoubtedly involved – are those circumstances in which the industry appears to be providing helpful support, with no strings attached, by assisting with the publication of scientific reports and journals, sponsoring scientific conferences or presentations at such conferences, recruiting scientists to join them on research committees or boards or to conduct reviews or simply providing funds for university-based scientists. The influence in these cases is more subtle but no less powerful. An example of a publication supported by the drinks industry was the book *Health Issues Related to Alcohol Consumption*, which provided no information about who paid for the publication, how much the authors were paid or whether they had any conflicts of interest. Only later did it emerge that the publication was supported with funds from the drinks industry. A further example was a book on the prevention of alcohol-related harm entitled *Drinking in Context: Patterns, Interventions, and Partnerships*, which represented a collaboration between drinks industry organisations, including the International Center for Alcohol Policies (ICAP), and health bodies, such as the International Harm Reduction Association, and which had high profile launches in several countries, including at the Houses of Parliament in London. It subsequently came in for much academic criticism for only focusing attention on specific groups, such as 'hard core drunk drivers' and pregnant women drinkers, and for failing to promote public health measures which might harm the interests of the industry by threatening a reduction in per capita consumption (Babor 2009).

More commonly industry will provide support in the form of hosting a conference on industry premises, hosting the conference dinner or offering travel support or honoraria. Researchers are easily seduced by such offerings, and specialist scientific groups and organisations – usually short of money – are often all too willing to accept support of these kinds. Sometimes the support is obvious but in other cases it is undeclared or obscure. Some of us who have worked in the field of gambling studies have been impressed with how common this form of industry support is (Adams 2008; Orford 2011). I have been met with surprise when refusing to speak at a scientific meeting to be held in a casino. On another occasion, when due to speak at the annual conference of the UK national gambling charity, GamCare, I was persuaded against my better judgement to revise the original title of my talk on the grounds that it would have discouraged gambling industry representatives from attending – an important consideration since GamCare is largely funded by contributions from the industry.

Under the heading of 'efforts to influence public perceptions of research, research findings and alcohol policies', the seven ways of being co-opted article refers to a series of cases in which scientists or their institutions have been paid by the industry either to critique research which is contrary to industry interests – for example, research concluding that exposure to alcohol advertising is associated with increased alcohol use by young adults – or to write in support of research suggesting some health benefits of drinking. In the UK the Portman Group has given rise to a number of controversies. In one instance selected academics were offered sizeable fees to write anonymous critiques of a World Health Organisation book on alcohol policy.

Powerful commercial gambling interests are promoted in much the same way. An example is support which a number of academics in the field have given to a new idea which they call 'adaptation theory'. This so-called theory runs counter to much accepted wisdom in the public health field. The latter states that increased access of citizens to a dangerous activity leads to an increased take-up of that activity in the population and that this increased take-up leads to increased incidence and prevalence of problems related to that activity (Lund 2008). Adaptation theory, on the other hand, proposes that liberalisation which increases access to an activity such as gambling, whilst it may initially give rise to greater problems, does not do so in the medium to longer term because populations adapt to the presence of risks and learn to avoid them or deal with them (LaPlante and Shaffer 2007). Although this theory was relatively new, it was actively promoted by a number of high-profile academics and, not surprisingly, was taken up by the gambling industry. The latter, knowing that the greatest threat to unbridled industry expansion is awareness of the addictive potential of their products, draws great comfort from an idea, despite the thinness of the evidence for it, which suggests that increasing the supply of their products will not be as harmful as some might have supposed. Again there is a transparency issue here. The fact that development of adaptation theory was partly supported by the gambling industry is not declared when it is spoken about in public forums where gambling policy is being debated; to find this out it is necessary to look at the acknowledgements in small print at the end of academic articles and then check whether named sponsors are part of the gambling industry.

Researchers have sometimes claimed that their research is quite unaffected by the source of funding, but the evidence suggests otherwise. One report found that review articles on passive smoking by authors with, often undeclared, affiliations with the tobacco industry were a hundred times more likely to report the absence of a relationship between passive smoking and health than was the case for articles written by those without such affiliations (Barnes and Bero 1998, cited by Edwards and Bhopal 1999). At the same time evidence was coming to light that the US Tobacco Institute had paid four-figure sums to authors of letters criticising a report of the Environmental Protection Agency which had declared passive smoking to be carcinogenic (Edwards and Bhopal 1999).

The whole question of industry research funding and sponsorship becomes murkier when the matters being researched are less clear-cut or when industry influence is less direct and more subtle. The Irish branch of Diageo, for example, gave €1.5 million to an Irish university, partly to fund a study of health risk associated with Irish young adults' binge drinking. The corporation's chief executive was honest about its motives. He was quoted in the *Irish Times* as saying, 'the company did not want problems with binge drinking to lead governments to place higher taxes on its products and thus eat into revenues' (cited by Babor 2009, p. 38). Lately the British government has welcomed the same company's offer of a grant towards a campaign to advise pregnant women about the dangers of over-drinking, an offer which has attracted criticism for showing typical industry focus on just a part of the problem they help to create – a part that promises to win them plaudits but which offers little threat to their commercial interests.

In the alcohol field there exist at least three organisations funded mainly from industry sources with the purpose of supporting research. The European Research Advisory Board (ERAB), to take one of them, was established in 2003, is funded by European brewers, and offers research grants up to €120,000 as well as travel grants and awards for young researchers.

Such organisations are sometimes lorded as exemplary ways of channelling industry money for independent research. In the case of the ERAB, for example, the business of soliciting and reviewing grant applications and awarding grants is conducted by an advisory board consisting of academics with expertise in a range of relevant medical and social sciences. They are responsible to the board of directors which consists of people drawn from business, including the beer industry, public relations, the legal profession, banking and medical sciences. To a naive researcher or to members of the public to whom these arrangements are unknown and unquestioned, or to members of parliament committed to public-private initiatives, this may seem a sound arrangement for ensuring independence. To a power theorist, on the other hand, this is a fairly transparent recipe for subtle but pervasive influence of the powerful drinks industry. There are a number of questions which students of power relations would be bound to ask. How are members of the scientific committees of such organisations chosen? Would someone with a track record for criticising the industry or for asking awkward questions be as likely to be selected as someone without such a reputation? And, if such scientists were chosen, would they be likely to accept? In what ways, subtle though they may be, do the organisations' directors influence what kinds of research come to their scientific committees?

At least one of these organisations puts out calls for research on particular topics, and besides that the whole machinery for soliciting applications is bound to contain partly veiled messages about the kind of research that is likely to be supported. The key question is not whether the industry is heavy handedly dictating to the scientific community but rather whether it is subtly and insidiously biasing the whole research agenda. This would occur if there were a bias towards favouring certain research topics – and the seven ways of being co-opted review is quite clear that each of the three alcohol organisations specifically attempts to fund research on topics favourable to the industry such as the health benefits of moderate drinking – but also by discouraging other research topics. It would be surprising if it were otherwise. Given a choice between research on the relationship between impulsive personality and binge drinking and research which analysed the internal documents of a drinks company for signs of targeting its products at young people, it would be surprising if the bias was not towards the former.

What has happened recently in the UK regarding the funding of gambling research is another case in point. Following the Gambling Review Body report in 2001, gambling research and the very few services which exist for problem gamblers have mainly been funded by the Gambling Industry

Charitable Trust out of voluntary contributions from the gambling industry. The Trust was later renamed the Responsibility in Gambling Trust, several of whose trustees were senior executives of gambling trade organisations. In 2008 the Gambling Commission reviewed these arrangements (Gambling Commission 2008). It seemed to have received the message that those arrangements might result in bias. This led to three separate bodies being set up: one to determine national research and treatment strategy (the Responsible Gambling Strategy Board, RGSB), another to raise funds from the industry and a third to disperse those funds (RGF). Unfortunately, however, the new arrangements failed to deliver the independence that was promised. For one thing, the RGF complained of interference by the industry fund-raising body. More seriously still, the RGSB was clearly not independent of industry influence. By the time I came to draft the present chapter, the main strategy board of ten members contained three who were either current or former senior gambling industry people or who were involved in advising the industry. Even the research panel, which, in any case, is responsible to the board, included a member who, until very recently, had been the chief executive of one of Britain's top gambling companies. Despite the Gambling Commission's awareness of the dangers of bias it appeared to have set up new arrangements whereby industry influence on the research agenda would continue in a more covert form. A similar tripartite system for gambling in New Zealand has been criticised on similar grounds (Adams 2011). By the time the final draft of the present chapter was prepared, Britain's tripartite system had fallen apart: the RGSB remained, but the functions of raising funds and dispersing them had been united in the form of an industry-led Responsible Gambling Trust. Any pretence of independence had been sacrificed.

The foregoing suggests that influence on research is impersonal, all to do with research topics and applications for funding. But the 'seven ways' review article raises the spectre of a much more personal form of influence. It is one that accords with my own observations. Is it possible, the reviewer asks, that a scientist's objectivity might be compromised, not just by receiving honoraria and travel funds, but by 'the opportunities to fraternize with industry executives at international meetings' (Babor 2009, p. 37). I suspect that those in the world of business, including those who work for large corporations, are much more aware than are researchers of the importance of fraternisation. Just as it has been shown that men's talk changes if just one woman is present, so must researchers' talk change if one industry executive is present. I have been in a position to compare the nature of discussions which take place at meetings where the alcohol industry is not represented with those taking place at meetings about gambling where that industry is well represented. What is on and off the agenda for discussion differs substantially. In the latter of those two settings talk which criticises the industry is inhibited. That very basic and understandable social psychological process, whereby topics for discussion are promoted or inhibited depending upon who is present, is fundamental in my view to understanding how dangerous consumption industries attempt to wield their power. That is why these industries put so much effort into being at the conferences, being represented on the boards, having a presence wherever it matters, hosting the conference dinner and offering young researchers the opportunity to travel to an international conference.

Discourses that support power

The massive legalised alcohol and gambling industries wield power of several different kinds. Recalling the discussion of the different faces of power in Chapter 2, it is evident that they are of sufficient size and clout often to be able to have their way with governments by lobbying hard, offering things that governments need and threatening to take business elsewhere if conditions are unfavourable. This is the first and most obvious face of power: A can get B to do what A wants because A has resources upon which B is dependent. It is legal and comparatively civilised. No threat of violence is necessary but the exercise of power is quite direct and fairly obvious. Much of the power of these legitimised industries, for example, power over the research agenda, shows the more subtle, second face of power – preserving a privileged position by keeping off the agenda those questions which would be most challenging to that position.

But, as power theorists have shown us, power is most effectively exercised, often without debate or even recognition that power is involved at all, if the status quo can be accepted by all concerned, particularly by those who are disempowered by it (Lukes 2005; Kay et al. 2010). If powerful interests can control the way people think and talk, getting them to accept the 'discourses' which support their position, their power is even better secured. The addictions field offers a splendid example of the way language is used to support certain positions and, hence, to serve certain interests. In the case of the legal dangerous consumptions like alcohol and gambling, increasingly encouraged in the later part of the twentieth century in line with free market ideology, it is now corporate interests which are served by these hegemonic discourses. I suggest that the following five discourses dominate current official thinking about the legal, commercially supplied potentially addictive products, alcohol and gambling. I identified them first in relation to gambling specifically (Orford 2011), but they equally apply in the case of alcohol. *Drinking and gambling are harmless forms of leisure activity and entertainment (the harmless entertainment discourse)*. Let us look at each one of that cluster of discourses in turn, beginning with the one that speaks of activities such as gambling and drinking as harmless forms of amusement. This has become one of the most powerful elements undergirding support for removing restrictions on the sale of these products and, where necessary, making legal, forms of provision that were previously illegal. This discourse represents one of the principal ways of thinking which the drinks and gambling industries would like the public to sign up to. There are a number of strands to this way of thinking. One is that most drinking and gambling is modest, moderate, on a small scale. Closely related is the idea of drinking or gambling as simply a bit of fun, an idea which representatives of the gambling industry are particularly keen to promote. Official endorsement of this discourse came in 2001 when the British government transferred lead responsibility for gambling from the Home Office to the Department for Culture, Media and Sport (DCMS), a relatively new department, dubbed by its first Secretary of State as the "Ministry of Fun" (Miers 2004).

Another strand to the harmless amusement discourse was well put by the Amusement Caterers' Association, giving evidence to the Betting, Lotteries, and Gaming Royal Commission of 1949–51, when they argued that gambling was a 'wholesome entertainment that is perfectly innocuous' (cited by Miers 2004, p. 118). To this day the gambling machine industry maintains the idea that machines requiring low stakes and offering small prizes should hardly be seen as gambling at all but rather as 'amusements', a traditional part of the family seaside day out. Promotion of its products by the alcohol industry goes further, of course, linking alcohol in its advertisements with sophistication, prestige, success, athleticism, sexiness, virility and even health and happiness.

Alcoholic beverages and forms of gambling are products or commodities just like any other and their provision is just like any other form of legitimate business (the ordinary business discourse). Hand in hand with the language of harmless leisure entertainment goes the just-an-ordinary-business discourse – the idea that alcoholic beverages and gambling products are ordinary commodities like any other. One leading British historian of gambling has pointed out how big was the change in thinking from the late 1960s, when the main British gambling legislation of the later twentieth century was enacted (the Gaming Act of 1968), to the late 1990s when the Gambling Review Body (GRB) was set up, which led to the Gambling Act of 2005.

In his view, gambling in the 1960s was, 'most emphatically not regarded as performing any desirable or any productive economic function' (Miers 2004, p. 395). When the GRB was set up in December 1999, the responsible Home Office minister stated explicitly:

> Much of our current gambling legislation is over 30 years old. Social attitudes have changed and the law is fast being overtaken by technological developments. The Government wants to get rid of unnecessary burdens on business, while maintaining protections necessary in the public interest. (cited by the Gaming Board 2000, p. 3)

The report of the GRB, which made numerous recommendations for removing restrictions on gambling, was welcomed with delight by betting companies whose share prices rose instantly, and also by the government. In the subsequent DCMS proposals for legislation, the discourse of ordinary, not-to-be-restricted business predominated. For example, it was proposed to remove, 'unnecessary barriers to customer access to gambling'; 'gambling products [would be] more visible and accessible'; gambling debts would for the first time be enforceable by law, 'like other consumer contracts'; casino operators would be freed from the existing controls which, 'unnecessarily discourage innovation and restrict customer choice'; and there was an aspiration that Britain would be 'world leader' in online gambling. In summary gambling was to be seen as, 'an important industry in its own right, meeting the legitimate desires of many millions of people and providing many thousands of jobs' (Department for Culture, Media and Sport, 2002, paras 4.2, 4.4, 4.7, 4.23, 4.52), 'creat[ing] a more open and competitive gambling sector . . . [giving] better choice for consumers and enhanced opportunities for business both in the UK and abroad' (Department for Culture, Media and Sport, draft Gambling Bill: Regulatory Impact Assessment 2003, cited by Miers 2004, p. 482).

The provision of alcoholic beverages and opportunities to gamble contribute positively to a nation's cultural and economic capital (the cultural and economic enhancement discourse). Supporting the ordinary business discourse is another, now often heard, argument which states that gambling – and the equivalent argument in the case of alcohol is so common that it hardly needs emphasising – far from threatening the life of communities or a whole nation, is something that enhances it both economically and in terms of leisure opportunities and cultural life in general. Although such claims have certainly not gone unchallenged, they have been made in countries around the world when new casino complexes have been proposed; for example, in Atlantic City in the USA, Hamilton in New Zealand, Niagara Falls in Canada, and Blackpool in England (Orford 2011). Much was made of the way in which Britain's first regional casino, if it came to Blackpool, would rejuvenate this now somewhat run-down iconic English seaside resort. Anticipating the Hamilton casino, the Waikato Times opined that, 'finally Hamilton will be a real city', and after the casino opened it offered its view that, 'Hamilton is no longer a boring provincial city. It's a go-ahead place, a metropolitan city which offers its populace a choice in what they can do' (cited by Adams 2008, p. 137). As in other countries, the National Lottery in Britain, run by a monopoly provider under government licence, has been heavily promoted by emphasising the contributions it makes to the National Lottery distribution fund and, hence, to national 'good causes'.

Citizens should be free to choose how to use their leisure time, including being free to drink or gamble as they wish (the freedom to choose discourse). The freedom to choose how to behave without interference, and particularly without interference by the state, is another key element in this powerful amalgam of discourses. It draws from a deep well of belief in freedom as a cornerstone of the concept of the rights of citizens in free countries. When it comes to now legal forms of consumption such as consuming alcoholic beverages or engaging in gambling, prohibition has a bad reputation and is generally unpopular. Giving the appearance of opposing freedom to choose therefore invites being cast in the role of 'radical puritans', spoil-sports, or supporters of the 'nanny state', motivated by a desire to restrict other people's pleasures (Adams 2008). In Britain at the end of the Victorian era, when temperance sentiments were strong and the Anti-Gambling League almost succeeded in getting horse race betting banned altogether, the secretary of the Anti-Puritan League complained to the Home Secretary about the 'grandmotherly interference of self-righteous faddists . . . [and the] meddlesome attempts . . . to interfere with the national sports and pastimes of the people' (cited by Miers 2004, p. 257). Almost a hundred years later in his book *Gambling and the Public Interest*, a book in which the freedom to choose argument features strongly, gambling professor Collins (2003, pp. 33, 40) states that 'interfering with people's freedom of choice to protect them from harming themselves goes against and goes beyond the legitimate role of government in a free society' and that 'government has no business interfering with the exchanges of goods and services between willing buyers and willing sellers'. In New Zealand, the chair of the charity Gaming Association declared, 'Gambling is part and parcel of life in New Zealand and Australia. Our people are industrious, self-reliant and able to make their own decisions about their lives' (Adams 2008, p. 75). Spokespeople for the alcohol and tobacco industries, too, are fond of championing individuals' rights to make their own choices, even if they involve taking risks with health, opposing restrictions on advertising of unhealthy products on the grounds of commercial freedom of speech and criticising regulatory policies as the intrusion of 'big government'.

Consumers have a responsibility to protect their own health and well-being, and that of others close to them, by drinking sensibly or gambling responsibly (the personal responsibility discourse). Sitting well with notions of alcohol or gambling supply and consumption as ordinary business, harmless amusement and free choice is the idea that consumers have an obligation to consume these products 'sensibly' or 'responsibly'. In the case of gambling, the most recent addition to the cluster of pro-liberalisation discourses speaks of 'responsible gambling'. This is a concept now widely signed up to by not only much of the gambling industry but also governments, gambling regulators and even by organisations whose aims are the treatment and prevention of gambling addiction. The expression is used as if it is clear and unproblematic but the truth is otherwise. For one thing, no clear limits have been agreed within which gambling might be defined as responsible, although some have been suggested (Currie et al. 2006).

But the main issue over the concept of responsible gambling is the assumptions it makes about where responsibility for any harmful effects might lie. As one economics professor says, much of what has been written about responsible gambling 'emphasizes *players'* responsibility for their own gambling decisions' (Miers 2004, p. 487, his emphasis). As he points out, suppliers have responsibilities as well as consumers, and where the balance between the two should be struck has been a debate within the field of consumer protection more generally. It is often assumed that consumer protection is best served by ensuring that consumers are 'informed'. In the case of gambling the idea of 'informed consumers' is problematic since much of the information – some of it highly technical – about how games operate and what exactly are the odds of winning and losing are not transparent and very few jurisdictions require that gambling operators publish odds pertaining to different games or different machines. Since the odds are necessarily stacked against the player, it could be argued that full transparency about the odds of winning and losing, combined with education about statistical probability, would be bound to undermine efforts to market gambling.

One of the implications of the responsible gambling and drinking discourse, interpreted to mean that the lion's share of the obligation to behave responsibly falls on the consumers, is that the large majority consume the product responsibly, leaving only a small, even 'tiny', minority who do not or cannot use the product responsibly. Statements about responsible gambling often, therefore, involve a minimising and marginalising of those thought to be at risk. As one commentator from New Zealand puts it, this part of the argument involves 'narrowing the responsibility down to a small group of people that cause the problems and arguing that their indiscretions cannot justify restricting the freedom to gamble for the public as a whole' (Adams 2008, p. 70).

The marginalisation of those harmed is clear, for example, in the submission of the American Gaming Association (AGA) to the Australian Senate, arguing against restrictions on the operation of gambling machines. Such restrictions, they argued, would 'reduce the enjoyment of the other ninety-nine per cent of people who play the gambling machines for recreation' (AGA 2008, p. 1). This small minority who threatened the enjoyment of the majority were, 'troubled people... [with] alarming levels... [of] comorbidity... [suggesting] a disturbing picture of the individuals who are unable to control their gambling'. This 'blaming the victim' (Ryan 1971) position is recognisable in pronouncements of the alcohol industry on the subject of prevention. The American Medical Association (AMA) found there to be a consistent theme:

> [The argument is that] Environmental strategies (like decreasing the number of alcohol outlets in an area, limiting advertising, increasing alcohol taxation) do not work and the individual drinker (or the underage individual with his or her parent) bears the sole responsibility for any problems that occur. The individuals the industry seeks to blame for problems with its products are also their best customers, and the industry's marketing budgets, which dwarf its expenditures on educational programs, are tailored to reinforce and encourage heavy drinking behaviour. (AMA 2002, pp. 8–9, cited by Singer 2008, p. 103)

Along with the four other discourses described previously, this provides a powerful combination of ways of thinking which serves to legitimate the expanding activities of industries that are legalised to provide potentially addictive products. Alongside the selling of their products they have sold the ideas that their businesses do not differ from any others, that the commodities they deal in are not only harmless if used properly but are positively beneficial for individuals and communities, that the freedom of citizens to use their products as they choose is a fundamental right not to be interfered with, and, perhaps most important of all, that those who do experience difficulty using these commodities are failing to show due responsibility. It is this collection of ideas, which cloaks these industries in an apparel of respectability, which Singer calls the 'official discourse'. Challenging it is not easy because,

... the official discourse is ubiquitous and it is empowered; it is the voice of convention, the voice of authority, the voice of the law. It is reproduced across central social institutions from schools to places of employment and from sermons given in houses of worship to presidential speeches broadcast on television. It shapes the language we speak and the categories we learn and use to think about the world. It is, quite simply, embedded in our culture. (Singer 2008, p. 28)

Power relationships in the illegal drugs trade

The global illicit drug market is colossal. According to some estimates, annual sales world-wide have been approaching half a trillion US dollars. This is truly big business. In fact, those who have studied and written at length about the trade in illegal drugs, such as the anthropologist Merrill Singer (2008) and documentary film producer and activist Tom Feiling (2009), have argued that, in many ways, it is not at all unlike business pursuits which stand on the right side of the law. Although purveyors of legal but dangerous or polluting commodities try to portray themselves as completely benign, and are mostly accepted as such by the media and the public, whilst the popular perception of illegal drug trading sees it as utterly different, at worst a malignancy in the body of society or at best a 'terrible parody of entrepreneurial success' (Feiling 2009, p. 57), in fact in many ways they are rather alike. For one thing, large corporations, such as those in the alcohol or gambling businesses, often exert their power, as we have seen, in ways that may be legal but which have the effect of bypassing or hindering democratic processes which aim to promote public health or environmental protection. Nor, as everyone now knows, do corporations always stay on the right side of the law, although when bribery or other forms of 'corporate crime' are discovered, the matter is often settled out of court. Such crime is less well publicised than illegal drug trading and corporate crime is not a high priority for research funding. Furthermore, numerous businesses, large and small, in many countries of the world, operate at the interface of the legal and illegal business sectors. Either they are actively engaged simultaneously in dealing in illicit drugs and other illegal commodities of one kind or another or they are involved in laundering of money earned through the sale of drugs. Businesses of many kinds, including restaurants and casinos, are ideal for processing large quantities of relatively small denomination notes. At a further stage of the money-laundering process, much aided by the globalised financial system, tax havens and the setting up of 'shell companies' are part of the process of obscuring what is going on. Many of those involved may genuinely be unaware of this but many are undoubtedly displaying what lawyers now call 'wilful blindness', studiously disregarding all the evidence pointing to the fact that what is being dealt with is illegal money.

When the focus turns to those who are engaged directly in the trade in illegal substances, what impresses observers of that trade is how business-like it appears. Being illegal and unregulated, it differs from legal trading in at least two respects. First, the exercise of power can be more blatant, more 'naked', more coercive. Exploitation of the weak is rife and conflicts between traders are more likely to be settled by violent means. Secondly, much effort has to be expended on keeping trading out of sight of the authorities, amounting at higher levels of the drug trade to the allocat-ing of extensive resources to intelligence gathering. But otherwise what is striking is how entrepreneurial it all seems. Whether it is the trade in heroin from Afghanistan to neighbouring countries, the wider middle-east, Africa and Europe, or in cocaine from Colombia and other Latin American countries up into North America, or in methamphetamine from Myan-mar to neighbouring countries such as Thailand and on to Australia and Europe and North America, or Jamaican trade in marijuana, or the trade in a rapidly expanding number of synthetic drugs with which legislators can scarcely keep pace, the methods used impress observers as being much like those employed by their legal counterparts (Singer 2008; Chin 2009; Feiling 2009). The use of terms such as 'cartel', 'mafia' and 'drug baron' obscure the similarities with legal trading. One of the features which has most impressed commentators on the illicit drug trade is its ability to adapt in the face of changing market conditions, which, in the case of illicit drugs, includes not only changing tastes and prices but also changes in police practices and national and international policies pursued as part of the 'war on drugs'. For example, the drugs trade has quickly found new methods and routes for transporting drugs between countries; witness the increasing sophistication of cocaine transportation from South to North America – less use of individual carriers or 'mules' and more use of small planes and fast boats. Traders have quickly switched from one drug to another in response to official crackdown on a particular commodity or the development of a new product which can be more easily and cheaply transported or for which there is a new market; for example, the switch from opium and heroin to methamphetamine production in Myanmar or the discovery of the commercial value of crack cocaine. The observation has been made that 'drug capitalism' has responded to the attempts to destroy it – largely unsuccessful – and the development of modern communication technologies and business practices by moving from a hierarchically organised business model to one that is much more decentralised and flexible, outsourcing many aspects of the complicated process of growing, producing, transporting and selling, finding niche markets and micro-branding its products (Singer 2008; Feiling 2009).

The value of the drugs trade to producer countries can be of enormous significance. Feiling (2009) gives the example of the cocaine trade passing through Jamaica in 2003; worth over $US 3 billion a year, it was equivalent to the island's tourist trade three times over. But relatively little of the profit goes to the farmers who grow the coca bushes. He cites figures suggesting that just 1 per cent of the price that cocaine fetches in the USA goes to the farmer in the originating country such as Colombia, 4 per cent to the cocaine manufacturers, 20 per cent to smugglers and the rest to the chain of distributors in countries where cocaine is retailed – hardly fair trade. Farmers in low-income, drug-producing countries are often so poor that their meagre incomes can be multiplied several times over by cultivating opium or coca rather than maize, rice or onions, and if their land is owned by powerful people with an interest in the drugs trade, they may have no option. The position of workers on very low wages in heroin, cocaine or methamphetamine factories or 'labs' is, if anything, even worse. There may be few other alternatives for earning the same income and the conditions under which they are working are often extremely unhealthy:

> Working in an illicit trade, it is hard for drug lab workers to organize; certainly it is all but impossible to pressure the government to come to their aid, as is sometimes possible in legal industries. As a result, they are at the mercy of their bosses and their subordinate social position may literally be etched in their bodies in the illnesses they suffer from the kind of work they do. (Singer 2008, p. 213)

Some of the poorest and least powerful of those involved in the drugs trade carry the greatest risk of being apprehended. Whether it is poor Jamaican women in British prisons convicted for their small parts in smuggling cocaine, the countless black or Hispanic USAmericans imprisoned for drug offences, or young people, involved in the drugs trade in a small way from a very early age, killed by police on the streets in Rio, it is the 'foot soldiers' who are in the front line. That is perhaps always the way with illegal trade: the bigger players have the power to remain hidden while those whose powerless position can be exploited cannot. Much the same was true when off-course horserace betting was illegal in Britain: the bookmakers rarely got apprehended while their runners were often caught (Chinn 1991).

An illicit trade of such size could not exist without the widespread involvement of powerful individuals and groups. Colombia is perhaps the best known example where huge sums were spent bribing high-placed politicians and members of the judiciary and military and where a complex relationship existed between drug traders, FARC (Revolutionary Armed Forces of Colombia) fighters and government supported paramilitaries. Feiling (2009) lists other beneficiaries of the drugs trade, including the huge numbers of police devoted to drug control in the USA, those who build and staff the bloated prison system, and even politicians who gain power by talking tough about drug control. Even the US government, which talks as tough on drugs as anyone and which coerces other countries into accepting its hard line on drugs, has been accused of turning a blind eye to illicit drug trading in countries like Panama and Afghanistan when it suited its interests to do so. The web of powerful interests that supports the colossal drugs trade is tangled indeed.

There are, of course, bigger social forces at play – macro-social factors such as poverty in islands like Jamaica, the weakness of a national economy such as that of Mexico, lack of integration and stability in a country like Colombia, and the effects of de-industrialisation and urban decline plus the involvement of immigrant groups as drug dealers and consumers in countries such as the USA and UK. It is hard to avoid the conclusion that poverty and instability, both where drugs originate and where they are consumed, have much to do with the success of the drugs trade. Singer (2008) likens it to an hourglass: large numbers of poor farmers and lab workers at the top and large numbers of consumers at the bottom, the latter often relatively powerless to begin with and certainly made more so if they become addicted. In between are relatively small numbers of 'illicit drug capitalists who reap the real profits' (p. 172). Like Bourgois, whom we met in the previous chapter, she views drugs – by which she means both the legal and illegal kinds – as a response to and a way of maintaining

> ... an unjust structure of social and economic relations ... drug users serve an important social function as objects of blame: they, not structures of inequality in employment, housing, education, and ownership, are responsible for the social ills that plague everyday life. (pp. 230–2)

Feiling (2009, p. 67) is of a similar opinion: 'Blame is at the heart of the war on drugs ... As long as the focus stayed on drug sales and drug abuse, inner-city residents could be blamed for the poverty that they had been driven into'. The idea of 'a culture of poverty' was used to support this blaming position, and the concept of a community's 'social capital' has been accused of serving the same purpose. Here again, power relationships and commentaries on them give rise to confusions and paradoxes. *Narcocorridos* offer one example. They are songs popular among certain groups in Mexico and the southwest of the USA, strongly disapproved of by some for their apparent lording of the illicit drugs trade and described by Feiling (2009, p. 140) as celebrating not the trade itself but rather 'the power the drugs trade has given to the powerless'. For some Mexicans, used to having an all-powerful neighbour across its northern border, the cocaine trade and the often successful exploits of cocaine smugglers, seemed for once to reverse the usual power relations.

An example from southeast Asia

Many of the features of the illicit drug trade, just described, are very well illustrated by the report of a unique piece of research carried by Chin (2009) in part of the notorious 'golden triangle' area in southeast Asia. Over a period of several months in 2001 more than 400 interviews were conducted in the semi-independent Wa state in the eastern part of Myanmar – referred to throughout Chin's book as Burma – bordering on China and Thailand. Three hundred of those interviews were with opium farmers, fifty or so with drug users, thirty-five with drug producers/dealers, more than twenty with Wa leaders, and ten with other key informants. On subsequent trips in the following years, twenty further interviews were conducted with law enforcement officers in Burma and neighbouring countries. The Wa area, poor and virtually inaccessible, isolated and torn by war for many years, became a main source of heroin for western markets in the 1990s and in the late 1990s and early 2000s a major source of methamphetamine. Opium had long been a crop grown in the area and its refining into heroin was financially very rewarding for people at all levels of society. The later switch to methamphetamine production came about for a number of reasons, including international pressure to control the heroin trade – at one time there was even fear that the USA might bomb the area – and the crackdown on methamphetamine production in Thailand, as well as competition for the US trade from Latin American countries. Relations with Thailand worsened as the latter country cracked downed ruthlessly and violently on methamphetamine use and trading in 2003 (the then Prime Minister of Thailand became known in Britain in the next few years only by virtue of his ownership of one of England's main football teams).

In addition to the route through Thailand, that across the border into China and thence to Hong Kong had been a transport route for heroin and the Wa had already been in trouble with the Chinese, who, from the mid 1990s, had adopted the principle of the 'four prohibitions' – of drug abuse, trafficking, cultivation and manufacturing. Their citizens crossing the border into the Wa area in order to gamble at the casino was another source of conflict. The attitude of the Wa authorities towards opium, heroin and methamphetamine production had been at the least ambivalent. Crop-substitution and attempts to promote legitimate business, including alcohol and tobacco production, were followed in 2005 by the passing of a much more stringent set of drug control laws. Even opium growing, formerly relatively open and scarcely discouraged, had gone partially underground, away from the roads, and when Chin's book was written in the late 2000s it seemed that drug production, far from having been eradicated in the area, was still a flourishing trade.

At the bottom of the drug trade pecking order were the Wa hill farmers growing opium, usually alongside other crops, in harsh working conditions and living in extreme poverty. Chin calculated that in 2000 the average household income from sale of their opium crop was just over $US500 and that the figure had fallen to little more than half that amount in 2001. Farmers explained that they grew opium as a means of basic survival or as the only means they had to improve their lives a little. Many had no education or training or opportunities to engage in any other type of employment and most were doing what they had done for 10 or 20 years or more and what their parents had done before them. Many felt exploited by the local government opium tax, which required them to return a certain amount of opium each year, the amount often determined in a way that was felt to be unfair. Chin was impressed by the dire existence of Wa villagers, particularly by the suffering experienced by women and children, and by the limited role which they played in the international drug trade:

> Even though there is a booming drug trade in the Wa area, it obviously does not bring much benefit to the ordinary Wa people. The drug trade enriches only a small number of people, mostly Wa leaders and their families and those Chinese entrepreneurs affiliated with the Wa leadership . . . It is clear that ordinary villagers in the Wa area do not play any role in the accumulation and transportation of opium, the refining and trafficking of heroin, and the manufacturing of methamphetamine . . . Ordinary Wa farmers living in the remote villages do not play any role in the decision-making process or in the implementation of these activities. (Chin 2009, pp. 43, 46)

Chin also interviewed local opium traders, some whom he referred to as 'low-level' traders, who bought and sold relatively small amounts, doing their business in the local market place or in people's homes. Unlike the intermediary or 'mid-level' traders, they would never meet those engaged in the trade on a larger scale. Many of the low-level traders were women, some of whom had started in the trade as teenagers, often with the support of family members. They explained their involvement in the opium trade in terms of the need for money, lack of other business opportunities, the fact that relatively little start-up money was required, that many other people they knew were involved in the trade, and that it was at the time perfectly legal in the area. Compared to opium farmers, low or mid-level traders made a fortune, averaging about US$5000.

Once opium was converted into heroin or precursor chemicals, such as ephedrine, were used to produce methamphetamine, the poor played a vital role in transportation. These were usually poor Thai or Chinese people living close to the Burmese border. One was a Chinese woman who had moved from Burma to Thailand as a child:

> When I was seventeen, I smuggled heroin from Tachilek [Burma] into Mae Sai [Thailand] for my father. My younger sister went along with me, and we smuggled half a kilo every trip. We divided half a kilo of heroin into four packages and my sister and I would each hide two packages on our bodies. We did that right before we went to school and during lunchtime we would go again to bring in the other half kilo. My father would threaten to withhold our allowances if we did not help him. My mother would yell at my father for asking us to do these things. At that time, it was no big deal, even though it was illegal. The worse that could happen to us if arrested was to pay a fine. (Chin 2009, p. 107)

As Thai and Chinese governments started to crack down on the drugs trade, the risks for such couriers increased, including jail sentences or judicial or extra-judicial execution. Some of the poor people Chin met, involved in one role or another in the lower levels of the drugs trade, were themselves addicted. Indeed, Chin observes that, besides the notoriety southeast Asia has earned as a main source of drugs which reach the West, the devastating effect of addiction on individuals and families has been neglected – in the Wa area of Burma, Yunnan province in China and in Thailand, where Bangkok's Klong Toey community, a particularly poor area of the city, became Thailand's central methamphetamine pill market.

The drugs trade is of course a complex one involving the coordination of many people and organisations playing different parts. The southeast Asian trade has been described as an example of a horizontally organised one consisting of separate parts without an overall umbrella organisation. Take, for example, the trade in methamphetamine just between the two neighbouring countries of Burma and Thailand. Chin described the following nine roles that were involved. Someone had to import or traffic precursor chemicals and machines into Burma from China or India. Someone had to act as organiser/investor/producer, initiating a manufacturing process and overseeing the production operation. That person needed another person or people who functioned as protector or partner, providing a factory location, money and/or protection. Once the drug was produced, there needed to be wholesalers on the Burmese side of the border who bought and sold speed pills and someone responsible for transporting them from the factories to the border. Cross-border transportation was managed by a trafficker who was not directly involved in the transportation and a courier who actually carried the pills across. Once in Thailand the trade requires wholesale distributors and retailers.

Like Singer, Chin became convinced that the complex drug trade, such as that in methamphetamine or heroin, was possible only if large numbers of people with power and influence, including politicians and otherwise legitimate business people,

> ... simply take advantage of their connections, opportunities, and business acumen to move the heroin from one place to another and, in the process, reap a huge profit. Most of them are not professional criminals, nor members of a criminal organization, but owners of legitimate businesses in Rangoon, Bangkok, Kunming, Hong Kong and New York. (p. 126)

Whereas the heroin trade was discreet, and personal involvement rarely openly admitted, the involvement in the opium trade of low- and high-ranking government officials, army officers, other rich and influential people, and their family members, was scarcely hidden. As one influential Wa leader told Chin:

> It is completely legitimate to buy and sell opium here. I, myself, will buy opium and resell it for a higher price. I mean, the trade is just a very normal thing for us to do. Nobody here questions the ethical and legal aspects of the trade... For me, this is just a business: moving a commodity from one market to another to make money. This mode of operation is not for everybody; it is only for those who are in power and those who are well connected. (p. 79)

Cautious Wa leaders would confine their drug business to opium whilst the less cautious engaged in heroin and/or methamphetamine trading. In international drug trade terms most were not getting very rich on the proceeds but for many it was seen as the only way of buying a new house. Only a handful of people, predominantly ethnic Chinese born in Burma, Thailand or China, were getting really rich. One 'kingpin' of the methamphetamine business, a military commander in the southern Wa region, was specifically targeted by the US State Department, who announced a $2 million reward for information leading to his arrest or conviction. When Chin asked Wa leaders about him, they tended to stress the large donations he had made to support public works in the area, including building a high school and a new library. He was said to have given up drug trading and now to be one of the people who was serious about banning drugs. On the whole the big players escaped the law through the use of their influence and the difficulty of obtaining evidence of their illegal drug trading.

Chin's book provides ample evidence for the thesis that the line between legal and illegal trade in substances of addiction is a thin one and one that is constantly shifting. Wa government documents have acknowledged that in the early 1990s business people were allowed to set up heroin refineries. Over the first five years of that decade the government was said to have collected a total of 30 million yuan (equivalent to between 3 and 4 million US dollars) in heroin refinery taxes. In the following few years, as production shifted in the direction of methamphetamine, approximately 8 million yuan was collected yearly as methamphetamine production tax. Its manufacture in that period, according to Chin, provided leaders in the area with a golden opportunity to achieve three important goals: to generate money for infrastructure projects, to decrease reliance on opium in response to international pressure, and to placate the Chinese government by reducing the amount of heroin entering China. Methampetamine was described to Chin as being the 'engine of economic growth' in the Wa area at the time.

> What we fail to see is that the drug trade can be, in certain parts of the world, a legitimate and logical endeavour for many people to simultaneously improve their living conditions and build a state . . . it is not possible to permanently eliminate the drug problem without solving the political and economic problems that are responsible for the development of the drug trade in the first place. (p. 7)

And in Britain

A study in Britain of a not dissimilar kind but on a smaller scale focused on drug supply networks in British South Asian communities. Interviews were carried out with drug offenders who were in custody as well as drug dealers and users who were unknown to official agencies. Other interviews were carried out with key informants with relevant knowledge and with law enforcers and treatment staff in both Britain and Pakistan. That study also concluded that, whilst the British South Asian trade, like the drugs trade in southeast Asia and elsewhere, was characterised by fragmentation, mobility, and lack of overall coordination, there were clear differences of level. Those at the upper level, described in the report as 'corporate-style suppliers', were not confined to particular local areas. The middle level of 'socially bonded businesses', was seen as one in which the drug trade was associated with other illicit activities. The lowest or 'local' level was populated by small, freelance dealers who found it difficult to transcend their local areas or to get out of the drug market and start a legitimate business. The majority of those involved at this lowest level,

> ... had experienced [occupational] instability, low wages and unrewarding or menial occupations. Most had found occupational opportunities in the informal economy and engaged in semi-legitimate income raising activity... Class A drug dealers operating at the local level were perceived largely as marginalized and powerless. 'They do not have a clue about trafficking routes and division of labour'. Theirs was described as a repetitive, monotonous occupation. (Ruggiero and Khan 2006, pp. 476–7)

We should be careful not to generalise, however. Even in one country, at one time, illicit drug markets can be quite varied, as one piece of research carried out for the Joseph Rowntree Foundation in the UK showed. Research focused on four urban areas, each high on indices of social deprivation, and each with drug markets in heroin and crack cocaine. Interviews were carried out with sizeable samples of drug sellers, police officers, other professionals knowledgeable about drug dealing and local residents. Although in all areas the drug markets were very active and highly lucrative, and open for business 24 hours a day, 7 days a week, they were not all alike. At one extreme, in Byrne Valley – not its real name – the market had been stable for a number of years and, compared to the other areas, was relatively calm. People described the area as tightly knit and most drug sellers were described as having been born and bred in the area. Drug selling, from all accounts, was a 'closed shop', in the hands of a small number of local families and their friends. Unlike in the other areas, there were no known problematic drug dealing houses. Most transactions were conducted in public places using 'runners' who, again unlike in other areas, were generally not users of Class A drugs themselves. As one informant said:

They [runners] have a massive role to play. Through growing up here most of the runners know the dealers so it's easy to start running. They are all young boys, they're getting younger [from] 9 to 16. They're all from the estate. (May et al. 2005, p. 11)

As one young man put it himself:

I had nothing to do; my dad asked me, it's [selling drugs] pretty easy money. I like it. I can buy things now and I get girls. I'm on bail though so I'll probably go down for a bit in the New Year, but I can work again once I get out. It's my rent money. (p. 40)

It was not only the young runners who benefitted financially from the local drug trade. Others benefitted, too, for example, from the thriving local market for stolen goods stimulated by a high prevalence of expensive drug habits, or, more directly, from money passed on to them by family members or friends in the drug trade. Another 'perverse benefit' that was noted was a certain degree of protection from other kinds of crime, attributed to drug traders' wish not to invite police interest in the area. A reading of this interesting report indicates, however, that it would be an over-simplification to see Byrne Valley's drug trade as contributing only positively to the area's sense of community and the empowerment of its residents. The impression given is that of a poor area with a tradition of 'getting by' in circumstances of adversity, suspicion of the police and the local council, a tradition of tolerance of deviance and of not 'grassing'. Drug, selling families were generally tolerated by others rather than liked or approved of. Meanwhile, violence was frequently directed at drug users:

Many young people in the area viewed users as 'fair game' to chase, throw stones at and generally harass. They were seen as creating many of the problems in the area and were blamed for a significant proportion of crime in the area. (p. 39)

The runners – mostly boys and male youths – also come across from this report as an exploited group. Although young men were said to be queuing up to be employed in this way, sometimes seeing it as a way to get a foot on the ladder into the trade, and although runners' weekly earnings put them on a par with the national median income at the time, they were paid only a fraction of what was being earned by the for-profit sellers, and they were largely in the dark about what was going on in the higher reaches of the market. It was unusual for participants at this level of the drug market to have any knowledge of the economics involved in distribution networks or market structures above street level.

At the opposite extreme to Byrne Valley was Midson Vale, a high-crime area, with generally poor housing, including three tower blocks scheduled for demolition. The illicit drug market was less stable than in Byrne Valley. Drugs were sold from drug dealing houses – around ten in number according to most respondents – as well as in a street-based market. Compared to Byrne Valley, the market was more 'open' to sellers from outside the area coming in to compete. This led to an increase in aggressive selling tactics and violent incidents. The report describes residents as cowed by their worries about violence. One vulnerable group in the area were some tenants whose properties became targets and who were coerced into letting their properties be used.

The other two areas were less easy to describe because their markets were in transition. One had a national reputation for drug dealing, local residents had achieved some success in campaigning, a number of dealers had been imprisoned and the market appeared to be somewhat in decline. In the other area the trends seemed to be in the reverse direction. But in all areas and by all groups of informants the drug trade was believed to be associated with violence. Drug sellers themselves believed violence was a risk and owning and carrying weapons was common amongst sellers. In Midson Vale runners were a less important part of the trade and sellers were vulnerable to robbery, including by members of a local gang who obtained money by 'taxing' sellers. Many residents in all areas were concerned about violence but an even larger number were concerned about the negative impact the drug market had on the general social and economic decline of their areas and their reputations. Those who lived near one of the dealing houses in Midson Vale and who felt the threat of violence experienced what the report calls a collective sense of powerlessness. Even in Byrne Valley many residents were described as feeling powerless in the face of such a deeply embedded market.

In this chapter it has only been possible to touch on the vast subject of how power is manifest in the supply of dangerously addictive substances and activities. What is quite clear, however, is that power is being exercised and power differentials exploited and maintained whether supply is legal or illegal. All the forms and faces of power described by power theory are here. The illicit drugs trade displays power relationships in a cruder, more naked, form. Coercion, often involving the threat of violence, is commonplace, and exploitation of the powerless by the powerful is more transparent. But the supply of legal products is also supported by the structures of power, including the power of legitimate governments which support and benefit from supply. Although the power of the alcohol and gambling industries is not difficult to reveal if one knows what to look for and where to look for it, much of the power behind the legal supply of dangerous products is subtle and hidden from the view of most people most of the time. It is often the 'second face' of power which is at work – the power to set the agenda and to keep off the agenda questions which would threaten provider interests. More effective, because it is less transparent still, is the exercise of 'third face' power – the ability to influence the very way in which we think and talk about our habits of consumption and the ways in which they are fed.

Amanda, Caroline and David are at the sharp end of gigantic and complex power systems. They like to believe that they are free agents; indeed, many people would hold them responsible for the difficulties which their consumption habits have got them into. The truth is more complicated. Many interrelated structures of power, and many other more or less powerful people, have played a part in creating and maintaining their addictions. In the following chapter, I explore the way in which power continues to play its central role when they, and others who have experienced addiction at first hand, try to reassert their autonomy and escape their addictions.

CHAPTER SIX

Reasserting control and power in the process of change and treatment

Up against the diminution of personal agency which addiction entails, backed up by the power of those who benefit from the supply of the addictive substance or activity, it is a remarkable fact that every year people in their tens and hundreds of thousands overcome their addictions. How is control reasserted, power re-established? Where does the motivation to change come from? On the face of it there appear to be two contradictory opinions about this. First, there is the view that change must come from the individual; it has to be a question of self-determination. In fact, that is probably the view about conquering addiction which holds sway in the public imagination: no one except the addicted person him- or herself can do it. In some ways that view is very convenient for the rest of us; it's his or her problem not ours. It is also the position on the question of addiction change espoused by many professionals and to be found in many academic accounts of how people give up addiction. The most prevalent theory is a cognitive one: people make changes because they start to think differently about drink, drugs or gambling and the roles they play in their lives. This was the view that impressed me most when I was preparing my book *Excessive Appetites* (Orford 2001). I formed the view, as many others have done, that making a change to one's addictive behaviour was, in most important respects, just like making any other life decision, albeit in this case a particularly difficult decision. Others have written about, 'weighing the perceived costs and benefits of continuing to drink and deciding that the adverse consequences outweigh the benefits' (Sobell et al. 1993, p. 222). It is like carrying out a private cost–benefit analysis. Others have talked of addiction change in similar terms, using expressions such as 'resolving', 'appraisal', 'contemplation of change', 'commitment to change' or 'breaking down denial' (Janis and Mann 1977; DiClemente and Prochaska 1982).

The power of others to support change by standing up to addiction

But that individualistic, mental understanding of the change process inadvertently downplays the role played by other people. There is another view of the process of re-establishing control which acknowledges the power that other people have to support personal change. In fact, most models of behaviour change of health relevance, such as *the theory of reasoned action* (Fishbein and Ajzen 1975), take account not only of the person's beliefs and intentions but also of what significant other people think and of prevailing norms and expectations within the social groups of which the person is a part. When it comes to health behaviours which carry serious social costs, such as excessive drinking, drug-taking or gambling, the reactions of other people are likely to be difficult to ignore. One prominent early addiction social scientist put it this way:

> The recovery personnel of prime significance are the associates, the significant others . . . the crucial persons for recovery are the daily life associates through time . . . methods crucial for recovery . . . are those processes and structures and interrelationships and attitudes and behaviours of the person and of the relevant surrounding others which rebuild control . . . recovery itself comprises the moulding of such changes into a pattern of life, life through time, life with meaningful others, life more satisfying to the person, to his associates, and to the community. It is that moulding through time, persons, and society, which is the core of treatment. (Bacon 1973, pp. 25–6)

What parts do others play in the restorative process? In this chapter, I want to suggest that power provides us with a concept that helps stitch together a large number of loose threads. In Chapter 3 it was argued that disempowerment was what characterised the typical experience of close family members, friends and colleagues affected by someone else's addiction. But, as was clear from the stories of David, Amanda and Caroline in Chapter 1, the group of those who are required to react to another person's addiction covers a far greater range of people and institutions, including doctors and nurses, police and judges, social workers and probation officers, teachers, bosses, housing authorities and many others. All, in one way or another, are likely to experience the feeling of impotence in the face of addiction. Finding a way to stand up to the power of addiction is always difficult. It can be thought of as creating a serious dilemma or, perhaps more accurately, a series of dilemmas (Orford 2012). Studies of how families solve those dilemmas have suggested that there are three distinct ways of responding in the face of other people's addictions. Broadly speaking, there are three options – to *put up with it, withdraw from it,* or *stand up to it* (Orford et al. 2010c). In fact, these three ways of coping with addiction probably correspond with three options for coping with any ongoing social difficulty which is experienced as highly stressful (Hirschman 1970), although in the case of responding to another's addiction, the circumstances created are often extremely stressful and threatening in multiple ways – emotional, financial and social – and the coping options take on a special colouring peculiar to addiction.

Putting up with addiction

Putting up with someone else's addiction can take a number of forms: inaction in the face of the problem, or the acceptance of things as they are, support for the addicted person without change, or self-sacrifice by restricting oneself or putting oneself out to accommodate the excessive drinking, gambling or drug-taking. Women in traditional marriages, subservient to their drinking, drug-taking or gambling husbands, provide perhaps the clearest examples. But putting up with addiction is one of the most common reactions, whoever it is and whatever the relationship to the person addicted. There are many reasons for putting up with addiction, including not wishing to rock the boat, finding it difficult to be hard with the person addicted, coercion on the latter's part, attitudes of tolerance towards drinking, drug use or gambling or simply feeling helpless in the face of addiction's power.

Withdrawing from it

The second way of reacting to addiction – withdrawing from it – is perhaps even more common, although it is less of an option for close family members, such as parents and partners, than it is for others. It involves putting distance, spatial, emotional, or both, between oneself and the addicted person. For family members, it can mean separation. For those whose relationship with the addicted person is not so close to start with – for example, a work colleague or a close friend – it may simply mean keeping out of the way or allowing the relationship to grow cool and distant. For professionals, faced with addiction, but lacking the motivation or confidence to deal effectively with it, withdrawal may involve passing the case on to someone else or simply neglecting the problem. For those close family members whose lives have become very affected by someone else's addiction, the withdrawing option involves an element of gaining or regaining independence. This includes worrying less, doing more of what one wants to do, getting involved in other things, escaping or getting away, concentrating on sorting oneself out and thinking of getting a new and better life for oneself and others one is responsible for.

Standing up to it

Accepting addiction or keeping out of the way of it may be the commonest reactions, but they are not the only ones. There are ways of standing up to it, including directly confronting the addicted person and his or her addictive behaviour, trying to control the person's behaviour, supporting that person, for example, by encouraging change or assisting the seeking of help, refusing to be threatened or hassled by it, and protecting one's own interests and those of other dependents, especially children. All such reactions are difficult and involve dilemmas. In Chapter 3 the controversial tough love approach was described. Its problematic nature lies in its attempt to combine standing up to a relative's addiction with continuing support for the addicted person. Affected family members are indeed at the sharp end of coping with addiction, but standing up to addiction's power is by no means a task confined to family. In the rest of this chapter, I shall discuss a number of arenas in which that task has to be faced, beginning with the world of work.

The role of coercive power

The difficulty of standing up to addiction in the work setting is well illustrated by the case of Charles Kennedy, the British Liberal Democrat Party leader, discussed in Chapter 3 (Hurst 2006). That story contained elements of covering up what was going on, conflicts of interest, disagreements about how best to respond, prevarication and indecision about the right course of action – all quite typical of what happens when a person who is important to a social group is suffering from the effects of addiction. In short, there was no agreed policy for dealing with such circumstances and it took a long time and much anguish before the group could reach a resolution. Even then the outcome was probably not the one which might have been reached had there been in place a more effective agreed policy. That is why many large companies have explicit policies for helping employees whose job performance is adversely affected by their excessive drinking. Those who have written about company policies have described the need to combine help with discipline, kindness with firmness, support with confrontation (Trice and Sonnenstuhl 1990). The strategy has been described as 'constructive confrontation' or 'supportive confrontation', since it involves two parts. The first, the supportive element, involves setting up a social support network within the workplace, expressing concern and emotional support, assisting the employee in obtaining whatever treatment or advice is necessary and reassuring the employee that the job is secure provided appropriate help is taken and work performance improves. The second, the firm discipline component, involves reiterating expectations regarding satisfactory job performance, reminding the employee that if help is declined or discontinued or work performance remains unimproved, then a formal disciplinary procedure may be necessary, being prepared to instigate such a procedure if that happens, and finally dismissing the employee from his or her employment if all else fails. The power of the company, as employing authority, is being used here to try to oppose the power of the addiction. Companies of sufficient size, with well worked out alcohol policies in place, can act more constructively than an employer who simply agonises about the problem and ends up dismissing the employee without being able to help. The company with such a policy is not only acting more humanely towards the addicted employee but is also displaying self-interest because it is considered worth investing time and resources to help and retain a valued member of the workforce. In many ways an employer is in the same position as a worried family member who would like to help restore an addicted relative to his or her proper place in the family. The difference, of course, is that the employer's power, although circumscribed in its scope – with influence only over performance at work – is much clearer and probably easier to wield than that of an affected family member.

There are examples, however, of concerned family members working in conjunction with an external authority in order jointly to stand up to addiction. Scandinavian countries in the early to mid twentieth century provided some fascinating examples of how the tightly regulated liquor control systems in operation at the time could support affected family members. For example, in Helsinki, for some years from 1943 onwards, a purchase card was required to buy alcoholic drinks and all such purchases were registered. If purchases were thought to be excessive, investigations were carried out which could involve inspectors calling on a customer at home, even interviewing neighbours and obtaining information from police and social authorities. Purchase cards could be suspended for a maximum of one year.

Women customers were treated as being of great importance under this system, not because they were often excessive drinkers themselves but because
of their influence as purchasers of alcoholic drinks for their husbands and
as potential accomplices in controlling their husbands' drinking. One such
case was described as follows:

> Mrs B, a 28-year-old Helsinki factory worker, was interrogated in a liquor
> store in 1951. She had bought 58 bottles of Schnapps over the last 3 months.
> After a house call the inspector wrote: 'Mrs B is a tip-top woman... Her
> husband, a house-painter, drinks too much... In collaboration with this
> wife it should be possible to reduce Mr B's drinking'. (Jarvinen 1991,
> pp. 3–4)

Under a not dissimilar Swedish system in the 1920s and 1930s the control of
male relatives' drinking by their women folk was also a feature. It involved
liquor store surveillance, the use of alcohol ration books and fixed quotas
for purchases of alcoholic beverages. Indeed, the system even had a special
term for ration books held by married women: these were referred to as
'curative ration books' (Bruun 1985, cited by Jarvinen 1991).

Those long abandoned Nordic systems may now seem to us unacceptably coercive, inappropriately interfering with a person's free choice. But
coercion continues to play a much greater role in addiction behaviour
change than individualistic, cognitive models of change suppose. Indeed,
there is the view that change only occurs under a degree of coercion, either
from other people or from events. One saying had it that those addicted to
alcohol were only inclined to change when forced to on account of their
'livers, lovers, livelihoods or the law'. In fact, it seems likely that the two
motivational strands promoting change – individual-cognitive and social-
coercive – are almost impossible to disentangle. A number of studies have
shown this to be the case. One was a study of 300 clients entering treatment for addiction to alcohol, cocaine or other drugs. Some had entered
as self-referrals, whilst others were legally ordered to receive treatment.
But when asked in detail about the circumstances under which they had
entered treatment, a third of the former reported being coerced and a third
of the latter reported absence of coercion (Wild et al. 1998). Another study
of nearly a thousand treatment clients found that as many as 40 per cent
had received an ultimatum to enter treatment from at least one person.
The most common source was a family member, with smaller numbers
receiving ultimata from legal and healthcare professional sources (Weisner
1990).

Some forms of treatment deliberately make use of coercion. One, known simply as the 'intervention', explicitly utilises coercion from family members, helping them stage a confrontation with the addicted relative, during which attempts are made to reduce the relative's denial and engage him or her in treatment (Johnson 1986). Another, known as the 'pressures to change approach', trains partners of problem drinkers to deal with the impact of the problem on themselves and to talk to their relatives about entering treatment (Barber and Crisp 1995). Others use the power of the law. One approach which has been used with great promise, both in the USA and the UK, is known as the family drug and alcohol court method (FDAC) (Worcel et al. 2008; Harwin et al. 2011). This has been used in cases where a parent, usually the mother, has been brought to court by the local social services authority because a child is thought to be at risk and the parent is believed to have a problem of alcohol or drug addiction. What is special about this approach is that, unlike routine care proceedings, the parent is required to return to court briefly on a very regular basis – every two weeks – for a period of several months, during which time the court process is overseen by the same judge and the parent's treatment is managed by a specialist FDAC team. Impressive is the way in which the judge appears to embody both a firm, controlling and perhaps even coercive approach with the care and concern which might more often be expected of a counsellor or therapist. The following are observations of the judges made by two of the mothers who participated in an evaluation of the first such court to be set up in London:

> The judge today was very definite. I'm back in court in two weeks and I could lose my child then. You know where you stand. It is upsetting to be told I might lose her, but I'd rather know – it means I've got a goal to work towards. (Harwin et al. 2011, p. 87)
>
> At first I didn't like him because he was honest. He was saying it how it was and it was bad. It was horrible. But now I know it was the truth. (p. 88)

The word 'coercion', with its negative connotations, may not be the best for capturing what the FDAC programme aims to achieve. Power theorists have often used the word to refer specifically to 'punishment power' or the wielding of influence by the use of negative sanctions. Although this innovative court system undoubtedly relies in part on such sanctions, its influence rests in addition on the use of other forms of power, including those the theorists call 'expert power', 'authority', and 'reward power'

(Wrong 1979). The very explicit use of reward power has found favour in a number of treatment centres for the treatment of alcohol or drug problems in the USA. Alongside regular treatment, clients are given incentives for obtaining zero breathalyser readings or urine specimens which are negative for drugs. Consistent with the behavioural philosophy behind the approach, this is sometimes referred to as 'contingency management' (CM). In some examples of CM, additional advantage is taken of the excitement of having a gamble. For example, in one alcohol treatment programme a negative breathalyser reading was rewarded by the opportunity to draw from a bowl of slips of paper. Three-quarters of the slips were winning ones, mostly of small value – exchangeable for one dollar's worth of goods at the canteen or a bus token – but with a proportion worth 20 dollars and a few of higher value still (Petry et al. 2000). However, most CM has not involved a gambling element but has carefully arranged rewards to maximise the incentive element. In one typical example, a $1.50 voucher was given as a reward for the first negative urine specimen, with the value of the voucher for each subsequent consecutive negative specimen increasing by an additional $1.50. A positive specimen resulted in the voucher value for the next negative specimen being reset to $1.50 (Budney et al. 2000). In this and other CM programmes clients can earn vouchers worth several hundred dollars in a few weeks.

Those who write with enthusiasm about CM are keen to emphasise that vouchers are designed to be spent on goods and services which are consistent with a positive lifestyle free of alcohol or drug problems. For example, voucher earnings might be redeemed for such things as passes to film shows, sporting equipment or educational or vocational classes. Sometimes clinic staff retain veto power over all purchases, which are approved only if, in the staff's opinion, they are in keeping with the client's treatment goals of increasing drug-free pro-social activities. CM advocates stress the way in which this element of treatment helps to build on positive motivation rather than, as has often been the case, placing emphasis only on taking out of someone's life something that has undoubtedly served functions for the person, albeit at a cost. This, they argue, is good positive psychology. It helps to turn treatment, which for many may be a negative experience, into something which is more fun. They can certainly point to evidence that CM increases the proportion of clients who stay in treatment and the length of time during treatment in which clients remain alcohol or drug free (Budney et al. 2000; Petry et al. 2000).

Benign social influence for change

Social influence towards change is very explicit in the case of CM but it is ubiquitous, mostly in a less obvious way, in the addiction change process. It is often social pressure, in the form of other people standing up to addiction, which provides leverage for change. For example, in a longitudinal study of very heavy drinkers, successfully abstaining or cutting right back on drinking was often attributed to internalising social pressure to change one's drinking (Webb et al. 2007). Some received ultimata from family members and others received what amounted to the same thing from their doctors. Several participants in the study recalled having been brought face-to-face with others, or having heard stories about other people, which had served as dire warnings against continuing drinking unchanged. There is now considerable evidence from that study and others that social support for change is an important factor in overcoming a powerful addiction and that, contrary wise, social support for continued excessive consumption is a factor militating against change (McCrady 2004). In the study just mentioned, a major benefit of seeking specialist help was said to be the contact it brought with others, 'in the same boat', who had similar histories, current problems and future goals. For example:

> ... going to meet people in the same situation, similar age group, with families, with jobs, and just see how it's affecting them as well. Just to confirm my ideas, what, yeah why am I doing this? Why is this bothering me, you know why is alcohol bothering me? Because it is bothering other people as well, not just me. (Webb et al. 2007, p. 92)

Some participants in the study described how specialist help had enabled them to develop new support networks or use old networks to effectively manage their drinking. Since social networks and social identity are closely related, it is not surprising that some people felt that changing their social group felt like taking on a whole new identity. That idea of identity change was central to the change model developed in the course of a study of Californian heroin addicts which has since become a classic (Biernacki 1986). The 100 participants in that study had all overcome serious addictions without recourse to specialist treatment. Breaking away from the addicted world either geographically or symbolically had been crucial for most of them. The final stage of change had been a transformation of social identity, or what the author of that study referred to as 'becoming ordinary'. In some cases, this had been a matter of forging a completely new identity, whilst for others what was involved was a reversion to an old identity or the extending of an identity that had not been completely submerged during the period of addiction.

This idea of social support for change is deliberately used in the case of a number of newish forms of treatment. One of these is social behaviour and network therapy (SBNT) (Copello et al. 2009). The principle behind SBNT is that of mobilising a small network of family members and friends who can provide positive social support for change. The addicted person – referred to as the 'focal person' – identifies those thought to be potentially the most helpful who are then invited to join treatment sessions or to be available to provide the focal person with emotional, informational or material support. How this worked in practice was examined in one study of the use of SBNT with clients with drug addiction problems and with their social networks. Interviewed about their experiences of this form of treatment, clients referred to a mixture of pressure for change from important people in their lives and positive support for change from those who encouraged it. Although it is often said that attempting to control others' behaviour is likely to provoke resentment and is bound to fail, change was sometimes attributed at least in part to the exercising of control by others. For example, one client said

> A lot of it is family – my Mum and Dad really helped me out this time. My father was there when I needed him . . . [He] ferried me around and they never really let me out of their sight . . . Even now, Mum asks me if I'm using if I'm tired or not eating . . . [She] keeps an eye on me. (Williamson et al. 2007, p. 170)

Others emphasised the importance of avoiding the bad influence of those people, mostly other drug users, who were a negative influence because they encouraged continued drug use. For example,

> . . . if you're going to be serious about this you're going to have to stop seeing certain people . . . if I'm going to make changes, need to knock certain friends on the head; I don't particularly want to do it, but if I'm truthful it's something that has to be done. (p. 170)

Many successful changes to addictive behaviours, probably most, are made outside of treatment. In the longitudinal study of heavy drinkers mentioned earlier, a number of those who succeeded in reducing their drinking without the help of expert treatment were influenced by pressures to change stemming from their feelings that they were not meeting the responsibilities of their social roles, including that of being a good role model for their children. Observing the negative health and other drink-related experiences of relations, friends and acquaintances, and perceiving those experiences as a possible portent of their own fate, constituted another implicit form of social pressure. Witnessing friends and relations losing their driving licences because of their drinking was another source of motivation for change (Rolfe et al. 2005).

Some participants described reduction in drinking necessitated by changes in personal circumstances. They considered that they 'had to' change through having taken on extra responsibilities of a domestic, employment or educational kind, which were incompatible with continued heavy drinking. Some had taken on responsibilities for elderly parents or ill relatives while others had started new jobs or educational courses. Their explanation for changes in drinking was that they had no choice: in effect they felt they were no longer in a position to drink so much.

Other participants who made changes considered that they 'needed to' change, mostly because of health scares. Several made changes, recommended by their doctors, as a result of the discovery of high blood pressure, suspected liver damage, mild cardiac damage or other medical problems. This illustrates what the theorists of social power refer to as expert power. But the accounts given also illustrated the limitations of that particular form of specialised power: in a number of cases heavy drinking was resumed when further tests suggested that the damage had not yet been as serious as had been feared.

Although social influence, coercive or more benign, almost certainly plays a large role in addictive behaviour change, most of us like to think that we are the agents of our own life trajectories and are averse to the idea that we are controlled by powerful other people or events. Our longitudinal drinking study illustrated the great store which people set by self-sufficiency or willpower. Indeed, for some, handing over responsibility for their drinking to others was thought to be counter-productive or even shameful:

> The only person that can solve my problems is me . . . I'm very self-sufficient. If people tell me to stop drinking as much, my back gets up and I start drinking more, just because they are telling me to do the opposite . . . I see my problems as mine, they are nothing to do with anybody else . . . so the whole group therapy thing doesn't interest me at all. It's my problem and I will deal with it in my own way. It will be my decision to cut down and my method.

> If you can't do it yourself, then I can't see the point of involving other people . . . I would be a little bit ashamed of myself. I would just feel that it's like having a stranger in your life . . . telling you what to do. (Orford 2004, pp. 194–5)

Self-sufficiency remains important even for those who undergo treatment. A view of change as self-directed was often expressed by those who took part in the UK alcohol treatment trial (UKATT). It was put in a variety of different ways. For example, 'I couldn't have someone to hold my hand all my life', 'I realised I had to try myself', 'At the end of the day it is up to me', 'Change comes from within rather than without', 'I had to find my own motivation, not be told what to do', 'The main changes have come from within me, I have been quite determined to get myself well' and 'I've just made my mind up' (Orford 2004, p. 196).

Even what looks like self-help, however, may need the support of external authority. One of the ways of trying to restore control over an out-of-control form of consumption is to enlist, *oneself*, the help of others who have authority over one's behaviour or who control the supply of the commodity concerned. The latter is perhaps most clearly seen in the world of gambling in the form of the phenomenon known as 'self-exclusion' (referred to in Chapter 2) which helps gamblers who wish to do so to exclude *themselves* from a casino or other gambling venue for 6 or 12 months or even longer. The system can be formalised still further. In the US state of Missouri the State Gambling Commission holds a 'dissociated persons list'. Gamblers seeking self-exclusion can get their names put on the list by completing an application at one of three state-administered offices or at one of a number of casinos. There has even been a proposal that casinos should have 'self-exclusion educators', who would provide those wishing to self-exclude with information, advice and referral for counselling (Blaszczynski et al. 2007).

Less formal appeals for help in exercising control have probably always been an accompaniment to dangerous forms of consumption. An early recorded appeal was made by James Chalmers of New Jersey, who made the following sworn and witnessed statement in 1795:

> Whereas, the subscriber, through the pernicious habit of drinking, has greatly hurt himself in purse and person, and rendered himself odious to all his acquaintances and finds that there is no possibility of breaking off from the said practice but through the impossibility to find liquor, he therefore begs and prays that no person will sell him for money, or on trust, any sort of spirituous liquors. (Cherrington 1920, cited by Levine 1978, pp. 153–4)

Appealing to a higher authority

An alternative is to appeal to the authority of a higher power. The taking of pledges has a long history and is well described in Longmate's (1968) book, *The Water Drinkers*, about the Temperance Movement in Britain. He devoted a whole chapter to the influence on Irish drinking of one man, Father Mathew, in the 1830s and 1840s. It is estimated that he administered in the region of 2 million abstinence pledges in the course of his tours of the country. His power to facilitate behaviour change was demonstrated by such an adverse effect on the drinks trade that, when he attempted to extend his campaign to England, his meetings were broken up by representatives of the trade. The Pioneer Total Abstinence Association, started by another Catholic priest, Father Cullen, also using pledge taking, lives on in Ireland generations later. In other Catholic countries, also, the taking of alcohol abstinence pledges remains significant. In Mexico, for example, women often mention encouraging their problem drinking or drug-taking relatives to take an abstinence oath as a positive, and sometimes effective, way of helping to restore control. To be done properly, the oath is sworn, in the presence of a priest, and a witness or witnesses, to the Virgin Mary (the Virgin of Guadalupe). A study in an indigenous rural community in Hidalgo State in Mexico found that more than half of a sample of affected family members – mostly women partners, daughters, mothers and sisters – had tried on at least one occasion in the last three months to convince their excessively drinking relatives to take an abstinence oath (Tiburcio Sainz 2009).

Alcoholics Anonymous (AA) is surely one of the longest lasting and probably the most successful self-help organisation ever. In 2004 there were reported to be 58,000 AA groups in the USA and Canada, with a total of 1,284,000 members. From the USA, where it began, it has spread to over 50 other countries and spawned similar 12-step mutual help organisations dealing with other addictions such as those to gambling (Gamblers Anonymous, GA), drugs (Narcotics Anonymous, Cocaine Anonymous and Nicotine Anonymous), eating (Overeaters Anonymous) and sex (Sex Addicts Anonymous). For a number of years, many professionals were sceptical about AA's success rates, citing figures suggesting that many people found it difficult to relate to the AA philosophy and programme and arguing that many members transferred their dependence from alcohol to the organisation, remaining committed members for months or even years after achieving abstinence. AA itself, which values the autonomy of individual AA groups and is determinedly independent as an organisation, did not facilitate research about its effectiveness. But later research, particularly carried out in the USA, has tended to show that, for those who become members – clearly a large number – it is a very effective complement to professional treatment and, on its own, can be equally as effective as professional treatment (Humphreys 2004).

For present purposes the importance of AA, and other addiction 12-step groups that have been much less studied, such as GA, lies in their philosophy of how addiction is overcome. What particularly catches our attention is the use of the concepts of power and powerlessness and related terms such as 'surrender' and 'humility'. Working the 12 steps of the 12-step programme is central. The first three of the steps – sometimes referred to as the 'surrender steps' – are as follows:

> We admitted we were powerless over alcohol – that our lives had become unmanageable.
>
> Came to believe that a Power greater than ourselves could restore us to sanity.
>
> Made a decision to turn our will and our lives over to the care of God as we understood Him. (cited by Connors et al. 2008, p. 212)

These three steps are often said to be the most important: in fact some researchers suggest that Step 1 alone is much the most important. God, Him or 'a Power greater than ourselves' is mentioned in no less than 6 of the 12 steps. This has inevitably given the impression that AA is only for the religious, but AA emphasises that its philosophy is spiritual in a broad sense, not religious in any particular way, and that 'a higher power' can be defined to suit individual taste. In practice degree of religiosity appears not to be related to individual success in AA (Kelly et al. 2009).

The key ideas – admitting powerlessness over the object of addiction and surrendering control to some source of power beyond one's own will-power – are thought to be relevant to anyone who has become addicted. Here then is an apparent paradox: one which may be at the heart of addictive behaviour change. What can it mean? How is it possible that someone who has lost a large degree of personal agency when it comes to consuming a certain drug or engaging in a certain activity can take a big step towards restoring self-control by not only admitting to being powerless over consumption – which sounds fair enough – but then appearing to resign to some other authority what power one has left? The first step is the easier to understand. There are many references in AA literature, and in theories about how AA works, to the addicted person admitting to having been 'beaten' in the struggle to control consumption, to having been 'broken' in the process and life having become 'unmanageable' (Pearce et al. 2008). In AA this admission or confession is summed up in the declaration, 'My name is X, and I am an alcoholic'. In fact the literature on why people enter professional treatment for alcohol problems also suggests that it is the recognition that one's drinking problem has become a severe one, or perceiving life as uncontrollable as a result of drinking, that is the factor about which there is most agreement when it comes to trying to understand why people seek treatment (Orford et al. 2006). This conclusion was supported by the results of interviews my colleagues carried out, as part of the UKATT trial, to try to understand why people had been willing to receive treatment for their alcohol problems. Although many had also been prompted by triggering events, had obtained fresh information or had received pressure towards treatment from family members or other professionals, what was common to all was what we called a 'realisation of worsening, accumulating, multiple problems' connected with their drinking. They were worried about the harmful consequences of drinking, usually in more than one life area, particularly effects on family life and on their physical health, but also on mental health, on finances and in other areas such as work performance and dangerous driving. It was the sheer number of life problems that people were experiencing, the dominance of drinking in their lives, and in many cases the perception that this was getting worse, which were so striking. The following is an extract from one of the interview reports:

> C [client] has sought help for her drinking because of the way that she feels about the fact that she's drinking every day and has been over the last 18 months: 'I just know in my own mind that this isn't the way that I want to carry on', and, 'I want to go back to the way I was before'. By this she means to go out socially, have friends over to dinner, 'just be normal'. She also doesn't want her children to 'think this is normal', to be drinking every evening, and it's that that particularly concerns her: 'I don't want to have to have a drink every day'. She has been feeling this way for a while, over the past couple of months. 'I just kept putting it off', and 'I realised I wouldn't be able to stop on my own and if I didn't see someone about it, it wouldn't change'. Before then she just kept thinking that she could stop it herself, that next week she'd try and then when she realised she needed help, she thought well next week I'll phone. However, one day she woke up and she thought: 'If I don't phone now I won't do it'. (Orford et al. 2006, p. 169)

It is AA's Steps 2 and 3 which are the more puzzling. In my search for help in trying to understand the AA power paradox – that a person might actually gain control by offering to relinquish it – I came across an article which appeared in the early 1970s in the *Journal of Abnormal Psychology*. It was principally concerned with how a 'confirmed smoker' might become a confirmed ex-smoker, but it placed that particular change within a much more general framework of 'conduct reorganisation', whether that be in a religious, political or therapeutic context. Three central change processes were recognised: symbolic death, surrender and re-education (or re-birth). Change was likened to a conversion process which began when the previous social identity was acknowledged to be bankrupt. The addicted person 'surrendered' to the programme and specifically to an individual or group who provided a role model for the new self. This might take the form of a group of others, such as the AA social fellowship, or an 'abstract referent in a transcendental or theological system', such as a 'higher power', or an individual teacher or guide such as a doctor or therapist, priest or shaman, or AA sponsor, who had, 'the legitimate or coercive power to administer reinforcements and also the expert power to guide the participant into proper role behaviour' (Sarbin and Nucci 1973, p. 186).

Talk of symbolic death and re-birth may seem somewhat over the top when it comes to making what looks like a circumscribed habit change like giving up tobacco smoking. But it is worth bearing in mind that addiction in its more severe form – remembering that addiction lies on a continuum and can be mild, moderate or severe – can be devastating, indeed fatal. Bill Wilson, the founder of AA, once wrote, 'How well we of AA know that for us "To drink is eventually to go mad or die"' (Alcoholics Anonymous 1967, p. 98, cited by Piearce et al. 2008, p. 201). Addiction may have changed a person's life so thoroughly that only a profound change may be sufficient to get life back on an even keel. Since beliefs associated with major world religions constitute some of the most all-embracing codes about social conduct and the self, it should come as no surprise to find that giving up an addiction often has a spiritual element to it and is not infrequently accompanied by re-engaging with a lost religion or finding one for the first time. AA has its own origins in the Christian fellowship known as the Oxford Group Movement.

One attempt to resolve the power paradox involved in AA puts it this way:

> Conversion in AA perspective begins when one reaches and acknowledges a state of helpless desperation in the effort to maintain the false self and the illusion that one can manage one's drinking. Bottoming out comes when some combination of self-disgust and fright at the extent of one's absolute loss of control, the terror of recognizing the devastation of one's own and others' lives, and some dim hope that one can be released and restored, coalesce. Real change begins with the readiness to admit powerlessness, to accept a new identity as an alcoholic, and to embrace the humbling identification with a community of others who have also relinquished the

illusion of self-control and have admitted powerlessness . . . This shift means embracing a paradoxical truth: There is a kind of power that issues from acknowledged powerlessness. There is a capacity for choice and the exercise of will that is made possible by giving up the illusion – or the demand upon the self – that one can or should control everything. (Fowler 1995, p. 116)

Accounts of how AA works have frequently spoken of the need for whole character change, a kind of moral transformation or 'conversion', involving 'surrender' to a power beyond oneself, a retreat from egocentricity and self-centredness and a shift in the direction of greater humility, gaining a sense of purpose in life and the adoption of a more trusting, less exploitative approach to the world (Gusfield 1962; Pearce et al. 2008; Kaskutas et al. 2008).

An even more explicitly religious route to change was taken by British South Asian men studied by a Ph.D. student at Birmingham University. Her interviews with Sikh men who had made a reassessment of their drinking and lifestyle showed very clearly the role in the transformation process played by religious authority. The model which she developed had three parts: 'religious adherence', 'undergoing purification', and 'seeking redemption'. The first usually involved engaging with the local *gurdwara* (temple), taking vows to become an *Amritdhari* (a fully practising Sikh) and performing *sewa* (a form of service involving unpaid voluntary work). The second involved a holistic process of cleansing body, mind and soul, akin to a physical, mental and spiritual 'detoxification', getting rid of 'impure' thoughts and immersing one's mind in the Word of God. The third involved engaging in prayer and asking for God's forgiveness for past behaviour. The following quotations from two of her interviews illustrate the role of religious authority in the process of change for these men:

> Nearly twelve years I tried to cure myself, men tried to cure me . . . those in the medical society. After taking *amrit* I never had the feeling in my mind to drink and yet three days before I couldn't live without it. Call it a miracle or faith. In the *Gurbani* (the Holy Book) there lies something very powerful to the alcoholic person. The *Gurbani* power changed my life. (Morjaria-Keval 2006, p. 101)

> Ultimately the fear that I've got of being within the *amrit's* boundaries, the fear of breaking it, is what is gonna keep me on the straight and narrow. It's fear of God. I have agreed to live by God's terms and then if I'm going back on my word God will punish me. (p. 108)

In a book entitled *Quantum Change*, the results were reported of conversations with a large number of people who had volunteered the fact that they had experienced in their lives a sudden life-transforming experience. They were not confined to those who had been excessive drinkers or drug-takers, but many had been, and what they said about their sudden experiences is relevant here. Some of the changes are described by the authors of the book as quantum changes of the 'insight type', a sudden new way of thinking or understanding that seemed to grow out of often troubled life experiences. Others were decidedly 'mystical' in type and they refer to these as 'epiphanies', characterised by a vivid sense of being acted upon by something outside and greater than themselves. The following is one example:

> I had tried desperately and sincerely to stop drinking, but in my heart I knew there was a chance that I couldn't do it. It seemed beyond my control. That morning, however, I awoke from a terrible nightmare, and as I became awake enough to understand where I was, I knew with absolute certainty that I would never drink again. It has been almost a year and a half now, and I still feel exactly the same way. As a bonus, my mind feels at ease and life is wonderful to me for the first time in over forty-five years. (Miller and C'De Baca 2001, p. 133)

The use of expert power

The examples just given, including that of AA, are all instances of change occurring outside the formal treatment system. If we turn our attention to expert forms of professional treatment, we find something rather interesting. Those who have studied and thought carefully about the process of addictive behaviour change have concluded that forms of professional treatment and self-help which may look very different and which have different theoretical rationales in fact may work through a number of processes which are common to them all. Outcome results tend to show that what look like very different treatments produce really rather similar results. One of the biggest trials of treatment for alcohol problems in the USA found similar results from three very different forms of treatment. One form (cognitive behaviour therapy) worked on the assumption that what is important in treatment is the ability to cope with stresses and temptations; the second form of treatment (motivational enhancement therapy) assumed that the problem lies in motivation; the third treatment (12-step facilitation therapy) was based on the AA 12-step programme and assumed that alcohol addiction is essentially a spiritual disease. Very different though those three forms of treatment appeared to be to the professionals responsible for the trial, the results were almost identical (Project

MATCH Research Group 1997). A few years later a similar trial, UKATT, was carried out in the UK. Again, forms of treatment – two of them in this case – were employed which were thought to contrast in important ways. Motivational enhancement therapy, based on the idea of motivation, was used again. The alternative treatment, SBNT, referred to earlier, was based on the very different assumption that what is important in overcoming an addiction problem is the support that can be offered by close family members and friends. Again, despite the treatment rationales completely differing, the results were almost identical (UKATT Research Team 2005). Subsequently, a larger meta-analysis was carried out examining the results of those two trials and a number of others. That analysis concluded that, provided a psychosocial treatment is delivered with enthusiasm, efficiency and credibility, then the results will be equally good whatever the theoretical rationale behind it (Imel et al. 2008).

In fact, it looks very much as if one of the factors determining which form of treatment will be offered is simply fashion. In the 1960s aversion therapy was popular in the treatment of alcohol addiction. Those were the days when behaviour therapy was in the ascendant and there was great excitement at the possibility of being able to help people to alter behaviour which previously had seemed to be utterly intransigent. In the years that followed – often referred to as the years of the cognitive revolution in behaviour theory – cognitive therapy became fashionable. By the new millennium, something called 'mindfulness therapy' was becoming popular, based in part upon Buddhist teachings. This change probably had less to do with evidence that aversion therapy was unsuccessful and mindfulness therapy much more so and rather more to do with changing fashions and preferences amongst therapists and their patients and in the wider society they were part of.

So what happens when people make changes for the better in terms of their addictive behaviours, and is it reasonable to construe that change as being a reassertion of personal power? The philosopher John Locke defined power in terms of change – being 'able to make, or able to receive, any change' (cited by Lukes 2005, p. 69). Modern social theorists such as Sen (1984) and Nussbaum (2000) are more likely to think of change in terms of restoring human capabilities for full human functioning, such as the capability to have good health and to make positive rather than negative attachments. Psychologists are more likely nowadays to refer to mastery or self-efficacy.

It may be that the real significance of the power surrender process in AA is to facilitate submitting to a credible programme of behaviour change, supported by people with expertise, which provides a structure, encourages a statement of commitment to change, and which instils a feeling of hope that change is possible and will bring benefits. One well-known attempt to produce a 'transtheoretical' model of addictive behaviour change identified ten separate change processes that were thought to be common to most methods that had been helpful in the treatment of addiction (DiClemente and Prochaska 1982). One of these, rated as one of the most important by their study participants, and yet surprisingly overlooked in writings about professional therapy, was 'self-liberation'. The examples given suggest that self-liberation is about making confident commitment to change. Smoking examples were 'I tell myself I am able to quit smoking if I want to' and 'It was really a day-to-day commitment not to smoke and to stay away from cigarettes that helped me to quit smoking'. Self-liberation was even rated as highly important for those who had received aversion therapy. In that case the transtheoretical theorists were right, I suggest, in believing that, 'the ordeal of undergoing unpleasant procedures either reflected or increased . . . personal commitment' (DiClemente and Prochaska 1982, p. 141). Some further results of UKATT, referred to earlier, support this idea of the importance of confident commitment. After each treatment session we asked people what had been most helpful about the session that had just taken place. At the end of treatment and again nine months later, if positive change had occurred, we asked what had particularly been helpful. Examples of statements suggesting the importance of commitment were:

> It was a very positive session and I feel confident that I will be able to keep off drink, hopefully without any relapse.

> I was surprised how easy it was once I'd made up my mind . . . the fact that I've decided.

> I know I can stop. I am determined to get my life under control.

> I am stronger than the alcohol this time. (Orford et al. 2009b, p. 6)

'Motivational interviewing' (MI) has become very popular as a psychological counselling method for treating addiction by helping to build that commitment. Its non-confrontational approach and its respect for the views of the addicted person are part of the attraction. It can be used in a wide variety of situations and by many different kinds of professional. For example, it is a method recommended for social workers dealing with the difficult circumstances posed by parental alcohol or drug use which is thought to be putting children at risk. The report of a programme of research looking at how parental alcohol problems are dealt with by social services in London has been very critical of the lack of attention paid to such problems and the absence of appropriate social work training and methods (Forrester and Harwin 2011). Probably through no fault of their own, social workers were found not to be confident about assessing the role of parental alcohol and drug problems in causing child abuse or neglect. Social workers face the familiar problem, discussed earlier, of deciding how best to engage with someone with an addiction problem in order to help that person regain the control which she (or he) has lost through addiction. When what is at stake is a decision about who should care for a child, the process of engagement is likely to be fraught and full of feelings of suspicion and mistrust. One conclusion of the report was that social workers were best able to engage a parent in discussion about the possible ways in which addiction might be risking harm to the child, not by engaging in a frustrating confrontation but by making a sustained attempt to obtain the parent's point of view and to demonstrate to the parent that her point of view had been understood. MI fits that bill.

In their important book on the MI method, Miller and Rollnick (2002, p. 35) try to capture the essence of the method when they say, 'the counselor affirms the client's right and capacity for self-direction and facilitates informed choice'. It takes the form of a conversation, described by these psychologists as a negotiation, a sharing of ideas in a collaborative spirit. It avoids, if done properly, falling into a common mode of dialogue wherein the counsellor drifts towards confronting the addicted person and, in effect, engaging in an argument in the course of which the person's resistance to the idea of change is likely to be fortified rather than diminished. Its aim is to enhance the client's intrinsic motivation: his or her readiness, willingness and felt ability to change. It is not hard to understand why MI has become so popular. Standing up to addiction, encouraging people to change, is sufficiently problematic, and so easily becomes unpleasant and bogged down in fruitless dissension, that an approach which avoids that trap is bound to be attractive. It appeals to our belief in equality. Results suggest that it is a powerful technique but not one that depends on being tough or confrontational, using coercion or manipulation.

But the issue of power is not so easily dismissed. Miller and Rollnick are explicit that MI is in fact a directive form of interaction and intentionally so. It is much more, they explain, than simply reflective listening or non-directive counselling. The goal is certainly not to accept people as they are but rather to create or enhance a person's awareness of a discrepancy between aspects of present behaviour and how the person would ideally like to be behaving. This is done by cleverly chipping away at the client's resistance to change and helping him or her to think and talk in terms of change. Their book, and manuals for professionals explaining how to use the method, are full of tips about how to do this. It is an art form. An important principle is to bring into focus both sides of the conflict – to change or not to change – and not simply to represent the argument for change. Just one of many tactics which are recommended is for the counsellor to adopt the role of someone who is sceptical of the need for change, thereby hoping to provoke the client into expressing the contrary position.

In one chapter of the book, which for our purposes is one of the most interesting, the authors discuss ethical considerations surrounding the use of motivational interviewing. Whether the method represents the use of undue influence, manipulation, even trickery, is an issue which they say regularly comes up when they are training professionals to use the method. They acknowledge that there is always a power differential between counsellor and client. Although they provide an interesting discussion of this issue and do not attempt to sidestep it, they deal with it in a way which leaves many questions unanswered. Their solution is to recommend MI only when the conflict is intrinsic to the client: 'We believe that unless a current "problem" behavior is in conflict with something that the person values more highly, there is no basis for motivational interviewing to work' (p. 167). MI, they assert, 'by virtue of its reliance on discrepancy with intrinsic values, cannot work in violation of a person's autonomy' (p. 168). But they acknowledge that circumstances are often more complicated and the more they are so, the less appropriate MI may be. Sometimes a counsellor has been engaged by another party, such as a court system, an employer or a school. Sometimes the nature of the relationship between the two parties to the conversation means that the counsellor has some other source of power over the client – for example, the power to give or withhold benefits or to decide where a child should reside. In other instances the counsellor's aims may not be consonant with the client's simply because they have discrepant views about what is in the client's best interests. But, arguably, it is exactly those conditions which are the rule rather than the exception in the case of addictive behaviour. The power issue simply won't go away.

In this chapter, I have tried to show how issues of power are never far away when it comes to the process of overcoming an addiction. Sometimes the operation of power is quite explicit as, for example, when coercion is used to encourage change or when rewarding or punishing contingencies are used. In other instances, expert power is employed, as in medical or other professional expertise. Sometimes the operation of power is paradoxical, as in AA and other 12-step programmes, which encourage members to empower themselves to change by surrendering to the power of a higher authority. Even in those professional forms of treatment, such as motivational interviewing, which seek to minimise the therapist's use of coercive or confrontational power, it is evident that power is being employed, albeit in a benign and subtle way.

CHAPTER SEVEN

Facing up to the power of addiction and those who benefit from it

The exercise of power is present at every turn in the attempt to understand addiction. That is what I have tried to show in this book. Sometimes the operation of power is brutal and unmistakable. Those whose lives are threatened because they know too much about the illicit drug trade from which they seek to escape know well that sort of power (Chin 2009). Family members subject to frightening intimidation on account of the unpaid debts owed by their addicted relatives come face-to-face with it (O'Leary 2009). Those who are themselves addicted and homeless meet it regularly in the form of harassment, often violent, from police and the public (Rhodes et al. 2005). There are many other examples. But what is equally clear, as those who have theorised about power more generally have told us, is that power is a multifaceted thing (Clegg 1989; Lukes 2005). Naked coercion of a violent or threatening kind is only one of its faces. In many of its guises it shows us an apparently and often misleadingly more benevolent face. Reward power constitutes the clearest example.

In cases of addiction, is free will undermined, sovereignty forfeited, responsibility diminished?

The most obvious application of reward power lies in the inherent reward-ing properties of those substances and activities which have addiction potential by virtue of their mood- or mind-altering capacities. Many object to the idea of such a property being inherent in a drug or in an activity such as gambling, preferring to emphasise the contribution made by peo-ple's beliefs and expectations, the circumstances in which consumption takes place, and society's attitudes towards particular forms of consump-tion (Zinberg 1978). Whatever the mix, it is an important part of the present argument that the experiences of drinking, taking certain drugs and engaging in certain forms of gambling were, for David, Amanda and Caroline respectively (see Chapter 1), highly rewarding, at least in the earlier stages of their careers of consumption before the costs of that consumption began to accumulate and their habits became mixed blessings and the source of serious conflicts of interests. Although, later on, the folly of having been taken in by the benign appearance of the objects of their addictions became clearer to them, for quite some time it was the rewards of their consumption habits which impressed them most. Only with time did they have to face the reality of that reward as a form of power: they had not felt threatened or intimidated but rather had willingly subjected themselves, realising too late that they had voluntarily risked subordinating themselves to a potent force. This form of power, central to addiction, is, therefore, in an important sense a *hidden* form of power.

The surreptitious nature of this power is clear from David's, Amanda's and Caroline's stories. David acknowledged that he should 'cut back a bit' on his drinking but as the problems it was causing accumulated he started to experience a sense of dread at the thought that he might have to give up that important part of his life which centred on the pub. He found it hard to imagine drinking non-alcoholic drinks when others around him were drinking. Amanda's life also became more and more linked with that of other drug users and it was only later during her pregnancy that she had to admit how difficult it was to stop using. As Caroline's machine gambling escalated and her attention became more focused on playing the machines, her behaviour became more compulsive to the point at which she found she was unable to stop when she tried to do so, leading to her feeling depressed and entertaining thoughts of suicide. As Billy, quoted in Chapter 2, said about his heroin use, he was for some while 'having a good time' but later 'it turned around' and he found his drug use had pushed out from his life those other activities which he had previously found satisfying. In Chapter 2 it was suggested that what particularly characterised addiction was the way in which consumption expanded in importance in a person's life, took on unwarranted significance, became demanding, even an imperative, creating a relationship of unequal power in which he or she became dependent upon the object of addiction. The result was that a degree of personal agency had been forfeited, a part of one's sovereignty over behaviour given away. The irony was that in the earlier stages of developing the consumption habit it had seemed as if personal power, far from being eroded, was being enhanced. David felt stronger in the world, not weaker, when he drank, as did Amanda under the influence of her preferred drugs. Caroline experienced an illusion of control as she played the machines, falsely believing that she could influence whether they paid out.

This takes us back to the important question raised at the end of Chapter 2, the question of whether it is reasonable to suppose that personal agency is compromised in cases of addiction, and, if so, how we can best understand this. The ideas of two philosophers, Wallace (1999) and Levy (2006), were cited, one arguing that volition was impaired in the face of the visceral pleasures of consumption, the other arguing that addiction involved the fragmenting of basic autonomy due to the inconsistency of preferences and judgement. In 2011 there appeared a book, edited by Poland and Graham, in which a number of philosophers, psychologists, criminologists, and others expanded on their theories about addiction and responsibility. All had to grapple with the same mystery which faces addicted people and their families, friends and other associates all the time. Addictive behaviour is not robotic behaviour and when we are addicted to something we are not behaving like automatons. We appear to know what we are doing. Seeking out and consuming the objects of our addictions often appears deliberate and planful. It is not obvious that agency is undermined by addiction. Indeed, Morse (2011), in his chapter on addiction and criminal responsibility, makes it clear that, in law, addiction is mostly not a defence. In his view, it is quite right that we should not be criminally excused for having become addicted in the first place. Neither lack of information about the possibility of addiction, extreme deprivation which may confer vulnerability, the insidious nature of its development, nor the existence of peer pressure or other such factors are sufficient to absolve us from responsibility. However, it is noticeable that he makes no mention of the responsibility of the suppliers of those substances and activities to which people can become addicted – the subject of Chapter 5 in the present book. Nor does he appear to entertain the possibility that in many instances people have become addicted before the age at which we generally consider people to have reached a developmental stage of adult responsibility nor the possibility that some of those who become addicted as adults have genuinely done so in the lack of full information about the dangers involved in recreational activities which they have later found it difficult to moderate or give up. Amanda (Chapter 1) began her career as a user of illicit drugs at a tender age, as do many illicit drug users and most users of tobacco products. Caroline says that she did not understand how 'fruit machines' could be so addictive when she started playing on them, and the same might reasonably be said about many forms of gambling since the addictive potential of gambling is probably rather less well known than is the case for substances. We might even ask whether David, presumably well informed as an adult about the dangers of alcohol dependence, was really aware of what he might be letting himself in for as his drinking became heavier and more regular.

More difficult for the criminal law is the question of whether, once addicted, a person should then be held fully accountable for acts relating to acquiring and consuming the objects of his or her addiction. Relevant here is the legal concept of *duress*. Might it be said that an addicted person is in effect coerced into addiction-related behaviour, almost as if there was 'a gun to the head', and cannot reasonably be expected to resist? No, not according to Morse, since craving cannot be equated with the threat of death or injury; in fact craving might be seen, on the contrary, as an offer of pleasure to come. Even if one entertains the idea that an addicted person is acting irrationally under the dysphoric build-up of craving, tension and thoughts captured and focused, unable coherently to weigh options, it has to be acknowledged that in lucid, rational intervals it would be possible to take steps to avoid temptation. Therefore, although criminal justice may be a blunt instrument in cases of addiction, and might even sometimes be accused of cruelty, it is fair most of the time to hold people who are addicted responsible for the crimes they commit.

None of the other contributors to that interesting volume are bound by the constrictions of the law. All, in their different ways, conclude that addiction diminishes responsibility. Yaffe (2011) employs a variant of the duress argument based on the notion of 'the burdens of compensation'. It is not that the addicted person cannot refrain because she is coerced under duress at the time of committing an addiction-related act, but rather that, given her existing addiction, in order to refrain she would have to bear a greater burden than would be the case for a non-addicted person. He offers the analogies of a heavy sleeping worker who needs two alarm clocks, rather than the one which is sufficient for most people, and a sentry with a weak bladder who has to drink less than others do before going on duty. In other words, refraining is more costly or burdensome to someone who has acquired an addiction, which is seen as a kind of weakness. The argument is that opportunity to engage in activity without burden (buying only one alarm clock, drinking without concern before going on duty, or refraining from pleasurable consumption) is diminished for someone who has such a weakness. In his chapter Levy (the same Levy whose views we met in Chapter 2) employs the idea of ego depletion. This is the idea, based on results of some psychological experiments, 'that self-control resources are temporarily depleted when they are drawn upon and that when self-control reserves are low, engaging in tasks that require self-control becomes much more difficult' (Levy 2011, p. 98). An example, perhaps trivial but one which makes the point, would be the selection of an intellectually unchallenging television programme to watch when one's reserves are depleted at the end of a busy day. The argument here is not unlike that of Yaffe's 'burden of compensation'. Both contain the idea that when addicted we do not lose the capacity for judgement and choice; however, consistent choice to resist engagement in destructive acts of consumption is rendered more difficult, because such choice requires the continued drawing upon resources or facing costs which other, non-addicted people are not required to do.

But Levy's main idea, and it is one that fits my own view of addiction, which gives conflict a central role (Orford 2001), is that addiction diminishes responsibility – or in my terms undermines personal power or agency – by fragmenting or disunifying decision-making or choice. Levy adds to his earlier thesis that what goes wrong in cases of addiction is a breakdown of normal preference consistency: at times of heightened temptation, for example, in the face of relevant cues, the preference for consumption is stronger than that for abstinence. At other times, for example, immediately following some damaging event caused by over-consumption, the preference for abstinence is relatively stronger. In Levy's view it is not the case that judgement is impaired but rather that judgement is inconsistent, that preferences oscillate.

Ainslie (2011) offers a similar model of conflicted choice, although in his case the argument is based on an extension of the principle of delay discounting which was discussed in Chapter 2. He draws on evidence that the choice of longer-delayed but larger (LL) rewards over sooner-delivered but smaller (SS) ones is made more probable if several choices can be 'bundled' together: impulsiveness decreases when choices are made in whole series rather than singly. In this way, 'Processes that are congenial to each other cohere into the same process ... [creating] what is in effect a population of reward-seeking processes that group themselves loosely into *interests* on the basis of common goals' (Ainslie 2011, p. 64). He views the making of consistent choices in series as the key to an autonomous self. The opposite is someone who is in a state of *limited warfare* with herself, motivated by both long-term goals and, from time to time, by the attraction of shorter-term gratification. She is perpetually engaged in a process of negotiation between these two conflicting sets of choices, a process not unlike interpersonal negotiation between two parties in conflict, except that in this case the negotiation is intrapersonal rather than interpersonal. In this series of choices relevant to addiction, a number have special significance. Amongst these are commitments and pledges of various kinds which have the function of helping to bind future choices into a bundle which makes it more likely that future temptation will be resisted. Having the opposite effect are lapses which can have the effect of lowering expectations that future resistance will be possible, hence loosening the bundling of future choices which are contrary to the maintenance of addiction. Finally, continuing with the economic analogy on which this line of thinking is ultimately based, Ainslie views the resourcelessness that follows repeated defections in this intrapersonal bargaining process as rather like a budgetary crisis. When the addicted person cannot find the personal resources needed to stand up to her temptations to consume, he thinks of her as no longer responsible for her choices – but because of a kind of bankruptcy, not a disease. Although conceptions of addiction such as those of Levy and Ainslie can be criticised for being overly cognitive, I believe they help us understand a little better the mystery of how it is that addiction compromises responsibility.

Habit: between autonomy and necessity

Insightful though such conceptions are about the state of addiction, they have little to say about how that state is arrived at. Here the notion of habit is needed. In Chapter 2, I put forward a view of addiction based on the idea that it is essentially a disorder of habit leading to a conflict of motives and interests. The fact that objects of consumption which have addiction potential have the capacity to change mood in a rewarding way, combined with the many cues associated with consumption, the false or at least only partially true positive expectancies about the effects of consumption, processes of biased information processing, and the costs associated with increasing consumption and neglect of other life interests, sets in train a number of vicious cycles, with the result that interests are divided and the capacity for consistent rational judgement apparently diminished. In her book *Diseases of the Will*, Valverde (1998) traces the history of the idea of habit as applied to alcohol addiction. In late Victorian and Edwardian times in Britain, those who were concerned about the effects of excessive drinking on individuals and in society had less difficulty with the notion of habit than was to be the case later. By labelling inebriety as a habit, as a government committee of 1908 did, it was by no means being trivialised. At that time discourses on many topics related to health and education were full of references to monitoring and shaping one's habits, which were regarded as the foundations of character and hence of both individual worth and national prosperity. Since then, Valverde argued, both philosophy and the psy sciences had gone in other directions and the idea of addiction as a habit disorder – although briefly prominent in World Health Organisation thinking in the mid twentieth century – had mostly been considered insufficient to do justice to addiction.

Valverde has done us a valuable service by restoring habit to what I consider its rightful position. She argues convincingly that habit does the necessary job of reconciling freedom and determination. This, she says, is because habit, 'lies in the borderland between act and identity' (p. 69). Individual acts are what concern family members, the law and other onlookers, but it is personality and personal identity which have been of more interest to psychologists (other than behaviourists of the 1950s and 1960s, who were concerned with habitual behaviour but adopted a very deterministic view of it). But addiction lies between the two: actions may be less than freely chosen if they are direct offshoots of habit, but habits may themselves have been produced through the accretion of chosen actions. In her view we would have been better building on the work of the North American pragmatists, notably William James and John Dewey. They cut through what they saw as the unhelpful dualism of freedom and determination. James wrote of the formation and re-formation of good habits as an essential precondition of freedom and believed that overcoming habitual actions such as excessive drinking or taking opium was best done not by attempting to 'flex one's will by mental effort' but by intervening in the chain of behaviours and neural connections set up and 'worn into a groove' by previous repetitions (Valverde 1998, p. 36). He viewed habits as semi-conscious patterned acts that were neither totally willed nor completely automatic. Similarly, Dewey, according to Valverde, believed that habits were 'precisely those patterns of action that are neither fully willed nor utterly determined, occupying that space in between perfect autonomy and utter necessity' (Valverde 1998, p. 139).

Addiction can be seen, then, as the result of the development of a strong and harmful habit of consumption which has given rise to an internal conflict of interests and a disempowering of the capacity to consistently make choices regarding consumption which are in keeping with other life plans. But we must be careful in using such language that we do not accidentally make matters worse. Is there a danger that such a disempowerment view of addiction could be associated with perceiving those addicted as weaker, likely to be leading a chaotic lifestyle, as people who do not know what is in their best interests, in denial, unable to cope? As two social scientists, writing from Australia and New Zealand, put it, might they be seen as having succumbed to a drug such as heroin which 'is characterised as a devil in disguise . . . [which] takes hold: users are consumed and possessed

by it' (Brook and Stringer 2005, p. 322). In this way, users might be por-
trayed as 'essentially beguiled and lacking agency' (p. 320). The compassion
promised by taking this kind of perspective is, they argue, inherently patro-
nising. It creates a dividing line between 'them' and 'us', who are normal
citizens, strong, functional and self-governing. What is more, they suggest,
this can legitimise taking control of the lives of users in their own interests
and in the interests of others: in short, 'marking drug users with the stigma
of debility and delusion simultaneously creates an arena of domination, sit-
uating heroin users as appropriate targets for shows of strength, therapeutic
or otherwise' (p. 319). It closes off any acknowledgement that drug users
might know more about their drug of choice than anyone else. Those are
powerful arguments but in my view they may insufficiently acknowledge
the way in which addiction has fragmented free choice and compromised
the full exercise of personal agency. It must be admitted, however, that there
may be some disadvantages to the term 'addiction' which I have accepted
as a key term around which to structure the argument of this book. It
inevitably focuses attention on the individual. It is, after all, an individual
diagnosis. As such it is bound to encourage a formulation of what has
gone wrong which puts the failure of the individual to control his or her
behaviour at the centre of things and to push to the periphery concerns
about supply and social structure. This dominance of a psychobiological or
medical model must bear much of the responsibility for the field's blindness
to power issues.

There is no doubt, though, that the disempowerment associated with
addiction is compounded by the negative view of it held by the general public. Judgemental attitudes are not confined to those relating to illicit drugs.
Despite the passage of half a century during which alcohol dependence or
alcohol addiction has been medically accepted as an illness condition, the
term 'alcoholism' continues to be used in the broadcast media in Britain in
a way which often makes it clear that it is being used as a term implying
either moral judgement or ridicule. In the case of some types of illicit drug
addiction, negative attitudes take the form of overt stigma. In 2010 the UK
Drug Policy Commission produced a report, *Getting serious about stigma:
the problem with stigmatising drug users* (cited by News and Notes 2011),
which reported the results of a survey of nearly 3,000 UK adults. Although
more than 80 per cent agreed it was important for people recovering from
drug dependence to be part of the normal community, over 50 per cent
agreed that one of the main causes of drug dependence was lack of self-
discipline and willpower. An interesting paper published two years earlier
reported finding evidence of stigma amongst the 12 pharmacists and their

staff who ran the needle exchange service for drug users in one town in the south-west of England (Simmonds and Coomber 2009). Some pharmacists viewed injecting drug users as 'undesirable, scary and undeserving' (p. 124), likely to be demanding or to be shoplifters. They described how their staff felt threatened, resentful of wasting resources on the undeserving and morally judgemental, even when the pharmacists themselves did not share those views. In one pharmacy, shopfloor staff questioned drug users' eligibility for support, calling for a 'three strikes and you're out' approach to those who were viewed as abusing treatment programmes by continuing to use street drugs. Pharmacists feared losing 'general customers' who might be frightened by injecting drug users. When drug users themselves were interviewed as part of the same project, it was clear that they were conscious of stigma from pharmacists and their staff. In some circumstances the picture is grim. For example, the Campaign to Stop Torture in Health Care produced two reports in 2011 criticising centres in countries such as China, Cambodia, Mexico and Russia which claim to provide medical treatment for drug addiction but which are, in effect, detention centres where drug users often face physical abuse, poor living conditions, solitary confinement and forced labour (News and Notes 2011).

The hidden faces of power: agenda setting, use of discourses, and the shaping of free-choosing, responsible consumers

In earlier chapters we have met several forms of power which are hidden in more or less subtle ways. For a start, there are many examples of what Lukes (2005) referred to as power's second dimension – exercising power by controlling the agenda. This is most obvious when it comes to setting the addiction knowledge agenda: certain forms of evidence are favoured by the powers that be – those bodies that deliberate about research strategy, those who disburse funds for services and research and ultimately their political masters and whoever can lobby them most effectively. That is a powerful amalgam of influences which generally privileges certain forms of understanding of addiction and corresponding research questions. It generally highlights the importance of biological and psychological characteristics of individual people who may be vulnerable to addiction, as well as focusing on the supply of illegal substances, while downplaying social structural factors and the ways in which legally supplied substances and activities are provided. This topic-setting operation of power runs far beyond the world of research. It is not only research grant-giving bodies which structure the questions they ask around a predominant interest in vulnerable individuals and criminals and an avoidance of addressing the ways in which the social and economic status quo promotes the exposure of vulnerable people and communities to powerfully addictive activities. As citizens we are all party to this skewed agenda.

The legal alcohol and gambling industries exert their power overtly through lobbying, offering developments which local and national governments find it hard to refuse, or by threatening to take their business elsewhere. But they also dictate the subject matter by co-opting scientists and others, such as policymakers and service chiefs, who draw on scientific findings. This they do effectively by hosting, paying, supporting and fraternising and by doing their best to make sure that the membership of the boards of any relevant organisations over which they have any influence reflects their interests and is not troubled by those who might be critical of the industry or who might ask awkward questions. The most covert and insidious way in which this form of power is exerted is by supporting most vigorously those forms of research and service provision which are 'safe' because they focus attention on specific groups such as 'hard-core' drinkers or pregnant women drinkers, on particular patterns of behaviour such as binge drinking, on the benefits of consumption such as the benefits of very moderate drinking in preventing heart disease amongst older people (Babor 2009), on theories such as 'adaptation theory' (La Plante and Shaffer 2007), or on relatively ineffective (and possibly even counter-productive) forms of prevention, such as education in schools about sensible drinking or responsible gambling – none of which pose any great threat to the continued expansion of the trade (Babor et al. 2010).

More hidden still is power's third face – the power to control the way we think and talk about things, in this case about addiction. Power is most effectively exercised, the argument runs, when it is least obvious. The interests of the powerful are best served not by crudely and obviously incentivising conformity or disincentivising rebellion but by supporting people in voicing beliefs and opinions on the subject which help promote those interests. Chapter 5 suggested the existence of a number of discourses, now widely accepted and strongly promoted by the drinks and gambling industries, which collectively provide strong support for those industries' interests. They include discourses which say that drinking and gambling are harmless forms of leisure activity and entertainment, that the provision of opportunities to drink and gamble are just like any other form of ordinary, legitimate business and should not be over-regulated, that the provision of these products contributes positively to a nation's cultural and economic well-being, that citizens have a right to choose to drink or gamble as they wish, and that consumers have a responsibility to themselves and others to consume responsibly and sensibly. No wonder the providers of these potentially dangerous activities are enthusiastic promoters of such discourses. If the citizenry accepts them, and any hints of non-conformist counter-talk can be quickly and effectively opposed, then power can be wielded without it being obvious and without arousing much resistance.

Of those discourses, it is a combination of the last two – the freedom and responsibility discourses – which is the most powerful, underpinning the continued expansion of the provision of legalised commodities with addiction potential. The former argues that we should be free to choose how to consume such products without interference by other people or by the state. The latter speaks of individual responsibility to consume competently: those who do not consume in a 'normal', sensible fashion are 'weak' and have misused, even 'abused', the freedom to choose which we are all said to have. They are a tiny number, according to this discourse, and the harmless enjoyment of the large majority should certainly not be interfered with just because they are unwilling or unable to exercise control.

Are the majority, in any case, as free as we are said to be? Social theorists, such as Nikolas Rose (1999), who have tried to unpick what we mean by freedom (Seddon 2007), have concluded that freedom in the modern world is not all it may seem. Rose's thesis is that, in fact, far from being free agents, we are all tightly governed all the time. This governance, he argues, is actually effected *through* our own freedom. Since the nineteenth century, liberty has been closely regulated through 'practices of normality, rationality and sensibility' (p. 72). Freedom came with 'instructions as to proper forms of dress, conduct, cleanliness and deportment and the avoidance of liquor' (p. 73). Shame was an important means of obtaining conformity. The home and the place of work were the main sites for ensuring this *responsibilization*, this process of controlling,

> . . . the dangerous passions of adults, tearing them away from public vice, the gin palace and the gambling hall, imposing a duty of responsibility to each other, to home and to children, and a wish to better their own condition. (p. 74)

People's conduct was regulated, not by subjugation and the imposition of power, but rather 'through practices that "make up subjects" as free persons' (p. 95). In the twentieth century, freedom came to mean the capacity of an autonomous individual to realise his or her own desires and potential through one's own acts of choice. No longer were self-gratification and civility to be thought of as being in opposition; happiness and profit were now in alignment: we shape our own lives, 'through acts of choice in the world of goods' (p. 86). In fact, according to Rose, we are not simply free to choose but actually obliged to be free in that sense: 'competent personhood is thought to depend upon the continual exercise of freedom' (p. 87).

Seen in that light, therefore, freedom, even the freedom which the majority feel they exercise when consuming dangerous products responsibly, is an illusion. This is what Foucault called 'disciplinary power' and what has sometimes been referred to as the fourth face of power (Servian 1996). If the first face of power is unsubtle coercion or control, the second control of the agenda, and the third control of ideology and knowledge, the fourth can be thought of as control of the very subject herself. She becomes her own disciplinarian, taking over the role of keeping her behaviour under constant surveillance, a role that in former, simpler times might have been played by the community. As Bauman (1982, pp. 40–1, cited by Clegg 1989, p. 167) put it, the object of this fourth type of power,

> . . . was now the subject himself, his daily rhythm, his time, his bodily actions, his mode of life. The power reached now towards the body and soul of its subjects. It wished to regulate, to legislate, to tell the right from the wrong, the norm from deviance, the ought from the is.

The modern world then needs responsible consumers of products, including products that are dangerous. We conform to these expectations, believing we are making consumption choices freely, only dimly aware that we are being manipulated by forces far stronger than ourselves. Because some of the products we consume are dangerously addictive, many of us are casualties. Some of us are more at risk than others.

The disempowering effects of addiction are most likely to occur where resistance is weaker

Not everyone who is affected by addiction at first hand is poor or oppressed. But, as was argued in Chapter 4, addiction flourishes best where the power to resist it is weakest. Those with fewer resources of knowledge, money and status are at a disadvantage in resisting the apparently benign attractions of addictive substances and activities and are at a further disadvantage in trying to give up addiction when its malign effects become clear. In Chapter 4 a number of studies were cited which support the general argument that people who are relatively lacking in status or resources are more vulnerable to suffering the ill effects of excessive drug use, drinking or gambling, even when the sheer volume of their consumption, or the amount of money they expend on consumption, is no greater, or even in some instances less, than that of the better off (Romelsjö and Lundberg 1996; Wardle et al. 2007). Those of lower socio-economic position, immigrant and ethnic minority groups, indigenous and aboriginal people, and lesbian, gay and bisexual people are more at risk (D'Avenzo et al. 1994; McCabe et al. 2009). One explanation is that people with fewer resources or those of lower status more often than others consume dangerous products in ways which are risky. Such risky modes of consumption include binge drinking, of which the Russian *zapoi* is an extreme example (Tomkins et al. 2007), the sharing of drug injecting equipment and other unsafe practices (De et al. 2007). A further explanation, discussed in Chapter 4, is that once the risks associated with particular products, and ways of consuming them, become more widely known, and when help to counteract or minimise those risks becomes available, it is those with greater resources, who are then more likely to avoid engaging in risky practices and more likely to be able to moderate or give up such practices (Genberg et al. 2011). Social gradients, showing increasing rates of risky behaviour with increasing social disadvantage, may become steeper at such times or may start to appear where no such relationship existed before (Chilcoat 2009).

It is not just people whose behaviour is risky but also environments that put people at risk. From the work of Chein and colleagues (1964) in New York more than half a century ago to much more recent research in the USA and elsewhere, studies have shown higher rates of drug problems in the poorer areas of cities (Brugal et al. 1999). These area effects are not confined to the most obviously drug-filled environments associated with the most notorious drug scenes. Nor do they pertain only to illicit drugs: there is also evidence of area deprivation effects in the cases of drinking and gambling (Lambert et al. 2004; Welte et al. 2004). Authors of such studies have speculated about what characteristics of neighbourhoods render them particularly risky. It may be that drug use is more than normal and attitudes towards drug use more accepting in such areas. There may be more cues and temptations or more offers of drugs for sale. The risks may have more to do with social networks: in poorer neighbourhoods there may be a greater chance of having more drug users in one's network and a lesser likelihood of knowing people who are in regular employment and who are not drug users. An alternative explanation is that living in poorer areas is more stressful, putting residents more at risk of anxiety and depression and hence of risky engagement in alcohol or drug consumption or in gambling as a kind of self-medication for the oppressed (LaVeist and Wallace 2000; Lambert et al. 2004; Chuang et al. 2005). A further explanation is that active drug markets are fostered and supported more readily in economically deprived neighbourhoods. This fits with the evidence touched on in Chapter 4 indicating that the density of outlets for dangerous but legal commodities such as alcohol and gambling tend to be concentrated in areas of social deprivation, where people are on lower incomes on average and where there is often a concentration of ethnic minority groups (Marshall 2005; Huckle et al. 2008).

The last of those explanations is met with favour by those such as Philippe Bourgois (2003a) and Merrill Singer (2001), who have studied drug use in Harlem, New York, and Hartford, Connecticut, and also by those, such as Nick Davies (1997), who have commented on drug use in poorer areas of London and other British cities. Bourgois writes of the erosion of traditional working-class employment in Harlem and the way in which dealing in crack cocaine was filling the role of an underground economy as almost the only available equal opportunity employer. Singer speaks of the decline in availability of accessible, entry-level employment for those without skills following the decline of traditional heavy industry in Hartford, and Davies talks of illicit drugs becoming a very saleable commodity in poor city areas. This was confirmed in the Joseph Rowntree Foundation study of drug markets in 'Byrne Valley' and 'Midson Vale' (May et al. 2005).

As Australian community psychologists, Fisher et al. (2007, p. 260) explain, 'Power is not something that is fixed with an individual . . . it . . . is constituted within relations between people within broader historical, social, cultural, economic and political contexts'. In the case of addiction the power networks of relevance are formidable in size and extensity. Where trade is illegal the networks embrace many poor people and communities besides those who are personally addicted to its products. So large are the armies of poor farmers, illicit laboratory workers, mules, and runners that some have likened the situation to an hourglass, with a relatively small number of beneficiaries in the middle, benefiting from the exploitation of the powerless at either side of them – those involved at a low level in production and distribution at one end and the vulnerable and increasingly disempowered consumers at the other end (Singer 2008). In fact, as Chin's (2009) research in Myanmar, described in Chapter 5, suggests, the hourglass analogy may not be completely appropriate since the numbers of powerful individuals and organisations which benefit from the illicit drug trade is by no means small in size, including as it does many businessmen and women otherwise engaged in legal commerce, many individuals and families involved in criminal activity and politicians and whole governments which become dependent on the trade. When the business of supplying potentially addictive substances and activities is a legal one, the beneficiaries may be yet larger in number, the exercise of power more multi-layered and many-faceted and the sources of social oppression which confer vulnerability to addiction and erode personal power once addiction takes hold more hidden and even more difficult to challenge.

Singer (2001; 2008) has used the term *structural violence* to refer to the disadvantages inflicted by the social, political, economic and institutional order of power which confers addiction vulnerability, and Bourgois et al. (2004) have employed the term *structural vulnerability*. Both make clear that an understanding of addiction has to reach far beyond the assumption that addictive behaviour is simply a rational lifestyle choice or just a response to difficult, immediate life circumstances. Each implies that individual decision-making and choice are constrained by larger forces and indeed that drug using and dealing are likely to enhance rather than diminish the power of those forces.

The contagious spread of disempowerment to family members, friends, work colleagues, and communities

Amongst those most exploited and disempowered by addiction are close family members such as David's wife, Marian, Amanda's parents, Mercy and Gilbert, and Caroline's daughter, Karen (Chapter 1). As discussed in Chapter 3, this is the largest group of people directly affected by addiction, perhaps numbering several hundred million people worldwide. They range from wives, already living in poverty, further affected financially and in other ways by their husbands' excessive drinking in a country such as India, as described by Martha Nussbaum (2000), to the partners, parents, children and other family members of those addicted to drugs or gambling in the western world. So large is this group that their lack of collective voice should be seen as extraordinary and requiring explanation. Family members affected by addiction have mostly gone unnoticed, kept at arm's length by professionals and academics otherwise interested in addiction and, when they have been noticed, often blamed. A cruel accusation, inherent in some professional theories, has been that the interests of family members – the accusation has most often been directed at wives – are served by their relatives' addiction (Orford et al. 2005). The truth is exactly the opposite. If there is one constituency of people whose real interests are unequivocally undermined by addiction, it is closely affected family members. Those who are in the grip of their own addictions may be profoundly ambivalent. Many others benefit in some way from supplying or taxing the objects of their addictions. Even those who are professionally involved in regulating or policing supply or in treating addiction are dependent on it for their livelihoods. But affected family members are in a unique position: their only interest in addiction is in seeing it come to an end or in having its effects mitigated.

Why, then, have they and their interests been so peripheral, their voices so little heard? Is there a conspiracy to silence them or is their obscurity best explained as an accident, caused by a combination of their own reluctance to come forward and an understandable focus in the field upon the addictive behaviour of their relatives? The powerlessness of their position provides the explanation. Not only are the majority living in poor families in poor communities, but it is also the case that the large majority of family members whose lives are harmed by their relatives' addictions are women and children, the two groups universally prone to powerlessness according to social dominance theory (Sidanius and Pratto 1999). Furthermore, the very nature of addiction renders them more powerless still and undermines their capacity for collective action. David, Amanda and Caroline are not suffering from an illness which announces itself in the form of pain and a desire for treatment but rather from an ambivalent attachment to a supplied product which creates an atmosphere of denial, miscommunication, uncertainty and mistrust. Family members spend a lot of time worrying and waiting, uncertain whether their suspicions are correct or misplaced, cut off from clear information about what is wrong and what they might do about it. This form of demoralisation, characterised by many doubts and uncertainties, is mostly a hidden one. In the terms used by Sen (1984, 1985) and Nussbaum (2000), it is an experience which undermines some basic human capabilities such as experiencing bodily health, bodily integrity, an emotional life, affiliation, dignity and self-respect and play. Although addiction is unequivocally contrary to the interests of affected family members, the experience is a confusing one for them because it is unclear where responsibility for their troubles lies. It may appear that their drinking, drug-taking or gambling relatives have become all-powerful, but this is an illusion. Their relatives' power over their own behaviour has diminished and their powerlessness is contagious. These are not the most auspicious circumstances for going out into the world and engaging in collective action.

In a programme of research spanning a number of years my colleagues and I have identified three broad ways, described in Chapter 6, in which family members can respond to their relatives' addiction problems. They can put up with it, stand up to it or withdraw from it or, to use the slightly more formal language which we have often used in our academic reports, they can react with *tolerance, engagement,* or *withdrawal.* Of course, there is a multitude of more individual and nuanced ways of coping with an addiction problem in the family, but most can be subsumed under those three very broad headings. It is never easy for family members to decide how to react. Their lives are full of what I call 'addiction coping dilemmas' (Orford 2012). Different members of the same family, such as Jacqueline Doherty (2006) and her husband (see Chapter 3), may choose very different ways of coping, giving rise to disagreement and further misunderstanding and demoralisation. Family members have often found themselves maligned on account of the ways they are coping, as were Sara Coleridge, Caitlin Thomas and Baudelaire's mother (Chapter 3), on account of their attempts to stand up to their relatives' addictions by being assertive or by attempting to take back some control of their lives.

The contagion of powerlessness associated with addiction affects many other people beyond the confines of the immediate family. Members of the extended family also share the same sense of impotence and many of the same addiction dilemmas, especially in parts of the world where it is common for several generations and less immediate kin to live under the same roof or close by. Even in the western country where David, Amanda and Caroline lived, there were others who were closely affected, for example, David's and his wife's relations, Amanda's sister and Caroline's brother. In Chapter 3 examples were also given of the way in which close friends and work colleagues can share some of the same frustrations and dilemmas as close family members. Addiction has the capacity to drive wedges between people and to set up uncomfortable triangles. The relationships among Coleridge, his wife, Sara, and their friends, the Wordsworths, is a classic example. The relationships among Dylan Thomas, his wife, Caitlin, and his US colleague, John Brinnin, is another. Work organisations, political parties and sports teams are further examples, discussed in Chapters 3 and 6, of settings where addiction can create confusion, varying levels of awareness, disagreements about how to cope and often inaction as a consequence.

Although it is something that it has been possible to only touch on in this book, there is also the question of how addiction can disempower whole neighbourhoods or communities. This may be at its most starkly obvious in the case of some indigenous communities where the harmful effects of drinking has become a major issue, or in poor, inner-city neighbourhoods where illicit drugs are readily available, where low or middle level engagement in the drugs trade has become one of the sources of income for a number of people and where the prevalence of drug addiction is high. Bourgois (2003a) wrote of the terror felt by local residents in the crack-dealing area of New York where he was carrying out his research, and the Joseph Rowntree Foundation research into illicit drug markets in a number of English towns found that, irrespective of the type of drug market, local residents experienced fear of violence and a sense of powerlessness as well as an awareness that the reputations of their areas were suffering (May et al. 2005). But even in areas where addiction is better hidden, communities are affected, for example, because of such things as drinking and driving, late-night binge drinking or a concentration of gambling outlets on their high streets.

Exit, voice, loyalty: the options for coping with addiction

The simple three-way typology of coping with addiction in the family – putting up with it, standing up to it or withdrawing from it – may have application well beyond the family group. Might it equally apply to the ways we all respond to addiction whether as individuals, groups or whole societies and whether we are concerned about an individual friend or colleague or more generally about addiction in the workplace, in our neighbourhoods or in society generally? I have been encouraged in thinking of such a broader application of the three ways of responding by discovering a book published in 1970, written by Albert Hirschman, under the title *Exit, Voice, and Loyalty*. It turns out that there is more than a little correspondence between his exit, voice and loyalty and our withdrawal, engagement and tolerance. Hirschman approached his subject from an economic perspective. In fact, the subtitle of his book was *Responses to Decline in Firms, Organizations, and States*. But he wrote his book during a sabbatical period spent at the Center for Advanced Study in the Behavioral Sciences at Stanford University and got talking to the psychologists there. As he says in the introduction, he started out with a focus on commercial firms but came to realise that the ideas he was developing were relevant to all manner of organisations, large and small, including families. Many of his ideas are certainly reminiscent of things we have learned about families coping with addiction, and a number of them may help us think further about the dilemmas which addiction poses, not just for closely affected family members but for us all.

Hirschman's basic interest was in understanding the circumstances under which the customers and members of organisations behave in different ways in response to the 'lapses from efficient, rational, law-abiding, virtuous, or otherwise functional behavior' to which firms were prone (Hirschman 1970, p. 1). In particular, he wanted to know why people sometimes choose the exit option – for example, dissatisfied customers sometimes choose to stop buying a firm's products or discontented members of organisations sometimes up and leave – and why they sometimes choose instead the voice option, by expressing their dissatisfaction or by generally protesting. He was also interested to know when one or other of these two options would be the more effective in arresting and reversing the deterioration in the organisation's performance. If it is reasonable to think of addiction as something that detracts from an individual's full contribution to any organisation of which he or she is a member, hence threatening the quality or performance of the organisation as a whole, and knowing that choosing between trying to stand up to the addiction (voice) and withdrawing from it (exit) is a central dilemma for many family members and others, it really looks as if Hirschman might have a lot to offer us.

Exit, he argues, is often seen as a last resort, chosen only after efforts have been made to voice concern and encourage recovery. People, he suggests, weigh up the chances of staying and getting the organisation back on track. They may stay in the hope of change. They may be willing to make sacrifices because they want to 'do something'. This has obvious relevance for families struggling to cope with addiction, but in their case withdrawal is certainly not so clear-cut as withdrawing one's custom from a commercial supplier. For one thing, withdrawal may be partial, as in the case of a family member who reduces contact or communication with an addicted relative whilst remaining living under the same roof. He recognised that the family is an example of a type of organisation (church and nation were others) from which exit is relatively unlikely and where voice is comparatively likely. But what Hirschman meant by voice was mostly limited to making one's complaints known within the organisation or to those responsible for it. In the case of addiction it may be counterproductive, even unsafe, to complain directly to the addicted relative or colleague, and there may be no obvious other place to go to complain.

What Hirschman had to say about the third option, loyalty, is particularly pertinent to family members facing the dilemma of how to cope with addiction. Members sometimes stay put, he says, out of loyalty rather than being motivated to use their influence to bring about change and recovery. Their motivation may be to give the organisation a chance to recuperate.

Loyalist behaviour may on the other hand be unconscious; the member may be unaware of the deterioration and hence free from felt discontent and unlikely to exercise voice. Loyalty is particularly likely when a member has strong affection for or attachment to the organisation – as evidenced by use of the word 'our' (recall from Chapter 3 Jacqueline Doherty's statement that she would not have a word said by others against her son despite all the anguish which his behaviour had caused her). Although loyalty may be most effective when backed up by the threat of exit, in practice leaving may not be easy and often there exists loyalty with little possibility or thought of exit. Loyalist behaviour may be motivated by the anticipation that the organisation would go from bad to worse if the member left. This implies that the quality of the organisation would matter to the member once he or she left. In that case, full 'exit' is in a sense impossible, as, for example, it is for most parents of addicted offspring who never cease to think of themselves as parents and, therefore, as people who continue to have some caring responsibilities. Loyalists will argue for staying in post despite the suffering this may bring them and may well overestimate the influence they have in the organisation and the damaging consequences if they exited. The feeling that one needs to stay in case things get worse may strengthen as the organisation deteriorates further, and exit may become even less conceivable, whilst unhappiness may increase. Loyalty may appear irrational to an outsider and the longer the loyalist remains and recovery fails, the more he or she may look like a 'sucker'.

Hirschman also had much to say about how organisations encourage or discourage exit, voice and loyalty, and how they respond to them. Commercial firms may have monopoly market power and can, therefore, get away with inefficiency, exploitation and even brutality. The firm has no rival and the customer has no provider B to substitute for provider A. He equates the low exit/low voice case with totalitarian organisations and regimes under which voice is seen as mutiny and exit as treason. There are undoubtedly families in which the addicted member is acting as a tyrant, closing off a family member's possibilities for voice or exit. But in most families, and in organisations more generally, exit or voice may be discouraged in less dramatic ways. The organisation and its managers may discourage desertion or complaints or simply be insensitive when members or customers react in these ways. They may have a stake in self-deception. They may have ways of absorbing or minimising members' or customers' weapons of exit or voice. Attempts to voice complaints, for example, may be construed as mere 'blowing off steam': family members' complaints about addiction are often brushed off as merely humorous and not meant seriously. Devices may be employed such as imposing stiff penalties for exit, the latter particularly relevant to traditional groups such as the family. Hirschman's conclusion is that some combination of exit and voice is often the most effective way of exerting influence for recovery on an organisation of which one is a member or customer. However, he suggests that such a combination is found to be the case only rarely, partly because one or other mode of responding to poor performance becomes increasingly familiar as it is used and the alternative becomes increasingly underestimated.

Overcoming addiction by submitting to the power of others

The three broad ways of coping idea is equally relevant in the case of the many professional and nonprofessional people who become involved in trying to help people like David, Amanda and Caroline. In the face of addiction many potential helpers withdraw or keep their distance, as, for example, did most of the general hospital staff whom Amanda met. In Chapter 6 the case was made that some degree of coercion was much more frequently involved when people with addictions seek help than most theories of addiction change care to admit. This is obvious in such cases as the Family Drug and Alcohol Court (Harwin et al. 2011), company alcohol policies such the one David's company had (Trice and Sonnenstuhl 1990), the Family Intervention method (Johnson 1986) or the old Nordic systems of monitoring alcohol ration books (Jarvinen 1991), which were given as examples. But the argument was that an element of coercion from others, alongside the addicted person's own decision-making, nearly always plays a part. This can be thought of as the social system or social network – whether that is largely the family or the workplace or the social services department or some combination of those and other sources of coercion – standing up to addiction rather than tolerating it or turning their back on it. The further argument was that effective ways of taking this stand and helping people overcome their addictions usually involves some combination of being firm and being kind, a mix of both discipline and support, or what in the context of company policies has been referred to as *supportive confrontation* (Trice and Sonnenstuhl 1990). More generally still, it was argued that when addiction is sufficiently severe that a person feels helpless desperation, finding she cannot control her behaviour despite the accumulation of harmful effects, it is then that she is willing to submit herself – 'surrender' is the word Alcoholics Anonymous might use (Pearce et al. 2008) – to a therapist, teacher, guide, group or fellowship who can then use their legitimate, expert or coercive power to assist the change process. The exact form that the helping process takes, and the particular mix of forms of power involved, is much less important than the fact that addiction is being confronted in a way that combines care and control, support and discipline. The way this is done varies from religious transformation, as in the example I gave of Sikh men using their religion to overcome their drinking problems (Morjaria-Keval 2006), to *motivational interviewing* (Miller and Rollnick 2002), which is much more subtly directive and controlling than might at first appear to be the case, to the currently very popular *contingency management* which explicitly uses reward power alongside the rest of a treatment programme (Petry et al. 2000). There is strong evidence to support the view that it is not the precise form that treatment takes, nor the specific rationale for the treatment, which matters but rather the change processes which are common to them. What may be important is that people who have been experiencing addiction, with all the personal disempowerment and contagious spread of disempowerment to others which it involves, submit, with some combination of voluntarism and coercion, to a credible programme which, by applying the crucial support-discipline mix, encourages confident commitment to change (Orford 2008b). Those who have written about AA refer to the process of surrendering to the programme as 'humbling' (Connors et al. 2008). Those who enter professional addiction treatment naturally like to emphasise the personal cognitive element of change: the decision, the commitment, the seeing sense. Those who prefer not to seek help emphasise self-sufficiency, the importance of using one's own willpower, and speak of seeking help as handing over to others responsibility which should be theirs, even as something shameful.

This 'confident commitment to change', suggested as basic to the process of overcoming addiction, some have called 'self-liberation' (Prochaska et al. 1991). This suggests the relevance of ideas contained in *liberation psychology*. Although this school of thought draws heavily on liberation theology and radical educational practice in Latin America, and may therefore seem foreign to a field of study such as addiction, which has been dominated by western medicine and psychology, some of its core ideas are highly relevant. They include the notion that change is usually preceded by critical reflection, a 'critical understanding of themselves and their reality' (Martín-Baró 1994, p. 41), the ability to contemplate a different future rather than continuing with fatalism and resignation, growing understanding (*conscientisation*) of the way in which power relations have worked to one's disadvantage, and a changing image of oneself (a kind of 'coming out'). Transformative change may require outside help from 'catalytic agents' just as addiction change may require expert intervention and willingness to take part in a credible, structured programme of behaviour change. Giving up or moderating excessive gambling or alcohol or drug use is, in liberation psychology terms, only a partial liberation, however. It certainly involves critical reflection on and understanding of how one's life has been dominated by the habit of attachment to a powerful substance or activity, but it does not go that step further of developing consciousness about the social and structural determinants of addiction discussed in Chapter 4 or the ways in which the provider industries exercise their power which were discussed in Chapter 5. In fact, Alcoholics Anonymous and other 12-step organisations, as well as professional forms of addiction treatment, are explicitly uninterested in such forms of power. In the process, they inadvertently reinforce the personal responsibility discourse about addiction.

The assimilation of responsibility

The argument of this book has been that addiction can be viewed as a form of disempowerment, even oppression. But, arguably, the most oppressive thing about it is the way in which those who become addicted and those closest to them are only dimly aware of how they are being exploited for others' profit and how circumstances of disadvantage have conferred vulnerability on them. Those most closely affected, Amanda, Caroline, David and their immediate networks of family members and friends, continue to believe in their own free will and are prone to hold themselves or each other responsible. Writers on power and freedom understand this only too well. As David Smail (2005, pp. 32–3) puts it, the source of their vulnerability lies beyond their 'perceptual horizon'. Zygmunt Bauman (1988, p. 50) explains it in terms of 'extended chains of dependence' between those who initiate actions with disempowering effects and those who are disempowered by them:

> ... as a rule there is a long social distance between the command and its fulfilment, between the design and its implementation, a distance filled by numerous people, each with only a feeble knowledge of the original intention and final destination of the activity to which they contribute.

He was not referring directly, when he wrote that, to the long chains of interactions that link the production of dangerously addictive commodities and those who become addicted to them, but he could easily have been.

The result, according to Nikolas Rose (1999), is that people are engaged in 'an intense and continuous self-scrutiny, self-dissatisfaction and self-evaluation' (p. 93). They are increasingly held responsible for their circumstances. They have been 'responsibilized' (p. 139). Freedom is 'represented in terms of personal power and the capacity to accept responsibility' (p. 269). Those of us who advise or treat people with addiction problems or their families contribute to this. Writers such as Bauman and Rose have argued that in the modern age of 'advanced liberalism' those who cannot appropriately take advantage of the freedoms we have, including the freedom to choose how to consume, constitute a deviant minority who need guidance, monitoring and correction. Under these circumstances expert authority flourishes. The aim is to instil the capacity for self-mastery and self-determination. Experts find themselves entering into a kind of double alliance, both with the individuals they are tutoring and with the political authorities, translating the latter's concerns about such things as economic productivity and law and order into the vocabulary of medicine, psychology, social science, management and accounting. Rose refers to my discipline, psychology, having cast off its earlier behaviourist association with repressive techniques for eliminating undesirable behaviours and having tried to become an emancipatory technology helping people re-establish control and take responsibility for planning their own lives. Those who wilfully refuse to operate within these values of responsible self-management and civility – among whom Rose includes 'drug abusers' – are subjected to what he calls 'abjection'. A whole variety of professionals, including social workers, probation officers and education welfare officers, are charged with responsibility for managing this group of 'enduringly problematic persons in the name of community security' (p. 262).

An important effect is that the interests of people who are addicted to dangerous products have to be represented by others. They are not a 'single class on the basis of a consciousness of their shared expropriation' (Rose 1999, p. 259). They have no collective voice. It is the same for family members and others who are affected by addiction, as was pointed out in Chapter 3. The question was raised in that chapter: why do they – and the same applies to all of us – put up with addiction? It was suggested that we might be able to learn much about why we tolerate addiction by looking at what social theorists have had to say about how powerlessness is legitimised and how consent with oppression is maintained. Power theorist Steven Lukes (2005) thought there were several explanations. One was that the powerless were trapped without means of extricating themselves, much as Caitlin Thomas felt trapped in her marriage to Dylan. Another was that some degree of coercion was applied, for example, in the form of the kind of criticism and accusations which Samuel Taylor Coleridge levelled at his wife, Sara. But the real 'false consciousness' occurs when the powerless remain in ignorance of their true interests because of confusion or mystification or the absence of any effective way of understanding their circumstances which would empower them to take a stand. Although affected family members like Sara Coleridge and Caitlin Thomas could hardly be said to be unaware of what was going on and how their interests were being subordinated, what their cases do illustrate is how easy it is for family members, and others who are affected, to be mentally disempowered due to the assimilation of responsibility. Sara came to regret her assertiveness and even asked for forgiveness, and Caitlin was critical of herself for her 'carping and nagging'. Tests of system justification theory (SJT) have shown how easy it is for those in relatively powerless positions to justify the status quo, subscribing to such arguments as the one that says that the powerful are deserving of their position or the general argument that present arrangements are unchangeable (Kay et al. 2010). It has been suggested that the assimilation of responsibility is particularly relevant to women in traditional roles, trained and expected to be passive and subordinate, to react to their oppression with acceptance rather than discontent, with conformity, self-sacrifice and endurance rather than rebellion (Sen 1984). In Chapter 3 I asked whether it might be not unreasonable to think of those most affected by addiction as carrying psychologically the 'scars of bondage' or the 'mark of oppression' which figure in post-colonial theory, thereby contributing in some measure to their own powerlessness. If that seems a step too far, then perhaps it can at least be accepted that those affected by addiction have much in common with other groups of people who are socially disempowered, whether by being caught up as civilians in warfare, as immigrants to a new country, because of homelessness, unemployment or poverty, or simply by virtue of their sex or sexual orientation, or by some combination of those. Central to these experiences of disempowerment is a concatenation of stressful events, resources lacking or threatened, fear and lack of safety, openness to exploitation, precarious existence, feeling trapped, social exclusion and the need to maintain identity and respect (Orford 2008a). Compounding that experience are a number of elements which are also common to disempowered groups. There usually exists a group of oppressors responsible for social dominance and prejudice towards, and stigmatisation of, the disempowered. Support systems for disempowered groups are usually strained or non-existent. Structural explanations are either difficult for the disempowered to grasp or else they refer to matters beyond their control. There is a tendency for them to blame themselves, and they often experience feelings of shame and humiliation. Finally, it is difficult to create an identity as a group, and there is absence of an effective collective voice.

Finding collective voice: some case examples

Addiction creates a feeling of impotence in those who experience it at first hand themselves, and particularly for family members, friends and residents in communities who have to stand by and watch its spoiling effects. It often seems as if there is nothing that can be done. Efforts to stand up to addiction are mostly solitary, unsupported by others and often lead to a sense of failure and, in the longer term, to resignation. Exit/withdrawal or loyalty/acceptance too often seem to be the only options. It is all the more heartening, therefore, to find examples of effective collective action. It is with a few examples of such efforts to voice collective opposition to addiction that I want to end this chapter and this book.

To start with, there are numerous groups, small and not so small, many with a short lifespan, which have arisen because of concern on the part of parents and others about the harmful effects of drug addiction and misuse. In Britain, they have included Parents Against Drug Abuse (PADA: www.pada.org.uk), which has been active in the Wirral area of northwest England; Mothers Against Drugs, which began with a much publicised march through Glasgow in 2001, developing later into the Cranhill Community Project (www.cranhillcp.co.uk); and the UK Drug and Alcohol Action Programme (www.daap.org.uk), which, amongst other things, organised a Women Against Drugs Day as part of International Women's Day. Groups with a more specific focus include Mothers Against Meth-Amphetamine (http://mamasite.net), started by a doctor in the USA whose brother had died after becoming dependent on methamphetamine, and Mothers Against Cannabis reported in Britain in the Daily Mail in 2009. A particularly impressive example is the Family Support Network (FSN) of family support groups now to be found in Dublin and across much of the Republic of Ireland and Northern Ireland (Rourke 2005; O'Leary 2009). It originated with the setting up in 1995 of the CityWide Drugs Crisis Campaign which aimed to unite Dublin communities facing the problems caused by illicit drug use. Under that umbrella, family support groups came together to create the FSN, sharing their needs for information and support and making known their views on policy and the need for improved services for families and communities affected by drug mis-use. An important event was the holding of a Service of Commemoration and Hope on 1st February 2000, 'to commemorate all those who had died from drug use or related causes, to offer hope to the families of those still involved with drug use and recovery and to highlight the invaluable role of Family Support Groups' (Citywide Family Support Network 2005, p. 1). Similar services have been held annually since then.

Knowing how stigmatised users of illicit drugs have been, and how they have been made subject to criminal law often involving severe sentences, including, in certain countries at certain times, the death penalty, it is not surprising that drug users have often tried to empower themselves by joining together in groups campaigning for their interests and rights. An early example was the Dutch MDHG (Interest Association for Drug Users). In the early 1990s, probably influenced by activism learnt in the HIV/AIDS movement, the International Drug User Network (IDUN) was inaugurated, following the first International Conference on the Reduction of Drug-Related Harm. The aim of harm reduction rather than prohibition and criminalisation was key to IDUN and the subsequent series of annual harm reduction conferences has been important to the user movement. In 2006 the seventeenth such conference endorsed the inception of the International Network of People Who Use Drugs (INPUD: www.inpud. net) (Byrne and Albert 2010). In Britain, the organisation Release (http:// release.org.uk) campaigns against the stigmatisation of drug users (for example, its Nice People Take Drugs campaign) and against criminalisation and harsh treatment; and the Transform (UK) Drug Policy Foundation (www.tdpf.org.uk) campaigns against prohibition and lobbies for moves towards a decriminalisation policy.

The USA has seen much local and national campaigning against the expansion of gambling (Goodman 1995). The first US casinos of modern times came in without public consultation, but by the mid 1990s numer-ous local or state organisations had come into being with names such as CASI*NO* and NO DICE and Citizens Against Gambling Expansion, as well as the National Coalition Against Legalized Gambling. A number of organisations campaigned specifically for the right to have a referendum on any new casino proposal. Gambling Watch organisations have been formed in a number of countries, including the UK (www.gamblingwatchuk.org), to challenge the expansion of gambling and the reliance of governments and community organisations on gambling profits. There have been cam-paigns against gambling in countries where tradition has been against gambling: a large public protest against the legalisation of casinos at the

National Mosque in Kuala Lumpur, Malaysia, is just one recent example. In the UK, organisations started by people who have experienced gambling addiction themselves, such as GRASP (Gambling Reform and Social Perception Group: www.grasp-group.org) and StopGam (www.stopgam. com), have amongst other things campaigned to call attention to the effects of fixed-odds betting terminals which allow virtual casino-style gambling by machine in high-street betting shops.

One of the notable features of many of these campaigns has been the prominent part played by women and particularly by mothers. This is not so surprising in the light of the fact that a number of well-regarded general community development models hold that '*community empowerment, especially empowerment of women*, is the key to successful programs for social change that affect the quality of life and health of poor and powerless families and communities' (Kar et al. 1999, p. 1433, original emphasis). Kar et al.'s review of community empowerment projects involving mothers and other women from different countries across the world drew out a number of common ingredients for success. One was the significant role played by the leadership of one or a small number of people who were usually victims of disempowerment of some kind within their communities. Action usually began with a strong sense of discontent and motivation to change the status quo, maternal motivation to prevent harm to children being a common driver. Struggles by women for their children's well-being, safety and prevention from harm were particularly likely to meet with support.

Women and alcohol prohibition on a Pacific island

An excellent example of collective standing up to the harm caused by excessive alcohol consumption – and one in which women played the main parts – is to be found in the book *Silent Voices Speak: Women and Prohibition in Truk*, written by the Marshalls, Mac and Lesley (1990), from the University of Iowa. It describes the campaign for alcohol prohibition organised by women over a number of years on the island of Moen, part of Truk State in Micronesia in the Pacific. Although the island is small – a population of little more than 10,000 people at the time – and distant, what went on in the late 1970s and early 1980s is not only described in fascinating detail in the book but it also touches on a number of themes of general relevance for a study of the role of power relations in the control of dangerous forms of consumption. The historical background to those events began with the introduction of alcohol (and tobacco) to Truk in the late nineteenth century – late compared to much of Oceania. After the First World War, under Japanese control, the manufacture, possession and consumption of alcoholic beverages were prohibited, as they were throughout the Pacific during the colonial period. Under US governance after the Second World War, prohibition was eased a little to allow home brew to be manufactured for personal use. In the 1950s, as in other places where colonial governments had supported prohibition, the movement for independence was associated with a demand that indigenous populations should have an equal 'right to drink'. The Truk magistrates voted in 1954 that each island should have local option on the matter and in 1958 the Truk Congress voted to de-prohibit the sale of imported beer. One argument was that this would replace locally made 'unsanitary' locally produced drink. Another, of course, was the attraction of taxing beer imports. In 1960 the beer tax constituted no less than 41 per cent of the estimated total revenue available to the Truk Congress.

By the mid 1970s Truk had developed what the Marshalls described as a well-deserved reputation for being out of control where drinking and drunkenness was concerned. A stream of newspaper articles reported drunken violence and accidents and a public investigation concluded that a third of all arrests and of all suicides and a half of all homicides in Truk were alcohol related, that 40 per cent of hospital patients were there because of excessive alcohol consumption, and that alcohol was costing businesses a huge amount due to accidents, insurance claims, property damage and loss of productivity. The Catholic Mission began a programme in which drinkers pledged publicly in the presence of a priest and others to abstain for a specified period of time. A law was passed requiring drinkers to apply for an identification card, submitting information about any alcohol-related hospitalisations or criminal convictions, but this was not well enforced and was much ignored. The import of wine and distilled spirits had been added to beer and hours of sale were liberalised as time went on.

The first significant step in the campaign for the re-imposition of prohibition was a conference of Protestant church women, on the subject of alcohol in the Pacific Islands, held in Honolulu in 1976. It was attended by two women from Truk, both leaders in their church women's groups, as well as church women from the USA who spoke strongly on women's rights. The pattern of sex roles in Truk had been a very traditional one. Although after the Second World War women officially had equal legal rights to men, a large gap in educational enrolment still existed in the 1970s, no women had been elected to municipal or state legislatures, and nearly all the women's groups which had sprung up were focused on women's traditional domestic and family caretaker roles. As one commentator on Truk society wrote in 1981, 'Women were humble, obedient, generous, and submissive. It has been like this for a long time, and it continues, in large measure, to be the same' (cited by Marshall and Marshall 1990, p. 41). An article in the *Micronesian Independent* in 1975 put it more strongly: 'Micronesia's customs and culture have kept women in a position of near-slavery and servitude for centuries, and . . . it is now time to elevate women to a position equal with men' (p. 43). The Marshalls comment that, whereas men were expected to smoke and drink, women were not. Consuming alcohol was thought to be degrading for women. Until the women's campaign began, women had had little voice over alcohol regulation. No women had been involved in the decision to lift prohibition in the 1950s. As has probably always been the case, it was women who were most conscious of the harm that excessive drinking was causing:

> Women were opposed to the public violence that increasingly was the order of the day in their communities. Women were opposed to having their husbands come home dirty after drinking, without money to run the household until the next paycheck, or to having them gone for several nights while on a drinking binge. Women were tired of being berated or beaten by their husbands after the men had been out drinking. Women were categorically opposed to the deaths resulting directly or indirectly from drinking via homicide, suicide, drunk driving crashes, drownings, and alcohol-related illnesses (including ethanol overdose). Women were unwilling to see their children abused by their drunken fathers. (p. 66)

It was after a series of public disorder incidents involving a number of deaths that the opportunity arose for the women's campaign. Church leaders came together, including the women who had attended the Honolulu conference and the district administrator who was himself a lay minister, and the women present argued for a petition to ask the Municipal Council in Moen to hold a referendum on total local prohibition. Petitions were circulated throughout the island and public meetings were held at which women spoke out publicly – out of keeping with the traditional non-political role of Truk women. As a result a formal referendum was held: 93 per cent voted 'Yes' on the question, 'Should the sale or consumption of intoxicating beverages in Moen municipality be prohibited?' The prohibition ordinance took effect in January 1978.

Subsequent events convinced the women campaigners that they needed to remain constantly vigilant. For a start, because Moen was the only port of entry for Truk State, provision was made for the legal storage on the island of alcoholic beverages for shipment to other islands which had not opted for prohibition, hence producing a loophole that contributed to the development of an illicit market in alcohol. By 1979 the loss of income to Truk State was such that the women campaign leaders heard of moves by Truk to override the Moen ordinance. The women immediately went into action, holding meetings, circulating petitions urging state-wide prohibition, between them travelling to every house in every village with copies of the petition and successfully winning the support of powerful people such as the mayor and governor. When their request to present their case formally was turned down they moved to a form of protest which had not hitherto been seen in Truk. This was a demonstration and march to the legislative building followed by a sit-in on the lawn and the veranda every day for nearly a week before the speaker finally invited a group in to present their case. The courts upheld the principle of local option; for the moment the legislators' drive to override the Moen ordinance had been beaten back. But two years later another women's protest outside the council chambers, once again successful, was necessary in response to the municipal council's attempt to repeal the prohibition law on the grounds that it was unenforceable, that revenue was being lost and that profits were instead going to those successful in the illicit market. Again, another two years on, women held a longer protest, despite having little notice of the need to organise, in response to another council debate on lifting prohibition, this time prompted by the lobbying of a group of Moen businessmen who cited the negative impact prohibition had on tourism and government tax receipts. Again the women's protest was successful. As a result, by the time the Marshalls were completing their book, Moen had experienced legal alcohol prohibition for over a decade.

The Marshalls attempted to come to a conclusion about whether that decade of prohibition had been a success in reducing alcohol-related harm. Their conclusion was a mixed one. Public life was, they concluded, certainly more peaceful: overt public drunkenness had certainly been reduced. Women whom they spoke to were also clear that alcohol-related family violence had decreased markedly, that there were fewer family arguments over money spent on alcohol and that drinking was much less often a cause for divorce. Figures available to them suggested, however, that after a period of a few years whilst police remained vigilant and the illicit market was only developing, alcohol consumption had returned to much what it was and alcohol-related crime, accidents and ill health had returned to pre-prohibition levels. A new police chief in 1982 was openly critical of the prohibition law which he thought was unenforceable, and policing it was left to a small and poorly trained municipal island force. It was generally known that many policemen drank themselves and some were known to be involved in the illicit market or were easily bribed by drinkers. Most illicit market dealers were, according to the *Truk Chronicle*, 'respected men in respectable positions' (p. 96). Police were instructed by their Chief to leave drinkers alone unless drunks wandered into public places, and by 1985 at least four clandestine bars (speakeasies) were operating fairly openly on the island. Quite a few illicit market outlets were family businesses, often attached to a small general store. The Marshalls were aware of at least two cases in which a woman campaign leader was working for pro- hibition whilst her husband, son or brother was benefitting from illegal alcohol sales. By the time the Marshalls were writing their book the climate had swung back in the opposite direction again on the appointment of another new chief of police in 1986. Although the illicit market continued to thrive, it was carried on more discreetly, police were more active and all but one of the speakeasies had shut down. Despite the mixed evidence for its success, prohibition remained very popular on the island. Nearly a thousand islanders responded to the Marshalls' survey question in 1985, 'Is this a good law or a bad law?': 90 per cent, including almost all women, responded that it was good.

The Marshalls were struck by the parallels among the women's campaign on Moen Island, other women's campaigns against men's drinking in other parts of the Pacific and Papua New Guinea and the women's temperance campaigns in the USA at the end of the nineteenth century. At both times male drinking was a threat to women's well-being and to that of their families and communities and at both times women were excluded from political power and public life. In both cases campaigns against drinking were highly significant in the process of women obtaining greater rights more generally.

Mothers Against Drunk Driving

Another, but very different, example of women standing up to the harm caused by alcohol misuse is Mothers Against Drunk Driving (MADD: www.madd.org), founded in 1980 in California by Candice Lightner after her 13-year-old daughter was killed by a drunken hit-and-run driver in a suburban street in Vancouver. Since then MADD has grown into a large and highly influential organisation in North America, which cam- paigns against drunk driving and supports the victims of drunken driving. MADD Canada was founded in 1990. Amongst its greatest successes has been the campaign to have the legal driving blood alcohol limit reduced to .08 in every state throughout the USA. It continues to lobby for a further reduction in the limit for previously convicted drivers and for laws enabling stricter punishments for offenders. It has claimed responsibility for a reduction in drink-driving deaths since the 1980s. MADD also promotes the use of victim impact panels in which judges require offenders to hear victims or relatives of victims of drunken driving crashes relate their experiences. It also supports random alcohol testing of drivers and the installation of breath alcohol ignition interlock devices in all new cars. It has also joined the campaign for raising the minimum legal drinking age to 21, and claims to have been a major force in the success of that campaign in the USA.

MADD is not without its critics, however. Candice Lightner left her position in the organisation in 1985, stating later that MADD 'has become far more neo-prohibitionist than I had ever wanted, or envisioned... I didn't start MADD to deal with alcohol. I started MADD to deal with the issue of drunk driving' (e.g. www2.potsdam.edu). Others have criticised the organisation for having become an enormous bureaucracy, with an annual budget approaching US$50 million. Some have questioned its claim to have been responsible for the reduction in drink-driving deaths, although even critics mostly concede that it has had a great positive effect. Others, whilst being critical that it had become an overbearing bureaucracy, have nevertheless concluded that MADD can take credit for raising awareness of the dangers of driving while intoxicated and was almost certainly responsible for the drop in fatalities since the 1980s.

An example of indigenous people standing up to the drinks trade

Tennant Creek is a small town in Australia's Northern Territory. It is situated 500 km north of Alice Springs and 1,000 km south of the territory capital, Darwin. It was the location of a struggle over the sale of alcoholic beverages which played out in the 1990s and was watched with interest throughout Australia. Its notoriety spread further afield and the story of that struggle offers a number of lessons about relations of power as they affect alcohol and other potentially addictive forms of consumption. The story is told by Alexis Wright (1997/2009) in her book, *Grog War*.

Sixty per cent of Tennant Creek's population was indigenous, mostly living in camps on the outskirts of the town or in smaller rural 'outstations' in the area. These circumstances had come about after decades of conflict with white people and authorities, involving massacre, exploitation as cheap hands in the cattle business, virtual imprisonment in reserves and several forced relocations. With 15 retail liquor outlets, this small town with a population of about 3,500 was thought to have one of the highest rates of alcohol outlets in Australia. Several of those outlets served mainly aboriginal customers, often in an atmosphere that was crowded, noisy, lacking food and associated with fast, heavy drinking and frequent violence. 'Grog' was generally considered to have become a serious problem. For some licensees and other members of the non-aboriginal population the problem was drunkenness and street violence in the main street of the town and it had a harmful effect on the tourist trade. For many aboriginal people, the more important problem was the effect excessive drinking was having on family and community life. Many indigenous people were non-drinkers – a higher proportion than in the non-aboriginal population in fact – who suffered the consequences of others' drunkenness in the form of being pestered by drinkers, seeing the health of family members deteriorating and finances wasted on drink, witnessing alcohol-fuelled violence which often resulted in serious injury, and not infrequently experiencing partner and child abuse. Elders talked of the threat to traditional law and even to the very survival of some aboriginal groups.

The Tennant Creek grog war provides an excellent illustration of the way in which those who felt they were being disempowered by the way in which alcohol was being sold had to contend with the personal responsibility and freedom of choice discourses. Specifically, it was necessary to counter the argument that drink was an aboriginal problem. The counterargument was that alcohol was introduced by the white man; indeed, not many years previously it had been white miners and meat workers who were the ones getting drunk in the local bars. Alcohol abuse should be the responsibility of all. Aboriginal people did not want special measures which applied only to them, such as the curfew of earlier years and the territory 'two kilometres law' which forbade public drinking within 2 km of any alcohol outlet. What was needed, it was argued, was a total commitment to solving the problem from the town as a whole.

A legal report prepared for the Liquor Commission put the counterargument to the majority freedom discourse as follows:

> Limitations on individual freedom have long been justified in terms of prevention of harm to others or to the individual concerned, protection to the social order and promotion of the common good ... The claim that collective rights jeopardise traditional individual rights misunderstands the interdependent relationship between group and individual rights ... Alcohol abuse is threatening the very survival of many indigenous communities ... A limitation of the former individual right is therefore justified by the need to protect the latter collective good. (cited by Wright 2009, pp. 146–7)

This shift in thinking was part of a more general and profound social and political change that was taking place in Tennant Creek at the same time. The struggle over grog was just part of a bigger struggle including long drawn-out battles over the restoration of aboriginal land rights and the provision of improved housing and health services. A significant event was the formation of the Julalikari Council in the 1970s and its official designation as an Aboriginal Corporation in 1989. Julalikari is a Warumungu word meaning 'for the people'. It gained a positive reputation for its achievements, which included the setting up of the first Night Patrol in Australia, an aboriginal-run alternative to police action using indigenous mediation methods to intervene in evening and night time drunken incidents. In the early 1990s, the Council started to seek power in the town; for example, one of its members stood as a candidate for town mayor. The idea of an alcohol-free day had been one of the principal suggestions of the Julalikari Council for some time. Thursday was social security payment day and had the reputation of being the day when most alcohol was consumed and most trouble caused. The Council asked licensees to 'give us a break' so that social security payments could be spent as intended rather than on drink. On 24th March, 1994, Tennant Creek saw its first trial 'grog-free day'. There were many testimonies to the town being 'a different place' on that trial day, which was widely considered to have been a great success. There followed a twelve-month period of feverish activity during which both sides made representations to the NT Liquor Commission which proposed a three-month trial to include a grog free day and other variations to licensing conditions. Several events were considered by Alexis Wright to have been key. One was when members of the Julalikari Council took the unusual step, frightening to several of them, to travel to Darwin to raise their concerns with the Chief Minister. A second was a symposium held in the town under the revealing title, 'Tennant Creek, Tourism and Grog – Progression or Regression'. It was addressed by the Minister responsible for the Liquor Commission and by a senior research fellow and head of the substance abuse unit at the Menzies School of Health Research, who summarised the evidence on the harm caused by excessive drinking. Another was a Supreme Court hearing in Darwin held as a result of the licensees' objections to the proposal. The most important event of all was a five-day Liquor Commission hearing held in Tennant Creek. In a tense courthouse atmosphere evidence was heard from all sides, including that from the Julalikari Council and individual aboriginal people. A turning point was thought to have been the evidence given by one particular indigenous woman who spoke at some length about the deaths of her brothers and sisters as a result of their alcohol addiction.

Throughout the process licensees and their supporters 'fought tooth and nail' (p. 10). They organised a petition and a letter writing campaign. They questioned the representativeness of the Julalikari Council. They disputed the circumstances of the death of one of the sisters of the aboriginal woman who gave such effective testimony. They objected to the use of the word 'grog' as opposed to the word 'liquor'. They attempted to have the hearing adjourned on the grounds that legal issues had arisen which they had not anticipated and which required seeking further legal advice. What is particularly interesting in this story, however, is the use that was made of various arguments which we met in Chapter 5 and which tend to recur in defence of the unrestricted supply of products which cause addiction. Not surprisingly, one of the arguments used was that any new restrictions, such as a grog free day, would interfere with business and would therefore constitute an inhibition on the freedom to trade. Alternatives were suggested. They included a number, such as restricting aboriginal people to a maximum of six cans of beer a day, finding a location for them to drink out of the sight of tourists, and even the idea of moving the entrances to bars on to the back lanes and away from the main street, all of which missed the point that it was the effect of excessive drinking on family and community life which constituted the main argument for change. One suggestion was that if there was to be a grog free day, it should be Sunday, the slackest trading day. The representative of the local Chamber of Commerce suggested that what was needed was education and behaviour modification, not changes to licensing conditions. Another idea was that if drinking on Thursday was a particular problem, then what was needed was for people to be taught budgeting and housekeeping. It is difficult to imagine a clearer example of how responsibility can be attributed to relatively powerless consumers of dangerous products in an effort to protect the profits of the relatively powerful.

The Julalikari Council had asked for a six-month trial to include Thursday as an alcohol-free day, plus a number of other changes such as a restriction on pub opening hours to between noon and 8 pm, a total ban on the sale of cask wine, a restriction on the amount of takeaway alcohol allowed per person, no happy hours and a prohibition on third-party sales to 'the taxi service'. Following the hearing the Liquor Commission agreed to enforce a three-month trial to include a ban on sales of alcohol in front bars and takeaway outlets on Thursdays, on the sale of large, four- or five-litre, takeaway wine casks and on third-party sales. Alcoholic drinks could still be served in restaurants, lounge bars, motels and private clubs. The first three months of the trial would be followed by a further three months during which all bars and takeaway outlets would be allowed to open on Thursday for the restricted hours of 3 pm to 9 pm. An important element was the requirement that a liquor Inspector would be present in the town for a substantial part of the trial period. The trial began on 14th August 1995.

Despite rumours that drinkers were travelling to Alice Springs or Katherine in order to drink, or that money saved was simply being spent on gambling, the reports were that Tennant Creek was a different town on Thursday during the first three months of the trial, that problems such as domestic violence and rent arrears were reduced, that the purchase of food was up and that the trial was a success. That was certainly the view of the Town Council, which was thought by the Julalikari Council to be now unfairly claiming ownership of the trial. However, the changes were thought by many to have gone into reverse once the first three months were over. Many of these impressions were confirmed by a formal evaluation headed by the research fellow from Menzies University. Amongst the findings were the following: compared to equivalent periods before the trial, police activity on Thursdays was 55 per cent reduced in months one to three and 13 per cent reduced in months four to six; presentations at the local hospital were down 36 per cent and 21 per cent in those two periods; and admissions to the women's refuge were also down. Although all but one of the licensees refused to provide trade information, and insisted on carrying out their own independent enquiry, the evaluation team concluded that there was no evidence that the commercial sector as a whole had suffered, although standalone takeaway outlets had lost trade during the trial whilst the local hotels had partially compensated by opening lounge bars. An opinion survey showed that the majority of Tennant Creek residents thought the trial had been a success and were in favour of changes being made permanent.

That was also the conclusion of the Liquor Commission, who decided that the general thrust of the first three months' restrictions should be maintained. Front bars and takeaway bottle shops would be closed on Thursdays; the sale of wine casks over 2 litres would be banned; the sale of casks would be limited to one per person per day; lounge bars would not open until noon on Thursdays and Fridays, with food available; only light beer would be sold between 10 am and noon; and there would be no third-party sales to taxi drivers. What had seemed like a long struggle by local aboriginal people and the Julalikari Council which represented them had produced a successful outcome. The result was a unique licensing arrangement – sadly abandoned by the NT government by the time of the second edition of *Grog War* – thought by the Liquor Commission at the time to be a decision of 'importance to Tennant Creek, Australia and the world' (p. 212). A feature emphasised by Alexis Wright was the way in which the battle for change had been one that was equally undertaken by both men and women.

Standing up to drug dealing on an English housing estate

My last example concerns a very different type of community in a different part of the world. Part of its interest lies in the role played by men. It also illustrates the uncomfortable fact that standing up to addiction may be fraught with difficulty and controversy. The setting was a large social housing estate, Southmead, on the north side of the city of Bristol, England. Built in the middle of the twentieth century, by the 1990s it had become one of the poorest areas in the city, with a reputation for trouble, regularly receiving negative attention in the media and being the subject of official reports. The local secondary school had had a series of damning inspection reports and bad press publicity and was finally closed in 2000. The community action campaign which is relevant here was called the Voice of Southmead. It is described in the book *Searching for Community: Representation, Power and Action on an Urban Estate*, written by Jeremy Brent (2009), who worked on the estate for a number of years as a youth worker.

The background to the Voice campaign was increasing public awareness about drug dealing on the estate. The immediate spur to its formation had been media coverage of a court case involving a Southmead man found guilty of drug dealing to, and sexual abuse of, children as young as ten years of age, as well as another case going through the courts at the time of a man who was said to have established a 'drugs fortress' in the area. A most obvious way in which Voice differed from the Moen Island example given earlier – and from most examples of community action – was the fact that it was men who took the lead. Brent noted at the time, 'The men are meeting to do something about the drugs' (pp. 185–6). It turned out to be the biggest mobilisation of people ever seen in the area. Weekly meetings, attracting 50 or more people, were held through the spring and early summer of 1997, at the local rugby football club – a very active local club organised around what is in Bristol a popular working men's sport. At a meeting Brent attended, 60 per cent were men, but there had been a conscious decision to bring wives along to make meetings less threatening.

Two leaders quickly emerged, one a local man who was good at dealing with the media, the other a woman, one of whose sons was a heroin user and who was prepared to talk openly about her experiences. Brent comments that, 'The stories of drug use and personal family pain.... drew people together' (p. 197). Mass leafleting of the area was organised and a large public meeting was held. After an initial period of frenetic activity directed at combating drug selling, Voice expanded its activities: for example, running an open air concert, raising money to kit out local football teams and organising volunteers to run them, raising money for equipment and encouraging girls' sports.

Like the women of Moen and the Julalikari Council in Tennant Creek, the men of Southmead used controversial tactics and ran up against opposition. Voice was undoubtedly dependent on the use of male power. The image of the rugby club was one of male strength. This was used against drug dealers and there were worries about vigilantism and the possible use of violence. In fact, the group decided against the use of violence, although it continued to be a major issue. Violence never was used, 'although some drug dealers who were visited by large groups left the area very quickly, and the presence of a fear of a loss of control was significant' (p. 187). Their methods also brought them into conflict with, for example, a local project, started only a few years earlier, which had the aim of helping individual drug users. Those representing local social services and police authorities were naturally ambivalent although the following meeting note by Brent (p. 188) suggests that the police, at least, were not against what the Voice was doing:

Floor. (Lots of anger about the housing rights of drug dealers).
Social services/housing. We need to work within the law.
Floor. If 40 of us go round to dealers, with no violence, what do the police think?
Police. You can challenge what people are doing. (Brent, 2009)

Their activities also threatened to split the community by breaking the local unwritten rule of 'no grassing', although only about drug dealing. Later on the group met regularly with the police to pass on information about drug dealing. Leading figures said that they were prepared to lose friends over the issue. They were also charged with hypocrisy and accused of smoking cannabis themselves since an early decision had been to confine the campaign to the use of drugs classified in Britain as Class A, principally heroin and cocaine.

Voice of Southmead was widely praised as a model community action campaign. It had widespread coverage locally and nationally. The local

newspaper ran a long article: 'Fighting back . . . How the Voice of Southmead has helped turn the estate around'. The police reported a 32 per
cent drop in crime in the following year. But, as Brent noted, it was the
transformation of private suffering into a matter of collective responsibility
which was most notable:

> . . . the concerns of the families of drug users moved into the public realm
> and were no longer treated as a private shame – public responsibility was
> taken for the wellbeing of young people. A major effect of Voice of South-
> mead was this shift in the boundaries of public and private behaviour,
> creating new communal, public responsibilities while turning Class A drug
> use into unacceptable public behaviour . . . the actions of just a few hundred
> people caused changes that should not be undervalued. (pp. 192, 200–1)

That is a fitting note on which to end this exploration of the relationship
between addiction and power. Individual attempts to stand up to addiction
in the privacy of one's own home are heroic, often successful but often
demoralising and painful. Ways need to be found to help those who are
affected find more of a public voice, to discover ways of collectively standing
up to addiction, and in the process to re-establish the power that has been
forfeited to addiction and to those who profit by it.

References

Adams, P.J. (2008). *Gambling, Freedom and Democracy*. London: Routledge.

Adams, P.J. (2011). Ways in which gambling researchers receive funding from gambling industry sources. *International Gambling Studies*, 11: 145–52.

Ainslie, G. (2011). Free will as recursive self-prediction: does a deterministic mechanism reduce responsibility?, in Poland, J. and Graham, G. (eds.). *Addiction and Responsibility*. Cambridge, Massachusetts: The MIT Press, pp. 55–88.

Aitchison, J. and Brown, J. (1966). *The Lognomal Distribution*. Cambridge University Press.

Alcoholics Anonymous (1967). *As Bill Sees It*. New York: Alcoholics Anonymous World Services, Inc.

Alexander, B.K. (2008). *The Globalisation of Addiction: A Study in Poverty of the Spirit*. Oxford University Press.

Allport, F. (1934). The J-curve hypothesis of conforming behaviour. *Journal of Social Psychology*, 5: 141–81.

American Gaming Association (2008). Submission to the Australian Senate regarding the poker harm minimisation and harm reduction tax bills.

Anderson, P. (2007). A safe, sensible and social AHRSE: New Labour and alcohol policy. *Addiction*, 102: 1515–21.

Arendts, M. (2007). A view of European gambling regulation from the perspective of private operators, in Littler, A. and Fijnaut, C. (eds.). *The Regulation of Gambling: European and National Perspectives*. Leiden: Martinus Nijhoff, pp. 41–52.

Asher, R.M. (1992). *Women with Alcoholic Husbands: Ambivalence and the Trap of Codependency*. London: The University of North Carolina Press.

Ashton, H. and Golding, J.F. (1989). Smoking: motivation and models, in T. Ney and A. Gale (eds.). *Smoking and Human Behaviour*. Chichester: John Wiley & Sons, Ltd.

Australasian Gaming Machine Manufacturers Association (2007). Submission to the New South Wales government regarding the Gaming Machines Act 2001.

Babor, T.F. (2009). Alcohol research and the alcoholic beverage industry: issues, concerns and conflicts of interest. *Addiction*, 104 (Suppl. 1): 34–47.

Babor, T., Caetano, R., Casswell, S., Edwards, G., Giesbrecht, N., Graham, K., Grube, J., Hill, L., Holder, H., Homel, R., Livingston, M., Österberg, E., Rehm, J., Room, R., and Rossow, I. (2010). *Alcohol No Ordinary Commodity: Research and Public Policy*. Oxford University Press.

Bacon, S. (1973). The process of addiction to alcohol: social aspects. *Quarterly Journal of Studies on Alcohol*, 34: 1–27.

Barber, J.G. and Crisp, B.R. (1995). The "pressures to change" approach to working with the partners of heavy drinkers. *Addiction*, 90: 269–76.

Barnes, D.E. and Bero, L.A. (1998). Why review articles on the health effects of passive smoking reach different conclusions. *JAMA*, 279: 1566–70.

Barraclough, S. and Morrow, M. (2008). A grim contradiction: the practice and consequences of corporate social responsibility by British American Tobacco in Malaysia. *Social Science and Medicine*, 66: 1784–96.

Bauman, Z. (1988). *Freedom*. Milton Keynes: Open University Press.

Baumberg, B. and Anderson, P. (2008). Trade and health: how World Trade Organization (WTO) law affects alcohol and public health. *Addiction*, 103: 1952–8.

Berridge, V. (1977). Opium and the historical perspective. *The Lancet*, 9 July: 78–80.

Berridge, V. (1979). Morality and medical science: concepts of narcotic addiction in Britain, 1820–1926. *Annals of Science*, 36: 67–85.

Best, D., Manning, V., and Strang, J. (2007). Retrospective recall of heroin initiation and the impact on peer networks. *Addiction Research and Theory*, 15: 397–410.

Best, S. (2003). *A Beginner's Guide to Social Theory*. London: Sage.

Bickel, W.K., Miller, M.L., Yi, R., Kowal, B.P., Lindquist, D.M., and Pitcock, J.A. (2007). Behavioral and neuroeconomics of drug addiction: competing neural systems and temporal discounting processes. *Drug and Alcohol Dependence*, 90S: S85–S91.

Biernacki, P. (1986). *Pathways from Heroin Addiction: Recovery without Treatment*. Philadelphia: Temple University Press.

Blaszczynski, A., Ladouceur, R., and Nower, L. (2007). Self-exclusion: a proposed gateway to treatment model. *International Gambling Studies*, 7: 59–71.

Boehm, C. and Flack, J.C. (2010). The emergence of simple and complex power structures through social niche construction, in Guinote, A. and Vescio, T.K. (eds.). *The Social Psychology of Power*. New York: The Guilford Press, pp. 46–86.

Bourdieu, P. (2000 [1997]). *Pascalian Meditations*, trans. R. Nice. Stanford University Press.

Bourdieu, P. (2001 [1998]). *Masculine Domination*, trans. R. Nice. Stanford University Press.

Bourgois, P. (2003a). *In Search of Respect: Selling Crack in El Barrio*. Cambridge University Press (2nd edn).

Bourgois, P. (2003b). Crack and the political economy of social suffering. *Addiction Research and Theory*, 11: 31–7.

Bourgois, P., Prince, B., and Moss, A. (2004). The everyday violence of hepatitis C among young women who inject drugs in San Francisco. *Human Organization*, 63: 253–65.

Bratman, M. (2000). Reflection, planning, and temporally extended agency. *Philosophical Review*, 109: 35–61.

Brenner, R. and Brenner, G.A. (1990). *Gambling and Speculation: A Theory, a History, and a Future of Some Human Decisions.* Cambridge University Press.

Brent, J. (2009). *Searching for Community: Representation, Power and Action on an Urban Estate.* Bristol: Policy Press.

Brinnin, J.M. (1957). *Dylan Thomas in America.* London: Ace Books.

Brook, H. and Stringer, R. (2005). Users, using, used: a beginner's guide to deconstructing drugs discourse. *International Journal of Drug Policy*, 16: 316–25.

Brugal, M.T., Domingo-Salvany, A., Maguire, A., Caylà, J.A., Villalbi, J.R., and Hartnoll, R. (1999). A small area analysis estimating the prevalence of addiction to opioids in Barcelona, 1993. *Journal of Epidemiology and Community Health*, 53: 488–94.

Bryant, J., Hull, P., and Treloar, C. (2010). Needle sharing in regular sexual relationships: an examination of serodiscordance, drug using practices, and the gendered character of injecting. *Drug and Alcohol Dependence*, 107: 182–7.

Budney, A.J., Higgins, S.T., Radonovich, K.J., and Novy, P.L. (2000). Adding voucher-based incentives to coping skills and motivational enhancement improves outcomes during treatment for marijuana dependence. *Journal of Consulting and Clinical Psychology*, 68: 1051–61.

Bugenthal, D.B. (2010). Paradoxical power manifestations: power assertion by the subjectively powerless, in Guinote, A. and Vescio, T.K. (eds.). *The Social Psychology of Power.* New York: The Guilford Press, pp. 209–30.

Bynner, J. (1969). *The Young Smoker.* London: Her Majesty's Stationery Office.

Byrne, J. and Albert, E.R. (2010). Coexisting or conjoined: the growth of the international drug users' movement through participation with International Harm Reduction Association Conferences. *International Journal of Drug Policy*, 21: 110–11.

Cantinotti, M. and Ladouceur, R. (2008). Harm reduction and electronic gambling machines: does this pair make a happy couple or is divorce foreseen?. *Journal of Gambling Studies*, 24: 39–54.

Caulkin (2003). *Observer/Guardian Weekly*, 28 March.

Chein, I., Gerard, D.L., Lee, R.S., and Rosenfeld, E. (1964). *Narcotics, Delinquency and Social Policy: The Road to H.* London: Tavistock.

Chen, M.J., Grube, J.W., and Gruenewald, P.J. (2010). Community alcohol outlet density and underage drinking. *Addiction*, 105: 270–78.

Cherrington, E. (1920). *The Evolution of Prohibition in the USA.* Westville, Ohio: American Issue Press.

Chilcoat, H.D. (2009). An overview of the emergence of disparities in smoking prevalence, cessation, and adverse consequences among women. *Drug and Alcohol Dependence*, 104S: S17–S23.

Chin, K.L. (2009). *The Golden Triangle: Inside Southeast Asia's Drug Trade*. London: Cornell University Press.

Chinn, C. (1991). *Better Betting with a Decent Feller*. London: Harvester Wheatsheaf.

Chuang, Y.C., Cubbin, C., Ahn, D., and Winkleby, M.A. (2005). Effects of neighbourhood socioeconomic status and convenience store concentration on individual level smoking. *Journal of Epidemiology and Community Health*, 59: 568–73.

Citywide Family Support Network (2005). *Resource Pack: A Handbook for Families Dealing with Drug Use*. Dublin: Printwell Co-operative (2nd edn).

Clark, L., Lawrence, A.J., Astley-Jones, F., and Gray, N. (2009). Gambling near misses enhance motivation and recruit win-related brain circuitry. *Neuron*, 61: 481–90.

Clegg, S.R. (1989). *Frameworks of Power*. London: Sage.

Coburn, D. (2004). Beyond the income inequality hypothesis: class, neo-liberalism, and health inequalities. *Social Science and Medicine*, 58: 41–56.

Collins, P. (2003). *Gambling and the Public Interest*. Westport: Praeger.

Connors, G.J., Walitzer, K.S., and Tonigan, J.S. (2008). Spiritual change in recovery, in Galanter, M. and Kaskutas, L.A. (eds.). *Recent Developments in Alcoholism: Research on Alcoholics Anonymous and Spirituality in Addiction Recovery*. New York: Springer, pp. 209–27.

Cooper, M.L., Frone, M.R., Russell, M., and Mudar, P. (1995). Drinking to regulate positive and negative emotions: a motivational model of alcohol use. *Journal of Personality and Social Psychology*, 69: 990–1005.

Cooper, M.L., Russell, M., Skinner, J.B., Frone, M.R., and Mudar, P. (1992). Stress and alcohol use: moderating effects of gender, coping, and alcohol expectancies. *Journal of Abnormal Psychology*, 101: 139–52.

Copello, A., Orford, J., Hodgson, R., and Tober, G. (2009). *Social Behaviour and Network Therapy for Alcohol Problems*. London: Routledge.

Crane, Y. (2008). What are the costs and benefits of gambling in the United Kingdom?, in Coryn, T., Fijnaut, C., and Littler, A. (eds.). *Economic Aspects of Gambling Regulation: EU and US Perspectives*. Leiden: Martinus Nijhoff, pp. 119–78.

Crum, R.M., Lillie-Blanton, M., and Anthony, J.C. (1996). Neighborhood environment and opportunity to use cocaine and other drugs in late childhood and early adolescence. *Drug and Alcohol Dependence*, 43: 155–61.

Currie, S.R., Hodgins, D.C., Wang, J., el-Guebaly, N., Wynne, H., and Chen, S. (2006). Risk of harm from gambling in the general population as a function of level of participation in gambling activities. *Addiction*, 101: 570–80.

Custer, R. and Milt, H. (1985). *When Luck Runs Out: Help for Compulsive Gamblers and Their Families*. New York: Facts on File Publications.

Dahl, R.A. (1961). *Who Governs? Democracy and Power in an American City*. New Haven, Connecticut: Yale University Press.

Davey Smith, G., Bartley, M., and Blane, D. (1990). The Black report on socioeconomic inequalities in health 10 years on. *British Medical Journal*, 301: 373–7.

Davies, J.B. (1992). *The Myth of Addiction, an Application of the Psychological Theory of Attribution to Illicit Drug Use*. Reading: Harwood Academic.

Davies, N. (1997). *Dark Heart: The Shocking Truth about Hidden Britain*. London: Vintage.

D'Avanzo, C.E., Frye, B., and Froman, R. (1994). Culture, stress and substance use in Cambodian refugee women. *Journal of Studies on Alcohol*, 55: 420–26.

De, P., Cox, J., Boivin, J.F., Platt, R.W., and Jolly, A.M. (2007). The importance of social networks in their association to drug equipment sharing among injection drug users: a review. *Addiction*, 102: 1730–39.

de Bruijn, A. (2008). No reason for optimism: the expected impact of commitments in the European Commission's alcohol and health forum. *Addiction*, 103: 1588–92.

Department for Culture, Media and Sport (2002). *A Safe Bet for Success: Modernising Britain's Gambling Laws*. London: The Stationery Office.

Department for Culture, Media and Sport (2003). Draft Gambling Bill: Regulatory Impact Assessment.

de Quincey, T. (1897 [1822]). *The Confessions of an English Opium Eater*, in D. Masson (ed.). *The Collected Writings of Thomas De Quincey, Volume III*. London: Black.

DiClemente, C.C. and Prochaska, J.O. (1982). Self-change and therapy change of smoking behavior: a comparison of process of change in cessation and maintenance. *Addictive Behaviors*, 7: 133–42.

Ditton, J. and Hammersley, R. (1996). *A Very Greedy Drug: Cocaine in Context*. Reading: Harwood Academic.

Doherty, J. (2006). *Pete Doherty: My Prodigal Son*. London: Headline.

Dorn, N., Ribbens, J., and South, N. (1987). *Coping with a Nightmare: Family Feelings About Long-term Drug Use*. London: Institute for the Study of Drug Dependence.

Downs, C. (2008). The Facebook phenomenon: social networking and gambling, presentation at the conference Gambling and Social Responsibility Forum, September 2008, Manchester.

Dyall, L. and Hand, J. (2003). Maori and gambling: why a comprehensive Maori public-health response is required in New Zealand, University of Auckland, New Zealand, published online 15 September, 2003. www.problem-gambling. info.

Eadington, W.R. (2003). Values and choices: the struggle to find balance with permitted gambling in modern society, in Reith, G. (ed.). *Gambling: Who Wins? Who Loses?*. New York: Prometheus, pp. 31–48.

Edwards, G. and Gross, M. (1976). Alcohol dependence: provisional description of a clinical syndrome. *British Medical Journal*, i: 1058–61.

Edwards, R. and Bhopal, R. (1999). The covert influence of the tobacco industry on research and publication: a call to arms. *Journal of Epidemiology and Community Health*, 53: 261–2.

Estes, N.J. and Baker, J.M. (1982). Spouses of alcoholic women, in Estes, N.J. and Heinemann, M.E. (eds.). *Alcoholism: Development, Consequences and Interventions.* St. Louis: Mosby, pp. 231–8.

Fast, D., Small, W., Wood, E., and Kerr, T. (2009). Coming 'down here': young people's reflections on becoming entrenched in a local drug scene. *Social Science and Medicine,* 69: 1204–10.

Feiling, T. (2009). *The Candy Machine: How Cocaine Took over the World.* London: Penguin.

Ferris, P. (1995). *Caitlin: The Life of Caitlin Thomas.* London: Pimlico.

Fishbein, M. and Ajzen, I. (1975). *Belief, Attitude, Intention, and Behavior: An Introduction to Theory and Research.* Reading, MA: Addison-Wesley.

Fisher, A.T., Sonn, C.C., and Evans, S.D. (2007). The place and function of power in community psychology: philosophical and practical issues. *Journal of Community and Applied Social Psychology,* 17: 258–67.

Fisher, S. (1993). The pull of the fruit machine: a sociological typology of young players. *Sociological Review,* 41: 447–74.

Fitzgerald, J.L. (2009). Mapping the experience of drug dealing risk environments: an ethnographic case study. *International Journal of Drug Policy,* 20: 261–9.

Forrester, D. and Harwin, J. (2011). *Parents Who Misuse Drugs and Alcohol: Effective Interventions in Social Work and Child Protection.* Chichester: Wiley-Blackwell.

Fowler, J.W. (1995). Alcoholics Anonymous and faith development, in McCrady, B.S. and Miller, W.R. (eds.). *Research on AA: Opportunities and Alternatives.* Rutgers University Press.

Frank, J.W. (2000). Historical and cultural roots of drinking problems among American Indians. *American Journal of Public Health,* 90: 344–51.

Freire, P. (1972). *Pedagogy of the Oppressed.* Harmondsworth: Penguin.

Fryer, D. (1990). The mental health costs of unemployment: towards a social psychological concept of poverty? *British Journal of Clinical and Social Psychiatry,* 7: 164–75.

Gaming Board (2000). *Report of the Gaming Board for Great Britain 1999/2000.* London: Her Majesty's Stationery Office.

Gambling Commission (2008). Review of Gambling Research, Education and Treatment, final report and recommendations, available via the Gambling Commission website www.gamblingcommission.gov.uk.

Gambling Review Body, Department for Culture, Media and Sport (2001). *Gambling Review Report.* Norwich: Her Majesty's Stationery Office.

Genberg, B.L., Gange, S.J., Go, V.F., Celentano, D.D., Kirk, G.D., Latkin, C.A., and Mehta, S.H. (2011). The effect of neighbourhood deprivation and residential relocation on long-term injection cessation among injecting drug users (IDUs) in Baltimore, Maryland. *Addiction,* 106: 1966–74.

Giddens, A. (1991). *Modernity and Self-Identity: Self and Society in the Late Modern Age.* Cambridge: Polity Press.

Glautier, S. and Spencer, K. (1999). Activation of alcohol-related associative networks by recent alcohol consumption and alcohol-related cues. *Addiction*, 94: 1033–42.

Goffman, E. (1967). *Interaction Ritual.* Garden City, New York: Anchor Books, Doubleday.

Goodman, R. (1995). *The Luck Business: The Devastating Consequences and Broken Promises of America's Gambling Explosion.* New York: The Free Press.

Gorman, D.M., Speer, P.W., Gruenewald, P.J., and Labouvie, E.W. (2001). Spatial dynamics of alcohol availability, neighborhood structure and violent crime. *Journal of Studies on Alcohol*, 62: 628–36.

Graham, H. (2009). Women and smoking: understanding socioeconomic influences. *Drug and Alcohol Dependence*, 104S: S11–S16.

Graham, H., Hawkins, S.S., and Law, C. (2010). Lifecourse influences on women's smoking before, during and after pregnancy. *Social Science and Medicine*, 70: 582–7.

Gramsci, A. (1971 [1926–37]). *Selections from the Prison Notebooks of Antonio Gramsci*, trans. Hoare, Q. and Nowell-Smith, G. London: Lawrence and Wishart.

Griffiths, M. (1993). Fruit machine addiction in adolescents: a case study. *Journal of Gambling Studies*, 9: 387–99.

Griffiths, M. (1995). The role of subjective mood states in the maintenance of fruit machine gambling behaviour. *Journal of Gambling Studies*, 11: 123–35.

Griffiths, M. (2011). Technological trends and the psychological impact on gambling. *Casino and Gaming International*, 1: 77–80.

Gruenewald, P.J. (2007). The spatial ecology of alcohol problems: niche theory and assortative drinking. *Addiction*, 102: 870–78.

Guinote, A. (2010). The situated focus theory of power, in Guinote, A. and Vescio, T.K. (eds.). *The Social Psychology of Power*. New York: The Guilford Press, pp. 141–73.

Guinote, A. and Vescio, T.K. (eds.). (2010). *The Social Psychology of Power*. New York: The Guilford Press.

Gusfield, J. (1962). Status conflicts and the changing ideologies of the American Temperance movement, in Pittman, D. and Synder, C. (eds.). *Society, Culture and Drinking Patterns*. New York: John Wiley & Sons, Inc.

Harrison, L. and Gardiner, E. (1999). Do the rich really die young? Alcohol-related mortality and social class in Great Britain, 1988–1994. *Addiction*, 94: 1871–80.

Harwin, J., Ryan, M., and Tunnard, J. with Pokhrel, S., Alrouh, B., Matias, C., and Momenian-Schneider, S. (2011). *The Family Drug and Alcohol Court (FDAC) Evaluation Project Final Report*. Brunel University, www.brunel.ac.uk/fdacresearch.

Herd, D. (1994). Predicting drinking problems among black and white men: results from a national survey. *Journal of Studies on Alcohol*, 55: 61–71.

Hilton, F. (2004). *Baudelaire in Chains: A Portrait of the Artist as a Drug Addict.* London: Peter Owen.

Hirschi, T. (1969).*Causes of Delinquency.* Berkeley, CA: University of California Press.

Hirschman, A.O. (1970). *Exit, Voice, and Loyalty: Responses to Decline in Firms, Organizations and States*. Cambridge, MA: Harvard University Press.

Hollingworth, W., Ebel, E., McCarty, C., Garrison M., Christakis, G., and Rivara, F. (2006). Prevention of deaths from harmful drinking in the United States: the potential effects of tax increases and advertising bans on young people. *Journal of Studies on Alcohol*, 67: 300–8.

Hook, D. (2004). Frantz Fanon, Steve Biko, 'psychopolitics' and critical psychology, in Hook, D. (ed.). *Critical Psychology*. University of Cape Town, pp. 84–114.

Huckle, T., Huakau, J., Sweetsur, P., Huisman, O., and Casswell, S. (2008). Density of alcohol outlets and teenage drinking: living in an alcogenic environment is associated with higher consumption in a metropolitan setting. *Addiction*, 103: 1614–21.

Hughes, T., McCabe, S.E., Wilsnack, S.C., West, B.T., and Boyd, C.J. (2010). Victimization and substance use disorders in a national sample of heterosexual and sexual minority women and men. *Addiction*, 105: 2130–40.

Humphreys, K. (2004). *Circles of Recovery: Self-Help Organizations for Addictions*. Cambridge University Press.

Hurst (2006). *Charles Kennedy: A Tragic Flaw*. London: Politico's Publishing.

Imel, Z.E., Wampold, B.E., Miller, S.D., and Fleming, R.R. (2008). Distinctions without a difference: direct comparisons of psychotherapies for alcohol use disorders. *Psychology of Addictive Behaviors*, 22: 533–43.

Jacobs, D.F. (1993). Evidence supporting a general theory of addiction, in Eadington, W.R. and Cornelius, J.A. (eds.). *Gambling Behavior and Problem Gambling*. Reno: University of Nevada.

Jahiel, R.I. and Babor, T.F. (2007). Industrial epidemics, public health advocacy and the alcohol industry: lessons from other fields. *Addiction*, 102: 1335–9.

Jahoda, G. and Crammond, J. (1972). *Children and Alcohol: A Developmental Study in Glasgow*. London: Her Majesty's Stationery Office.

James, W. (1891). *The Principles of Psychology, Volume 1*. London: Macmillan.

Janis, I. and Mann, L. (1977). *Decision-making: A Psychological Analysis of Conflict, Choice, and Commitment*. New York: Free Press.

Jarvinen, M. (1991). The controlled controllers: women, men, and alcohol. Paper presented at the Symposium, Alcohol, Family and Significant Others, Helsinki, 4–8 March.

Jernigan, D.H. (2009). The global alcohol industry: an overview. *Addiction*, 104 (Suppl. 1): 6–12.

Johnson, V.E. (1986). *Intervention: How to Help Those Who Don't Want Help*. Minneapolis: Author.

Jones-Webb, R., Snowden, L., Herd, D., Short, B., and Hannan, P. (1997). Alcohol-related problems among black, Hispanic and white men: the contribution of neighborhood poverty. *Journal of Studies on Alcohol*, 58: 539–45.

Judge, K., Mulligan, J.A., and Benzeval, M. (1998). Income inequality and population health. *Social Science and Medicine*, 46: 567–79.

Kar, S.B., Pascual, C.A., and Chickering, K.L. (1999). Empowerment of women for health promotion: a meta-analysis. *Social Science and Medicine*, 49: 1431–60.

Karasek, R.A. (1979). Job demands, job decision latitude, and mental strain: implications for job redesign. *Administrative Science Quarterly*, 24: 285–308.

Kaskutas, L.E., Ye, Y., Greenfield, T.K., Witbrodt, J., and Bond, J. (2008). Epidemiology of Alcoholics Anonymous participation, in Galanter, M. and Kaskutas, L.E. (eds.). *Recent Developments in Alcoholism: Research on Alcoholics Anonymous and Spirituality in Addiction Recovery*. New York: Springer, pp. 261–82.

Kay, A.C., Banfield, J.C., and Laurin, K. (2010). The system justification motive and the maintenance of social power, in Guinote, A. and Vescio, T.K. (eds.). *The Social Psychology of Power*. New York: The Guilford Press, pp. 313–40.

Kelly, R., Magill, M., and Stout, R.L. (2009). How do people recover from alcohol dependence? A systematic review of the research on mechanisms of behaviour change in Alcoholics Anonymous. *Addiction Research and Theory*, 17: 236–59.

Keltner, D., Gruenfeld, D., Galinsky, A., and Kraus, M.W. (2010). Paradoxes of power: dynamics of the acquisition, experience, and social regulation of social power, in Guinote, A. and Vescio, T.K. (eds.). *The Social Psychology of Power*. New York: The Guilford Press, pp. 177–208.

Kerr C., Maslin J., Orford J., Dalton S., Ferrins-Brown M., and Hartney E. (2000). Falling on deaf ears? Responses to health education messages from the Birmingham Untreated Heavy Drinkers cohort, in Watson, J. and Platt, S. (eds.). *Researching Health Promotion*. Routledge: London, pp. 231–253.

Khobzi, N., Strike, C., Cavalier, W., Bright, R., Myers, T., Calzavara, L., and Millson, M. (2009). A qualitative study on the initiation into injection drug use: necessary and background processes. *Addiction Research and Theory*, 17: 546–59.

Knapp, T.J. (1997). Behaviorism and public policy: BF Skinner's views on gambling. *Behavior and Social Issues*, 7: 129–39.

Krishnan, M. and Orford, J. (2002). Gambling and the family from the stress-coping-support perspective. *International Gambling Studies*, 2: 61–83.

Kroll, B. and Taylor, A. (2002). *Parental Substance Misuse and Child Welfare*. London: Jessica Kingsley.

Lambert, S.F., Brown, T.L., Phillips. C.M., and Ialongo, N.S. (2004). The relationship between perceptions of neighborhood characteristics and substance use among urban African American adolescents. *American Journal of Community Psychology*, 34: 205–18.

Langer, E.J. (1975). The illusion of control. *Journal of Personality and Social Psychology*, 32: 311–28.

Langton, M. (1992). Too much sorry business. *Aboriginal and Islander Health Worker Journal*. March/April: 10–23.

LaPlante, D.A. and Shaffer, H.J. (2007). Understanding the influence of gambling opportunities: expanding exposure models to include adaptation. *American Journal of Orthopsychiatry*, 77: 616–23.

Laranjeira, R., Marquest, A.C., Ramos, S., Campana, A., Luz, E., and Franca, J. (2007). Who runs alcohol policy in Brazil? *Addiction*, 102: 1502–5.

LaVeist, T.A. and Wallace, J.M. (2000). Health risk and inequitable distribution of liquor stores in African American neighborhood. *Social Science and Medicine*, 51: 613–7.

Lefebure, M. (1986). *The Bondage of Love: a Life of Mrs Samuel Taylor Coleridge*. London: Victor Gollancz.

Lefebure, M. (1977). *Samuel Taylor Coleridge: A Bondage of Opium*. London: Quartet Books.

Legleye, S., Janssen, E., Beck, F., Chau, N., and Khlat, M. (2011). Social gradient in initiation and transition to daily use of tobacco and cannabis during adolescence: a retrospective cohort study. *Addiction*, 106: 1520–31.

Leon, D.A., Shkolnikov, M., and McKee, M. (2009). Alcohol and Russian mortality: a continuing crisis. *Addiction*, 104: 1630–36.

Lesieur, H.R. (1984). *The Chase: The Career of the Compulsive Gambler*. Rochester, Vermont: Shenkman.

Levine, H. (1978). The discovery of addiction: changing conceptions of habitual drunkenness in America. *Journal of Studies on Alcohol*, 39: 143–76.

Levy, N. (2006). Autonomy and addiction. *Canadian Journal of Philosophy*, 36: 427–47.

Levy, N. (2011). Addiction, responsibility, and ego depletion, in Poland, J. and Graham, G. (eds.). *Addiction and Responsibility*. Cambridge, Massachusetts: The MIT Press, pp. 89–112.

Longmate, N. (1968). *The Water Drinkers: A History of Temperance*. London: Hamish Hamilton.

Lovell, A.M. (2002). Risking risk: the influence of types of capital and social networks on the injection practices of drug users. *Social Science and Medicine*, 55: 803–21.

Lukes, S. (2005). *Power: A Radical View*. Basingstoke, Hampshire: Palgrave Macmillan (2nd edn).

Lund, I. (2008). The population mean and the proportion of frequent gamblers: is the theory of total consumption valid for gambling? *Journal of Gambling Studies*, 24: 247–56.

McCabe, S.E., Huges, T.L., Bostwick, W.B., West, B.T., and Boyd, C.J. (2009). Sexual orientation, substance use behaviors and substance dependence in the United States. *Addiction*, 104: 1333–45.

McCrady, B.S. (2004). To have but one true friend: implications for practice of research on alcohol use disorders and social networks. *Psychology of Addictive Behaviors*, 18: 113–21.

McCusker, C.G. (2006). Towards understanding loss of control: an automatic network theory of addictive behaviours, in Munafò, M. and Albery, I. (eds.). *Cognition and Addiction*. Oxford University Press, pp. 117–45.

McCusker, C.G. and Gettings, B. (1997). Automaticity of cognitive biases in addictive behaviours: further evidence with gamblers. *British Journal of Clinical Psychology*, 36: 543–54.

MacDonald, R. and Marsh, J. (2002). Crossing the Rubicon: youth transitions, poverty, drugs and social exclusion. *The International Journal of Drug Policy*, 13: 27–38.

Macintyre, S., Ellaway, A., and Cummins, S. (2002). Place effects on health: how can we conceptualise, operationalise and measure them?. *Social Science and Medicine*, 55: 125–39.

McClelland, D., Davis, W., Kalin, R., and Wanner, E. (1972). *The Drinking Man*. New York: Free Press.

McKennell, A. and Thomas, R. (1967). *Adults' and Adolescents' Smoking Habits and Attitudes*. London: Her Majesty's Stationery Office.

McNeill, A. and Sweanor, D. (2009). Beneficence or maleficence – big tobacco and smokeless products. *Addiction*, 104: 167–8.

Madden, G.J. Ewan, E.E., and Lagorio, C.H. (2007). Toward an animal model of gambling: delay discounting and the allure of upredictable outcomes. *Journal of Gambling Studies*, 23: 63–83.

Mäkelä, P. (1999). Alcohol-related mortality as a function of socio-economic status. *Addiction*, 94: 867–86.

Mäkelä, P. and Österberg, E. (2009). Weakening of one more alcohol control pillar: a review of the effects of the alcohol tax cuts in Finland in 2004. *Addiction*, 104: 554–63.

Marmot, M., Bosman, H., Hemingway, H., Brunner, E., and Stansfield, S. (1997). The contribution of job control and other risk factors to social variations in coronary heart disease incidence. *The Lancet*, 350: 235–9.

Marshal, M.P., Friedman, M.S., Stall, R., and Thompson, A.L. (2009). Individual trajectories of substance use in lesbian, gay and bisexual youth and hetero-sexual youth. *Addiction*, 104: 974–81.

Marshall, D. (2005). The gambling environment and gambler behaviour: evidence from Richmond-Tweed, Australia. *International Gambling Studies*, 5: 63–83.

Marshall, M. and Marshall, L.B. (1990). *Silent Voices Speak: Women and Prohibition in Truk*. University of Iowa: Wadsworth Publishing Company.

Martín-Baró, I. (1994). *Writings for a Liberation Psychology*. Aron, A. and Corne, S. (eds.). Cambridge, MA: Harvard University Press.

May, T., Duffy, M., Few, B., and Hough, M. (2005). *Understanding Drug Selling in Local Communities: Insider or Outsider Trading?* York: Joseph Rowntree Foundation.

Miers, D. (2004). Regulating commercial gambling. Past, present, and future. *International Gambling Studies*, 6: 95–104.

Mill, J.S. (1989 [1869]). On the subjection of women, in Mill, J.S., *On Liberty and Other Writings*, Collini, S. (ed.). Cambridge University Press.

Miller, W.R. and C'De Baca, J. (2001). *Quantum Change: When Epiphanies and Sudden Insights Transform Ordinary Lives*. London: Guilford Press.

Miller, W.R. and Rollnick, S. (2002). *Motivational Interviewing: Preparing People for Change*. New York: Guilford Press (2nd edn).

Minihan, M. (1967). *Dostoevsky: His Life and Work by Konstantin Mochulsky*. Princeton, New Jersey: University Press.

Morjaria-Keval, A. (2006). Religious and spiritual elements of change in Sikh men with alcohol problems: a qualitative exploration. *Journal of Ethnicity in Substance Abuse*, 5: 91–118.

Morse, S.J. (2011). Addiction and criminal responsibility, in Poland, J. and Graham, G. (eds.). *Addiction and Responsibility*. Cambridge, MA: The MIT Press, pp. 159–201.

Munafò, M. and Albery, I. (eds.). (2006). *Cognition and Addiction*. Oxford University Press.

Nashold, J. and Tremlett, G. (1997). *The Death of Dylan Thomas*. Edinburgh: Mainstream Publishing.

Nasir, S. and Rosenthal, D. (2009). The social context of initiation into injecting drugs in the slums of Makassar, Indonesia. *International Journal of Drug Policy*, 20: 237–43.

Newman, O. (1972). *Gambling: Hazard and Reward*. London: Athlone Press.

News and Notes (2008). Australia – New Alcopops sneak around tax. *Addiction*, 103: 2072.

News and Notes (2011). UK Drug Policy Commission releases report on the stigma of drug use/Reports identify abuse of drug users in rehabilitation centres. *Addiction*, 106: 860, 1712.

Niedhammer, I., Tek, M., Starke, D., and Siegrist, J. (2004). Effort-reward imbalance model and self-reported health: cross-sectional and prospective findings from the GAZEL cohort. *Social Science and Medicine*, 58: 1531–41.

Nussbaum, M.C. (2000). *Women and Human Development: The Capabilities Approach*. Cambridge University Press.

Nussbaum, M.C. (2011). *Creating Capabilities: the Human Development Approach*. Cambridge, MA: Harvard University Press.

Oakes, J.M. (2004). The (mis)estimation of neighborhood effects: causal inference for a practicable social epidemiology. *Social Science and Medicine*, 58: 1929–52.

O'Leary, M. (2009). *Intimidation of Families*. Dublin: Family Support Network.

O'Neill, T.D. and Mitchell, C.M. (1996). Alcohol use among American Indian adolescents: the role of culture in pathological drinking. *Social Science and Medicine*, 42: 565–78.

Orford, J. (2001). *Excessive Appetites: A Psychological View of Addictions*. Chichester: John Wiley & Sons, Ltd (2nd edn).

Orford, J. (2004). Time for change in thinking about addiction change, in Hänninen, V. and Ylijoki, O. (eds.). *A Volume in Honour of Anja Koski-Jänneksen*. Tampere, Finland: Tampere University Press, pp. 185–209.

Orford, J. (2008a). *Community Psychology: Challenges, Controversies and Emerging Consensus*. Chichester: John Wiley & Sons, Ltd.

Orford, J. (2008b). Asking the right questions in the right way: the need for a shift in research on psychological treatments for addiction. *Addiction*, 103: 875–85.

Orford, J. (2011). *An Unsafe Bet? The Dangerous Rise of Gambling and the Debate We Should Be Having*. Chichester: Wiley-Blackwell.

Orford, J. (2012). *Addiction Dilemmas: Family Experiences in Literature and Research and Their Lessons for Practice*. Chichester: Wiley-Blackwell.

Orford, J., Copello, A., Simon, A., Waheed, H., Fazil, Q., Graham, H., Mahmood, M., McNeil, S., and Roberts, G. (2010a). Offering a service to BME family members affected by close relatives' drug problems, in MacGregor, S. (ed.). *Responding to Drug Misuse: Research and Policy Priorities in Health and Social Care*. London: Routledge, pp. 164–77.

Orford, J., Dalton, S., Hartney, E., Ferrins-Brown, M., Kerr, C., and Maslin, J. (2002). How is excessive drinking maintained? Untreated heavy drinkers' experiences of the personal benefits and drawbacks of their drinking. *Addiction Research and Theory*, 10: 347–72.

Orford, J., Griffiths, M., Wardle, H., Sproston, K., and Erens, B. (2009a). Negative public attitudes towards gambling: findings from the 2007 British Gambling Prevalence Survey using a new attitude scale. *International Gambling Studies*, 9: 39–54.

Orford, J., Hodgson, R., Copello, A., Krishnan, M., de Madariaga, M., and Coulton, S. on behalf of the UKATT Research Team (2009b). What was useful about that session? Clients' and therapists' comments after sessions in the UK Alcohol Treatment Trial (UKATT). *Alcohol and Alcoholism*, 44: 306–13.

Orford, J., Kerr, C., Copello, A., Hodgson, R., Alwyn, T., Black, R., Smith, M., Thistlethwaite, G., Westwood, A., and Slegg, G. (2006). Why people enter treatment for alcohol problems: findings from UK Alcohol Treatment Trial pre-treatment interviews. *Journal of Substance Use*, 11: 161–76.

Orford, J., Natera, G., Copello, A., Atkinson, C., Mora, J., Velleman, R., Crundall, I., Tiburcio, M., Templeton, L., and Walley, G. (2005). *Coping with Alcohol and Drug Problems: The Experiences of Family Members in Three Contrasting Cultures*. London: Brunner-Routledge.

Orford, J., Sproston, K., Erens, B., White, C., and Mitchell, L. (2003). *Gambling and Problem Gambling in Britain*. Hove: Brunner-Routledge.

Orford, J., Velleman, R., Copello, A., Templeton, L., and Ibanga, A. (2010c). The experiences of affected family members: a summary of two decades of qualitative research. *Drugs: Education, Prevention and Policy*, 17 (Suppl. 1): 44–62.

Orford, J., Wardle, H., Griffiths, M., Sproston, K., and Erens, B. (2010b). The role of social factors in gambling: evidence from the 2007 British Gambling Prevalence Survey. *Community, Work and Family*, 13: 257–72.

Ortiz-Hernández, L., Tello, B.L.G., and Valdés, J. (2009). The association of sexual orientation with self-rated health, and cigarette and alcohol use in Mexican adolescents and youths. *Social Science and Medicine*, 69: 85–93.

Overbeck, J.R. (2010). Concepts and historical perspectives on power, in Guinote, A. and Vescio, T.K. (eds.). *The Social Psychology of Power*. New York: The Guilford Press, pp. 19–45.

Parke, J. and Griffiths, M. (2007). The role of structural characteristics in gambling, in Smith, G., Hodgins, D., and Williams, R. (eds.). *Research and Measurement Issues in Gambling Studies*. San Diego: Academic Press, pp. 217–48.

Parker, H., Baker, K., and Newcombe, R. (1988). *Living with Heroin: The Impact of a Drug 'Epidemic' on an English Community.* Milton Keynes: Open University Press.

Parrott, A.C. (1998). Nesbitt's paradox resolved? Stress and arousal modulation during cigarette smoking. *Addiction*, 93: 27–39.

Pearce, M.J., Rivinoja, C.M., and Koenig, H.G. (2008). Spirituality and health: empirically based reflections on recovery, in Galanter, M. and Kaskutas, L.A. (eds.). *Recent Developments in Alcoholism: Research on Alcoholics Anonymous and Spirituality in Addiction Recovery.* New York: Springer, pp. 187–208.

Pearson, G. (1987). *The New Heroin Users.* Oxford: Basil Blackwell.

Peretti-Watel, P., Constance, J., Seror, V., and Beck, F. (2009). Cigarettes and social differentiation in France: is tobacco use increasingly concentrated among the poor?. *Addiction*, 104: 1718–28.

Petry, N.M., Martin, B, Cooney, J.L., and Kranzler, H.R. (2000). Give them prizes, and they will come: contingency management for treatment of alcohol dependence. *Journal of Consulting and Clinical Psychology*, 68: 250–7.

Pfeffer, J. and Salancik, G.R. (1978). *The External Control of Organisations: A Resource Dependence Perspective.* New York: Harper & Row.

Philpott, H. and Christie, M.M. (2008). Coping in male partners of female problem drinkers. *Journal of Substance Use*, 13: 193–203.

Poland, J. and Graham, G. (eds.). (2011). *Addiction and Responsibility.* Cambridge, MA: The MIT Press.

Pomerleau, O.F. and Pomerleau, C.S. (1989). A biobehavioral perspective on smoking, in Ney, T. and Gale, A. (eds.). *Smoking and Human Behaviour.* Chichester: John Wiley & Sons, Ltd.

Prochaska, J.O., Velicer, W., Guadagnoli, E., Rossi, J.S., and DiClemente, C.C. (1991). Patterns of change: dynamic typology applied to smoking cessation. *Multivariate Behavioral Research*, 26: 83–107.

Project MATCH Research Group (1997). Matching alcoholism treatments to client heterogeneity: Project MATCH posttreatment drinking outcomes. *Journal of Studies on Alcohol*, 58: 7–29.

Reinert, R. (1968). The concept of alcoholism as a bad habit. *Bulletin of the Menninger Clinic*, 32: 35–46.

Reith, G. (1999). *The Age of Chance.* London: Routledge.

Rhodes, T., Singer, M., Bourgois, P., Friedman, S.R., and Strathdee, S.A. (2005). The social structural production of HIV risk among injecting drug users. *Social Science and Medicine*, 61: 1026–44.

Rivers, J.J. and Josephs, R.A. (2010). Dominance and health: the role of social rank in physiology and illness, in Guinote, A. and Vescio, T.K. (eds.). *The Social Psychology of Power.* New York: The Guilford Press, pp. 87–112.

Roberts, D. (1998). Self-determination and the struggle for Aboriginal equality, in Bourke, C., Bourke, E., and Edwards, B. (eds.). *Aboriginal Australia.* Queensland: University of Queensland Press, pp. 259–88.

Robinson, T.E. and Berridge, K.C. (1993). The neural basis of drug craving: an incentive-sensitization theory of addiction. *Brain Research Reviews*, 18: 247–91.

Rolfe, A., Dalton, S., and Orford, J. (2005). On the road to Damascus? A qualitative study of life events and decreased drinking. *Contemporary Drug Problems*, 32: 589–604.

Romelsjö, A. and Lundberg, M. (1996). The changes in the social class distribution of moderate and high alcohol consumption and of alcohol-related disabilities over time in Stockholm County and in Sweden. *Addiction*, 91: 1307–23.

Rönnberg, S., Volberg, R.A., Abbott, M.W., Moore, W.L., Andrén, K., Munck, I., Jonsson, J., Nilsson, T., and Svensson, O. (1999). *Gambling and Problem Gambling in Sweden*. National Institute of Public Health Series on Gambling, report number 2.

Room, R. (2004). Disabling the public interest: alcohol strategies and policies for England. *Addiction*, 99: 1083–9.

Rose, N. (1999). *Powers of Freedom: Reframing Political Thought*. Cambridge University Press.

Rosecrance, J. (1988). *Gambling Without Guilt: The Legitimation of an American Pastime*. Pacific Grove, CA: Brooks/Cole.

Ross, C.E., Reynolds, J.R., and Geis, K.J. (2000). The contingent meaning of neighborhood stability for residents' psychological well-being. *American Sociological Review*, 65: 581–97.

Rourke, S. (2005). *Citywide Drugs Crisis Campaign: A Decade of Achievement*. Dublin: Printwell Co-operative.

Rowntree, B. (1905). *Betting and Gambling: A National Evil*. London: Macmillan.

Ruggiero, V. and Khan, K. (2006). British South Asian communities and drug supply networks in the UK: a qualitative study. *The International Journal of Drug Policy*, 17: 473–83.

Russell, M.A.H., Peto, J., and Patel, U. (1974). The classification of smoking by factorial structural of motives. *Journal of the Royal Statistical Society*, 137: 313–46.

Ryan, W. (1971). *Blaming the Victim*. New York: Vintage Books.

Saffer, H. and Dave, D. (2006). Alcohol advertising and alcohol consumption by adolescents. *Health Economics*, 15: 617–37.

Saggers, S. and Gray, D. (1998). *Dealing with Alcohol: Indigenous Usage in Australia, New Zealand and Canada*. Cambridge University Press.

Sarbin, T. and Nucci, L. (1973). Self reconstitution processes: a proposal for reorganising the conduct of confirmed smokers. *Journal of Abnormal Psychology*, 81: 182–95.

Sargent, M. (1992). *Women, Drugs and Policy in Sydney, London and Amsterdam*. Sydney: Avebury.

Scott, J.C. (1990). *Domination and the Arts of Resistance: Hidden Transcripts*. New Haven, CT: Yale University Press.

Seddon, T. (2006). Drugs, crime and social exclusion: social context and social theory in British drugs – crime research. *British Journal of Criminology*, 46: 680–703.

Seddon, T. (2007). Drugs and freedom. *Addiction Research and Theory*, 15: 333–42.

Segal, B. (1998). Drinking and drinking related problems among Alaska Natives. *Alcohol Health and Research World*, 22: 276–80.

Sen, A. (1984). *Resources, Values and Development*. Oxford: Basil Blackwell.

Sen, A. (1985). *Commodities and Capabilities*. Amsterdam: North-Holland.

Sen, A. (1999). *Development as Freedom*. New York: Knopf.

Servian, R. (1996). *Theorising Empowerment: Individual Power and Community Care*. Bristol: The Policy Press.

Siahpush, M., Yong, H.H., Borland, R., Reid, J.L., and Hammond, D. (2009). Smokers with financial stress are more likely to want to quit but less likely to try or succeed: findings from the International Tobacco Control (ITC) four country survey. *Addiction*, 104: 1382–90.

Sidanius, J. and Pratto, F. (1999). *Social Dominance: an Intergroup Theory of Social Hierarchy and Oppression*. Cambridge University Press.

Siegrist, J., Starke, D., Chandola, T., Godin, I., Marmot, M., Niedhammer, I., and Peter, R. (2004). The measurement of effort-reward imbalance at work: European comparisons. *Social Science and Medicine*, 58: 1483–99.

Simmonds, L. and Coomber, R. (2009). Injecting drug users: a stigmatised and stigmatising population. *International Journal of Drug Policy*, 20: 121–30.

Singer, M. (2001). Toward a bio-cultural and political economic integration of alcohol, tobacco and drug studies in the coming century. *Social Science and Medicine*, 53: 199–213.

Singer, M. (2008). *Drugging the Poor: Legal and Illegal Drugs and Social Inequality*. Long Grove, Illinois: Waveland Press.

Smail, D. (2005). *Power, Interest and Psychology*. Ross-on-Wye: PCCS Books.

Sobell, L.C., Sobell, M.B., Toneatto, T., and Leo, G.I. (1993). What triggers the resolution of alcohol problems without treatment? *Alcoholism, Clinical and Experimental Research*, 17: 217–24.

Sooman, A. and Macintyre, S. (1995). Health and perceptions of the local environment in socially contrasting neighbourhoods in Glasgow. *Health and Place*, 1: 15–26.

Spears, R., Greenwood, R., de Lemus, S., and Sweetman, J. (2010). Legitimacy, social identity, and power, in Guinote, A. and Vescio, T.K. (eds.). *The Social Psychology of Power*. New York: The Guilford Press, pp. 251–84.

Sproston, K., Erens, B., and Orford, J. (2000). *Gambling Behaviour in Britain: Results from the British Gambling Prevalence Survey*. London: The National Centre for Social Research.

Swendsen, J., Conway, K.P., Degenhardt, L., Dierker, L., Glantz, M., Jin, R., Merikangas, K.R., Sampson, N., and Kessler, R.C. (2009). Sociodemographic risk factors for alcohol and drug dependence: the 10-year follow-up of the national comorbidity survey. *Addiction*, 104: 1346–55.

Thatcher, A., Wretschko, G., and Fridjhon, P. (2008). Online flow experiences, problematic internet use and internet procrastination. *Computers in Human Behavior*, 24: 2236–54.

Thomas, C. (1998). *Double Drink Story: My Life with Dylan Thomas*. London: Virago Press.

Thomas, C. and Tremlett, G. (1986). *Caitlin: Life with Dylan Thomas*. London: Secker and Warburg.

Tiburcio Sainz, M.A. (2009). Adaptación de un modelo de intervención para familiares de usuarios de alcohol en una comunidad indígena. Tesis Doctora en Psicología, Universidad Nacional Autónoma de México.

Tilly, C. (1991). Domination, resistance, compliance . . . discourse. *Sociological Forum*, 6: 593–602.

Tomkins, S., Saburova, L., Kiryanov, N., Andreev, E., McKee, M., Shkolnikov, V., and Leon, D.A. (2007). Prevalence and socio-economic distribution of hazardous patterns of alcohol drinking: study of alcohol consumption in men aged 25–54 years in Izhevsk, Russia. *Addiction*, 102: 544–53.

Townsend, P., Whitehead, M., and Davidson, N. (1992). *Inequalities in Health*. London: Penguin.

Trice, H.M. and Sonnenstuhl, W.J. (1990). On the construction of drinking norms in work organizations. *Journal of Studies on Alcohol*, 51: 201–20.

UKATT Research Team (2005). Effectiveness of treatment for alcohol problems: findings from the randomised United Kingdom Alcohol Treatment Trial. *British Medical Journal*, 331: 541–4.

Ussher, J. (1998). A feminist perspective, in Velleman, R., Copello, A., and Maslin, J. (eds.). *Living with Drink: Women who Live with Problem Drinkers*. London: Longman, pp. 150–61.

Valentine, G. and Hughes, K. (2010). Ripples in a pond: the disclosure to, and management of, problem Internet gambling with/in the family. *Community, Work and Family*, 13: 273–90.

Valverde, M. (1998). *Diseases of the Will: Alcohol and the Dilemmas of Freedom*. Cambridge University Press.

Velleman, R. and Templeton, L. (2007). Understanding and modifying the impact of parents' substance misuse on children. *Advances in Psychiatric Treatment*, 13: 79–89.

Wallace, J. (1999). Addiction as defect of the will: some philosophical reflections. *Law and Philosophy*, 18: 621–54.

Walters, G.D. and Contri, D. (1998). Outcome expectancies for gambling: empirical modeling of a memory network in federal prison inmates. *Journal of Gambling Studies*, 14: 173–91.

Wardle, H. (2011). Mapping the social and economic characteristics of high density gambling machine locations. London: National Centre for Social Research.

Wardle, H., Moody, A., Spence, S., Orford, J., Volberg, R., Jotangia, D., Griffiths, M., Hussey, D., and Dobbie, F. (2011). *British Gambling Prevalence Survey 2010*. London: The Stationery Office.

Wardle, H., Sproston, K., Orford, J., Erens, B., Griffiths, M., Constantine, R., and Pigott, S. (2007). *British Gambling Prevalence Survey 2007*. London: National Centre for Social Research.

Warner, J. (1994). 'Resolv'd to drink no more': addiction as a preindustrial construct. *Journal of Studies on Alcohol*, 55: 685–91.

Weatherburn, D. (2009). Dilemmas in harm minimization. *Addiction*, 104: 335–9.

Webb, H., Rolfe, A., Orford, J., Painter, C., and Dalton, S. (2007). Self-directed change or specialist help? Understanding the pathways to changing drinking in heavy drinkers. *Addiction Research and Theory*, 15: 85–95.

Weisner, C. (1990). Coercion in alcohol treatment, in Institute of Medicine (ed.). *Broadening the Base of Treatment for Alcohol Problems*. Washington, DC: National Academy Press.

Welte, J.W., Wieczorek, W.F., Barnes, G.M., Tidwell, M., and Hoffman, J.H. (2004). The relationship of ecological and geographic factors to gambling behaviour and pathology. *Journal of Gambling Studies*, 20: 405–23.

West, R. (2006). *Theory of Addiction*. London: Blackwell and Addiction Press.

Whitbeck, L.B., Adams, G.W., Hoyt, D.R., and Chen, X. (2004). Conceptualizing and measuring historical trauma among American Indian people. *American Journal of Community Psychology*, 33: 119–30.

Whitehead, M. (1988). *The Health Divide*. London: Penguin.

Wild, T.C., Newton-Taylor, V., and Alletto, R. (1998). Perceived coercion among clients entering substance abuse treatment: structural and psychological determinants. *Addictive Behavior*, 23: 81–95.

Wilkinson, R.G. (1996). *Unhealthy Societies. The Afflictions of Inequality*. London: Routledge.

Wilkinson, R.G. and Pickett, K. (2009). *The Spirit Level: Why Equality Is Better for Everyone*. London: Allen Lane.

Williams, R.J., Simpson, R.I., and West, B.L. (2007). Prevention of problem gambling, in Smith, G., Hodgins, D., and Williams, R. (eds.). *Research and Measurement Issues in Gambling Studies*. San Diego: Academic Press, pp. 399–435.

Williamson, E., Smith, M., Orford, J., Copello, A., and Day, E. (2007). Social behaviour and network therapy for drug problems: evidence of benefits and challenges. *Addictive Disorders and Their Treatment*, 6: 167–79.

Worcel, S.D., Furrer, C.J., Green, B.L., Burrus, S.W.M., and Finigan, M.W. (2008). Effects of family drug courts on substance abuse and child welfare outcomes. *Child Abuse Review*, 17: 427–43.

Wright, A. (2009). *Grog War*. Broome, W. Australia: Magabala Books (2nd edn).

Wrong, D. (1979). *Power: Its Forms, Bases and Uses*. Oxford: Basil Blackwell.

Xenophon, N. (2012). It's harder than it looks: gambling reform in Australia. Keynote speech, Fourth International Gambling Conference, Auckland, New Zealand, 22–24 February.

Yaffe, G. (2011). Lowering the bar for addicts, in Poland, J. and Graham, G. (eds.). *Addiction and Responsibility*. Cambridge, MA: The MIT Press, pp. 113–38.

Zeigler, D.W. (2009). The alcohol industry and trade agreements: a preliminary assessment. *Addiction*, 104 (Suppl. 1): 13–26.

Zinberg, N. (1978). *Drug, Set, and Setting: The Basis for Controlled Intoxicant Use.* New Haven: Yale University Press.

Zinberg, N., Harding, W., and Winkeller, M. (1977). A study of social regulatory mechanisms in controlled illicit drug users. *Journal of Drug Issues*, 7: 117–33.

Index

5797341R00154

Printed in Great Britain
by Amazon.co.uk, Ltd.,
Marston Gate.